Playing with Books

Playing with Books

A Study of the Reader as Child

JOHN MORGENSTERN

McFarland & Company, Inc., Publishers
Jefferson, North Carolina, and London

LIBRARY OF CONGRESS CATALOGUING-IN-PUBLICATION DATA

Morgenstern, John, 1950–
    Playing with books : a study of the reader as child /
John Morgenstern.
       p.   cm.
    Includes bibliographical references and index.

    ISBN: 978-0-7864-4295-9
    softcover : 50# alkaline paper ∞

    1. Children's literature — History and criticism.
    2. Children's literature, English — History and criticism.
    3. Children's literature, American — History and criticism.
    4. Childhood in literature. 5. Play in literature.
    6. Children — Books and reading. I. Title.
PN1009.A1M74   2009
809'.89282 — dc22   2008052166

British Library cataloguing data are available

©2009 John Morgenstern. All rights reserved

No part of this book may be reproduced or transmitted in any form or by any means, electronic or mechanical, including photocopying or recording, or by any information storage and retrieval system, without permission in writing from the publisher.

Cover photograph ©2009 Shutterstock

Manufactured in the United States of America

McFarland & Company, Inc., Publishers
  Box 611, Jefferson, North Carolina 28640
  www.mcfarlandpub.com

Acknowledgments

This book began with Chapter Two which is a slightly expanded version of an article, "Children and Other Talking Animals," published in *The Lion and the Unicorn* 24.1 (2000): 110–127 and I am grateful to the John Hopkins University Press for permission to reproduce. I am particularly grateful to Jack Zipes who recognized the value of the article and thus helped to get this project underway. Chapter One is a condensed version of two articles published in the *Children's Literature Association Quarterly*, "The Rise of Children's Literature Reconsidered," *ChLA Quarterly* 26.2 (2001): 64–73 and "The Fall into Literacy and the Rise of the Bourgeois Child," *ChLA Quarterly* 27.3 (2002) 136–45. I am grateful for permission to reproduce and would like to acknowledge the careful editing those articles received from Roberta Seelinger Trites. I also thank my colleagues Peter Schwenger, David Monaghan and Susan Drain who read and commented upon various parts of the manuscript. Finally, I would like to thank Tracey Daneau for her help in editing the proofs and preparing the index.

Table of Contents

Acknowledgments v
Preface 1

1. The Fall into Literacy 7
2. Children and Other Talking Animals 44
3. Playing with Books 65
4. The Children's Novel 89
5. The Nineteenth-Century Children's Novel 125
6. The Twentieth-Century Children's Novel 176

Conclusion 205
Chapter Notes 211
Bibliography 219
Index 227

Preface

I have been a long time writing this book so naturally my intentions have changed over time. As my title is meant to suggest, my primary subject is the nature of children's play and what it can tell us about the nature of their literature but it took me a long time to discover that. Originally it was to be called *Prescriptions for Failure: A Study of the Child as Reader* and some hints of my original intention still persist in the book I eventually wrote. The original book was going to be considerably more playful than this one since, at the time, I was somewhat enamored of deconstructionism. Paradoxically, as it became clearer that my subject was the play of children, the book became more and more serious and I became more and more a materialist critic. Perry Nodelman's *The Pleasures of Children's Literature* had something to do with this change since his insight that the fundamental quality defining the children's book is a tension between the idyllic and the didactic is the key that led me to a theory of children's literature and to a description of the rhetoric of the children's novel, a rhetoric derived from, if slightly different from, that of Barbara Wall's *The Narrator's Voice*. This change in direction may also have been influenced by the appearance of *An Introduction to Children's Literature* by Peter Hunt whose comments on the subject of the nature of children's literature can always be relied upon to be useful and sensible. For instance, he asserts that "as it is quite obvious to most people when a book *is* a children's book, it seems equally obvious that there must be some textual characteristics that the books all share" (12).

This observation seems equally obvious to me and the only people who seem confused about the matter are literary critics. In making this statement I would seem to be identifying myself as what Hunt has called a "childist" and, indeed, I do believe that children's books are different from adult books and the reason is that they are written *for* children who are different from adults. On the other hand, I am enough of a literary critic to wish to assert that some children's books are better than others just as some adult books are better than others. Moreover, the best children's books are the ones that can be enjoyed, in exactly the same way, by both children and adults. One reason I would wish to say this is because I still enjoy reading children's books with the same rapt pleasure I felt when a child. If the pleasure one feels is clearly different from the pleasure a child would feel then one is not dealing with a children's book but with some odd hybrid like *The Wind in the Willows*. In a good children's book, like *Alice in Wonderland*, the child and adult merge or collaborate in a way that looks in both directions simultaneously and, since children will become adults, it is probably a good idea to give them books that can positively contribute to that transformation. Like Terry Eagleton I am not afraid to call myself a "humanist" (93) and so can believe that children are better for being given better books, though what I mean by that is nothing more than a strong prescription of playfulness.

More practically speaking, my task is to locate those "textual characteristics" that all children's books share and I am going to do so by locating those characteristics in the actual material reality of modern childhood. Since what we are dealing with is the child as reader it would seem sensible to study literacy itself as the crucial phenomenon. Since the invention of the printing press we have seen a spread of literacy to the general population, an historical development that can account for both the appearance of children's literature as we know it and for the development of the modern conception of childhood. Clearly, one factor that distinguishes children from adults is their level of literacy, and common sense would suggest that this difference contributes to the difference in their books. Also the modern conception of childhood innocence is largely based on the fact that children must learn to read and are thus conceived of as pre-readers, which is to say, some kind of primitive Other. Thus it is, that I have entitled my first chapter "The Fall into Literacy."

It is also necessary to consider the material reality of the child's biological body. Many of the decisions that writers for children make in regard to both style and content are based on their pre-conscious remembrance of the socialization process. The process of repression itself can account for the things that are repressed in children's books, most notably sex, horror, and irony. In Chapter 2, "Children and Other Talking Animals," I attempt to account for the unique "taste" of a children's book by an exercise in what might be called psychoanalytical stylistics. But most important to the argument of this book is a discussion of the biological significance of children's play. In all cultures at all times children have had a genetic pre-disposition to play, and it is arguably the one thing that they do better than adults. Indeed, it seems to me that the fundamental difference between children and adults is that whereas children play, adults play games. It occurred to me that if one were to study what children actually do when they play one might arrive at a better understanding of what they do when they read a book. I have attempted to construct a rhetoric for the children's novel by considering the children's novel as a kind of toy that they play with. In understanding the children's novel as an object of play one can understand it as a distinct entity, similar to, but different from the adult novel.

The literature on play is vast and interdisciplinary and there are many competing theories but I have largely relied on Brian Sutton-Smith's *The Ambiguity of Play* in constructing my own views. Sutton-Smith is a scientist with 50 years' experience in the field but what his book is about is how science has not yet managed to conquer play and what presently exists are seven competing "rhetorics" on the subject. Of these various rhetorics, I am primarily interested in the rhetoric that derives from an analysis of the social play of pre-school children. To that subject Sutton-Smith devotes an entire chapter, "Child Phantasmagoria" (151–72), in which he talks about "the ludic construction and deconstruction of irreality"(166) and alludes to Derrida. For obvious reasons this is a view of play that is of special interest to the literary critic. He observes that "children's own play society" is "not about the direct representation of reality" but "is a deconstruction of that realistic society. It takes the world apart in a way that suits their own emotional responses to it. As such, their play is a deconstruction of the world in which they live" (166). I would translate this observation into the generalization that the play of children is paradoxical, parodic and perverse, using the term "perverse" in the sense that Gilles Deleuze uses the term in *The Logic of Sense*. Since Deleuze's philosophical premises are structured upon a reading of *Alice in Wonderland*, they are obviously quite pertinent to an understanding of the nature of children's literature.

Sutton-Smith goes on to point out, however, that "what tends to be underemphasized in such accounts is that ordinary children, in establishing their social play, must do many mundane things in order to play together. In this they are no different from animals or adults whose social play is highly repetitive and in a way highly conservative." Thus there is a "paradox about social play" in that it is "both conservative and innovative" (167). This paradox has been named Newell's paradox after the author of the first book on children's games, *Games and Songs of American Children* (1883). The fact that children in their play are both creative and conservative is a contradiction that has been often noted in order to call into question either generalization. But in fact, both are true and should not be understood as erasing each other but as constituting a vital paradox. Children in their play do deconstruct reality but they do so over and over again in exactly the same way. Moreover, this truth about children's play is recreated in their literature, in which the creative reappears as the idyllic and the conservative as the didactic. Play is the material reality that lies behind Nodelman's contention that a tension between the idyllic and the didactic is the defining characteristic of the children's book.

In the final paragraph of his book Sutton-Smith defines play

> as a facsimilization of the struggle for survival as this is broadly rendered by Darwin. Biologically, its function is to reinforce the organism's variability in the face of rigidifications of successful adaptation (as formulated by Gould). This variability covers the full range of behavior from the actual to the possible. Psychologically, I define play as a virtual simulation characterized by staged contingencies of variation, with opportunities for control engendered by either mastery or further chaos. Clearly the primary motive of players is the stylized performance of existential themes that mimic or mock the uncertainties and risks of survival and, in so doing, engage the propensities of mind, body, and cells in exciting forms of arousal. It is also very interesting to think of play as a lifelong simulation of the key neonatal characteristics of unrealistic optimism, egocentricity, and reactivity, all of which are guarantors of persistence in the face of adversity [231].

Sutton-Smith has made three generalizations, all of which are essential to the argument that is to follow. I would like to translate these scientific generalizations into a simpler language that makes clearer their ethical implications. First, biologically, play is the principle of creativity itself and the evolutionary foundation upon which Sense rests. Psychologically, play is a performance that gives pleasure and as such is the pleasure principle itself in opposition to the reality principle. And ultimately, and most simply, play is the principle of hope. In the face of their evident incompetence, children at play egotistically assert a competence that is both dangerous and stimulating and this constitutes the idyllic that the adult seeks. The idyllic is the assertion of unrealistic hopes just as the didactic is the assertion of the vanity of human wishes that such hopes lead to. The rhetoric of the children's book is based upon an attempt to balance these two tendencies.

Finally, I would like to say a word about the terminology I use. Above I have used the term "children's books" to describe my subject and in doing so I am following the general practice of most critics, indeed I am following Hunt, but that is too general a term since what I am most specifically interested in is the children's novel. Sometimes I will speak generally of "children's literature," especially when my primary concern is the history of children reading. Other times I will speak of the "children's book" when genre is irrelevant or when I am thinking of it as a material object but ultimately what I am most interested in is the children's novel. I have noticed that most critics seem to avoid that term and generally prefer to talk about "children's fiction," but I think that is a manifestation of the inferiority complex that plagues our discipline, as if novels are things that can only be written for adults.

My first inclination was to simply talk about the child novel in order to assert its exact parallel to the adult novel but I gave up that notion as simply too awkward. Unfortunately, the English language does not permit us to use "child" as an adjective in the same way as "adult." "Adult" can denote possession but "child" usually modifies something that is done to children or imposed upon them, as in child labor, child welfare, or child pornography. Also, strictly speaking, the term "child novel," if it were to be used at all, should be reserved for that rare but existent category of novels actually written by children.

So I settle for "children's novel" but in doing so I am insisting that it is a thing different from, but in no way inferior to, the adult novel. *Alice in Wonderland* is a children's novel and, moreover, one that creates the basic formula for all subsequent children's novels, a formula that can be clearly described and differentiated from that of the adult novel. Moreover, cogent reasons for the existence of that formula can be given. In the past, many generalizations about the nature of children's literature have been asserted and I will be repeating many of them though perhaps couched in slightly different terms. The problem with these generalizations is that they all tend to contradict each other. I hope, in what follows, to arrive at a level of generalization that will resolve those contradictions.

1

The Fall into Literacy

There is a general consensus that children's literature first appeared in the eighteenth century, a consensus that is based upon a number of complex factors but perhaps two can be identified as the most cited, the identification of John Newbery as the first printer to publish books specifically for children[1] and the reliance upon Ariès's *Centuries of Childhood* to provide a conceptual framework for theorizing the rise of children's literature. For example, in *Poetics of Children's Literature*, Zohar Shavit adopts Ariès's thesis that "until the seventeenth century children were not considered different from adults" and concludes that because "it was assumed that they had no special needs ... there was neither an established education system, nor were there any books for children" (5).[2] One problem with this theory is that there were books for children before the eighteenth century. Warren Wooden has pointed to the Boy Bishop phenomenon and the fact that Foxe addresses children in his *Book of Martyrs* (1563) as evidence that a concept of childhood existed in the early modern period and Gillian Avery has analyzed the voices of children as revealed by the schoolbooks and "godly" books of the same period. More recently Gillian Adams has made a case for a medieval children's literature and if she is right then the whole notion that we can locate some historical turning point that saw the "discovery" of childhood is seriously called into question.

I have never been very comfortable with the Ariès thesis not only because it does not fit the facts but because it seems unlikely at face value and, in the end, does not really explain anything. One of the unfortunate consequences of the Ariès thesis is that it has made it fashionable, at least among literary critics, to talk about children as if they were fictions that can simply be understood by studying their representation and the result does tend to be a proliferation of "discoveries" of different concepts of childhood. This fashion seems to continue despite the evidence amassed by Linda Pollock that many different attitudes about children have coexisted in every period from 1500 to 1900. In *Forgotten Children*, she conducts an exhaustive survey of diaries and autobiographies from that period in an attempt to refute Ariès and his followers, Ivy Pinchbeck and Margaret Hewitt, Edward Shorter, Lawrence Stone, Martin Hoyles and David Hunt, who, though critical of some of Ariès's argument, agree in accepting the thesis that a new conception of childhood appeared in the seventeenth century. She concludes that "the material analysed here does not support the evolutionary theories of the history of childhood" and that "instead of trying to explain the supposed changes in parent-child relationship, historians would do well to ponder just why parental care is a variable so curiously resistant to change" (271). In her article "Medieval Children's Literature: Its Possibility and Actuality," Gillian Adams, for obvious reasons, is interested in refuting the Ariès thesis and, after citing the considerable evidence amassed by Meradith Tilbury McMunn, C.H. Talbot, John Boswell, Shulamith Shahar, Barbara Hanawalt and Hugh Cunningham, she concludes that "medieval and early modern scholars are unanimous in discarding the Ariès thesis...; it is time for children's literature scholars to do the same" (3). I quite agree and, indeed, would go further than Adams in that I am not as convinced as she is that "Ariès's insistence on the social construction of childhood ... is an essential contribution to the study of past children's literatures" (2). My own position would be closer to that of Peter Fuller whose article, "Uncovering Childhood," attempts to analyze, from a Marxist perspective, the "miniature adult" motif as it appears from the medieval period to modern times. I agree with him that any attempt to deny the unchanging biological nature of childhood in order to assert that "childhood is a product of history, alone" (77) is merely another form of idealism.

Having said that, however, I think there was a change in the conception of childhood in the eighteenth century, a change caused by the spread of literacy. As literacy spread, both in breadth (the number of people schooled in literacy) and in depth (the number of years spent in school), the nature of childhood changed in two ways. First, the

1. The Fall into Literacy

social reality of childhood changed as, more and more, childhood became associated with institutionalized schooling in literacy. Second, the nature of adult subjectivity changed as a gap opened between the literacy of adults and children, a gap that children's literature was invented to fill. Just as literacy made history possible so it made possible a nostalgia that increasingly defined adult views of childhood. Also, the spread of literacy was a precondition for the rise of the novel and it is no accident that this development coincided with the rise of children's literature since the appearance of an adult literature for a mass audience precipitated out, as a separate category, a literature for children.

I do not want to overdramatize this development. We know that books were written for children before the eighteenth century and we know that children read books before the eighteenth century (two categories that may overlap but are not identical) but these works are often dismissed by two arguments. Books of the first category are dismissed on the grounds that, although they are written for children, they are works of instruction rather than delight. We are asked to believe that before the eighteenth century children's literature was a desert of didacticism and only after Newbery (or Perrault) were children allowed to take pleasure in their literature, whereas, in most cases, what we are actually dealing with is a lack of historical imagination and a failure to understand the nature of the pleasure that children once took in works that are no longer to our taste.[3] The second category of works that are dismissed as children's literature are the chapbooks, works that we know children took pleasure in but which we dismiss because they were not specifically written for them. In *Small Books and Pleasant Histories*, Margaret Spufford provides an account of the nature and size of the audience for chapbooks and extends their period of historical influence back to the late sixteenth century. She also makes it clear that not only did children read the chapbooks but in some cases they were specifically marketed for children, a fact that makes it difficult to claim that Newbery was the first to publish specifically for children.[4]

But even if scholars were willing to concede that there is evidence that children's literature exists as early as the sixteenth century, I suspect that most would balk at extending the history of children's literature back further mainly because most recognize, at least implicitly, what I have been suggesting in the previous argument: the history of children's literature is intimately connected to the history of printing. Darton, who gave us the first complete history of children's books, was a publisher himself and his research is constantly informed by the realities of the publishing business. When he bluntly informs us that "the Middle Ages never invented a real children's book" (52), we can hear the printer in him speaking. Even more explicitly, Mary Thwaite identifies the invention of printing as the reason that "children's literature, as we now understand it, became a possibility" (1). She does not actually explain why this is so but presumably it is because books in general were so rare in the Middle Ages that to produce a manuscript solely to give pleasure to children was too frivolous an undertaking. She observes that "books especially designed for children were as yet as rare as swallows in a northern winter. The few made for youth in medieval days were strictly utilitarian and instructional, intended for budding grammarians, novitiates of the Church, or courtiers-to-be" (1).

It is this assumption that Gillian Adams attempts to refute in her article "Medieval Children's Literature: Its Possibility and Actuality." She has two arguments based upon two very different definitions of "literature." On one hand, defining children's literature as anything written for children, she proceeds to defend didacticism and to argue that "there is no reason why texts used for educational purposes should not also qualify as literature, whether they appeal to us or not" (7). On the other hand, operating on the much narrower definition of literature as *belles lettres*, she surveys the medieval curriculum to discover a "separate literature" existing "between the elementary texts and the medieval equivalent of Shakespeare and other works in today's high-school canon, the optional material in a curriculum otherwise dominated by classical and late Latin texts: the poems, fables, and stories adapted or specially written for children" (11). So, somewhere between the primer and the canon, there was a non-didactic medieval children's literature, texts that "are a far cry from *Fun with Dick and Jane*" (18).

I see no reason why there should not be children's literature in the Middle Ages and the long list of internal and external criteria that Adams uses to interrogate texts seems reasonable but her assertion that "books for children must have been part of" the trade in "buying and

1. The Fall into Literacy

selling codices" (8) is not backed up by the kind of autobiographical and material evidence that allows us to make reasonable deductions about what children actually read in the seventeenth century, that is, what they actually spent their sixpence to purchase. The fact that that particular question cannot be legitimately asked of the Middle Ages indicates there is a break in the historical continuity of pre-printing and post-printing cultures and the insight of Twaite that links the appearance of children's literature to printing cannot be simply dismissed.

The invention of printing produces a new understanding of literacy. Although Adams points out that literacy in the Middle Ages was not restricted to the clergy and was increasingly found among the aristocracy and merchant class, it is still true that training in literacy was professional training limited to a small proportion of the population. Even Harvey Graff, who is a critic of the "printing myth" and emphasizes the continuities between medieval and post-printing literacies, estimates only "5 to 10 percent male literacy"(106) by the end of the fifteenth century. I do not see how it would be possible for a society to even conceive of achieving universal literacy before the invention of the printing press. Of course, universal literacy is not inevitable, nor was it always seen as desirable, but in England it took only 400 years after the introduction of printing to achieve universal literacy. True, the small group of professional readers from the Middle Ages does not disappear after the invention of printing, though it does undergo certain transformations, but, more importantly, there now begins to appear a mass audience of general readers. It is this spread of literacy to a mass audience of general readers that is the foremost cause of the phenomenon we call the rise of children's literature.

As literacy spread, it began to affect how childhood was perceived and even Pollock, who is so skeptical of the Ariès thesis, has to admit that there was "an increased emphasis on the *abstract* nature of childhood and parental care from the seventeenth century onwards" and that "from the eighteenth century on, parents began to be more concerned with 'training' a child" (269). In other words, the child was being viewed as a "problem" in a way that it had not previously been viewed. Pollock thinks this is a "very minor" change and explains it as follows:

> It is possible that these developments were related more to the growth and

spread of literacy as well as increasing expertise with writing as a form of communication than to any significant transformations in the parent-child relationship [269].

Pollock does not explain why the spread of literacy would have this effect but perhaps she is alluding to Stone's concern that his thesis would be "seriously undermined" if "a growth in the capacity to express emotions on paper" creates the illusion of greater "affect" in the eighteenth century (13). Also, as literacy spread, more autobiographies were being written and they were becoming increasingly detailed; thus, they include more details about children and create the illusion of increased concern. Another explanation is that the spread of literacy results in more books being written about children and their training and in more parents reading them with the result that the child is increasingly seen as an abstract object of study. Yet another explanation and the one I intend to pursue is that literacy itself is the "problem."

It is difficult for us to see literacy as the "problem" that altered the way people viewed children in the eighteenth century because today we all take it for granted that children are going to learn to read. In order to understand the modern conception of childhood, we first need a history of literacy and schooling. We need to know how people learned to read, when they started and when they stopped and how large a proportion of the population availed themselves of the instruction available. Ariès gives seven as the age at which a "tardy weaning" is completed and children enter "the great community of men" (411) but Pollock cites Hanawalt (Childrearing, 18) to support her contention that even in the late medieval period "between the ages of 8 and 12 ... children were still living at home, being trained for the work they would eventually perform as adults" (54–55). Pollock's autobiographical evidence suggests "that there was no set age for going to school" (240) but there are many examples of children beginning as early as four. It is not always clear what kind of school she is talking about. Her most detailed evidence from the seventeenth century pertains to William Morris, the timing of whose educational career does not seem all that different from what is normal today. He was sent to a dame school at four but "did not seem to learn much there for at 7 he was sent to a tutor for six months to learn how to read." At eight he attended a local grammar school and at thirteen was sent to a boarding grammar school. At eighteen he went to university (242–43). For most of the population all that would be available would be the pre-grammar school education prior to the age of eight, either at home or in 'petty schools.' In *The Rise of the Schooled Society*, David Wardle, claims that "children left these schools very young — certainly by eight or nine years — and entered unskilled or semi-skilled trades" (4). Wardle also mentions 'writing schools' where pupils were "prepared for apprenticeship to highly skilled crafts, for posts in offices, warehouses and so on. Such pupils were unlikely to be indentured before they were twelve or fourteen years old" (4).

Clearly there was considerable variation in when and how one learned to read depending upon class, gender, availability of schools and personal circumstances. The assumption that one began school at a fixed age and proceeded by fixed stages was not yet institutionalized, but there is a general consensus that ideally the process takes place between the ages of four to eight, unless it should be extended for the purpose of training for a profession, which would include training in writing.[5] This supposition is supported by an interesting document dated 1548. In a call for universal schooling in literacy, William Forrest writes:

> As in honest arts we would have occupied
> every man after his vocation,
> so would we have youth to virtue applied,
> that are not ready for occupation
> of handcraft to use th'administration;
> infants I mean under eight years of age,
> their time I would thus to be put in usage.
> At four years old let such to school be set
> to gather and learn some literature
> by which they may after know their due debt
> to him that is author of each creature,
> by reading in books his will and pleasure [Cressy, 95].

This is clearly a utopian ideal in sixteenth-century England but it seems reasonable to suppose that it is a proposal based upon the social realities of the time. If one were to be schooled in literacy then one generally received one to four years of instruction between the ages of four to eight.[6] The next question is how large a proportion of the population received such instruction.

There is now a general consensus that earlier estimates of general literacy in the period between 1580 and 1800 have been much too low. Studies of the chapbook industry tend to support the need to revise estimates upwards since it is unreasonable to suppose that chapbooks would be produced in the numbers that they were if there were not readers to buy them. Even using the normal method of measuring literacy by signatures, there were impressive literacy figures among the lower classes. Of course, as Spufford observes, "literacy was economically determined. Between 1580 and 1700, 11 per cent of women, 15 percent of labourers, and 21 per cent of husbandmen could sign their names, against 56 per cent of tradesmen and craftsmen, and 65 per cent of yeomen" (21). She also points out that since reading was always taught before writing "reading was a much more socially diffused skill than writing" (27). Growth in literacy between the end of the sixteenth century and the end of the eighteenth was not without periods of stagnation and decline but, according to Roger Schofield's research using marriage registers, by the middle of the eighteenth century 40 per cent of women and 60 per cent of men could sign their names (446). In *Popular Education in Eighteenth Century England*, V. E. Neuburg, like Spufford, points out that considerably more people could read than could write and he argues that the assumptions of Ian Watt and R. D. Altick about the illiteracy of the lower classes ignore the evidence of the chapbooks and "the extent to which they circulated" (97). Moreover, it would have been unrealistic for the Society for the Promotion of Christian Knowledge to produce large numbers of "tracts addressed to soldiers, sailors and hackney coachmen" (98) if it could not be safely assumed that they could read them. Unfortunately there is no quantitative evidence to support these assumptions except for a single parish register analyzed in appendix iii of his book. Starting in 1767, a register was kept of names of children who were charges on the parish of St. Mary Islington and it indicates whether the children could read. Although Neuburg warns against rashly drawing conclusions based upon one parish, his analysis does reveal a surprisingly high level of literacy:

> To summarize these figures: very nearly five hundred children aged five or over appear on the list of Parish Poor Children between 1767 and 1810 when information about reading ability was (except for two years) entered

in the Register. About three-quarters of the children are shown as readers, and there is no significant difference between boys and girls in this respect [173].

Neuburg thinks it "reasonable to assume that most of these children came from the poorest section of the labouring class" and that "we might infer that reading was at least no less widespread further up the social scale" (173). I think it would be safe to assume, as does Graff, that "among the middle class, literacy was virtually universal" (239); moreover, schooling was probably extended longer. Stephen Duck did not leave school until he was fourteen (Neuburg, 39) and although this extended schooling was certainly the exception among the laboring class, it was probably the norm for the middle class. The middle class now also comprised a larger proportion of the population as "there was a marked rise in the numbers and wealth of shopkeepers, independent tradesmen, and administrative and clerical employees" who, as Watt argues, were now brought "within the orbit of the middle-class culture, previously the reserve of a smaller number of well-to-do merchants, shopkeepers, and important tradesmen" (41). These are the circumstances that gave rise to the novel. They are also the circumstances that gave rise to children's literature as we know it.

In summary then, in England in the late sixteenth century there was an increase in interest in education and a general increase in prosperity, and as a result "the generation of school age in the 1560's and 1570's, to which generation Shakespeare belongs, experienced a significant upsurge in its ability to read and write. By the end of the sixteenth century we may estimate that almost a third of the male population was able to write" (Cressy, 9). And if a third of males could write probably considerably more could read. It was this situation that gave rise to the chapbook industry. By the end of the eighteenth century, as the chapbook industry began its decline, there was universal and extended schooling in literacy among a large middle class and, if Neuburg's parish register is to be believed, 75 per cent literacy among lower-class males and females, though that is certainly higher than the average for the country. Somewhere in those 200 years a crucial change took place, a change that has been analyzed inaccurately as the "discovery" of the child.

We have been asked to believe the absurd proposition that before the seventeenth century no one considered children to be different from adults. Actually there was one significant way in which children and adults did not differ. As far as the chapbook industry was concerned they were equally part of the semi-literate, mass audience that had one to four years schooling in literacy. There was no reason to single out children as a distinct audience with their own taste in literature since there was no significant difference in their reading ability and that of most adults. It is only when there is a significant difference between the literacy of adults and children that children can be conceived of having a different taste in literature. In England, sometime between the end of the sixteenth century and the end of the eighteenth century, children ceased to be perceived as part of a large, semi-literate audience and came to be perceived as pre-literate, that is as people who must be schooled in literacy. Children's literature as we know it becomes possible when a culture begins to assume that every child is going to learn to read. It is impossible to give a precise date to such a cultural transformation but the year 1699, the year of the founding of the Society for Promoting Christian Knowledge, might serve as well as any.

Everyone knows how the rise of a large, middle-class audience led to the rise of the novel but I do not think it has been emphasized enough how closely this phenomenon is related to the rise of children's literature; indeed, it might just as accurately be referred to as the rise of adult literature. Once one has acquired the level of literacy necessary to read a novel one is less likely to be satisfied with a chapbook. Of course, the middle-class rejection of chapbook literature is a product of snobbery. Middle-class parents did not want their children to read the same books as the lower classes and literacy itself increasingly becomes a mark of class distinction. Snobbery aside, however, the linguistic and rhetorical complexity of the novel requires a more sophisticated literacy than is demanded by a chapbook. In *The Tatler*, Steele's comments on the reading habits of his godson reveal what happens when children are thought of as pre-literate:

> I perceived him a very great historian in Aesop's Fables: but he frankly declared to me his mind, "that he did not delight in that learning, because he did not believe they were true"; for which reason I found he had very much turned his studies for about a twelve-month past, into the lives and

adventures of Don Bellianis of Greece, Guy of Warwick, the Seven Champions, and other historians of that age [*The Tatler*, 95; 1709].

His patronizing, ironic tone makes it clear that he considers a taste for such stories to be childish. The joke is interesting in that the child naively assigns a historicity to these romances at a time when the adult novel is beginning to claim a historicity, or realism, that defines it as a genre separate from romance.[7] The joke is based upon the assumption, still common today, that children cannot distinguish between fact and fiction. As early as 1709, for a sophisticated man of letters, the chapbook stories are children's literature and the child is defined, at least partially, in terms of the difference in his taste in literature. We can see in Steele's comment the actual historical process that began to assign romance, folktale and fantasy to children as their own special literature, a process that constructs children as uniquely "imaginative," endowed with a "sense of wonder."

When Newbery came out with *A Little Pretty Pocket Book* in 1744, he knew quite well that children were reading chapbooks. He also knew that their middle-class parents disapproved of them and so he shrewdly came up with a compromise. The formula he devised is actually stated in *The Fairing*. After recounting the story of Puss in Boots, Dick Wilson is required to defend it against Sam Sensible's objection that it is "a Fairy Tale, in which there is not the least Appearance of Probability" (114). Dick proceeds to elaborate on "the Moral" of the story and, in the end, the Newbery compromise is articulated: "it was agreed, that Fairy Tales should never be read but on Fair Days, when People are inclined to have their Heads stuffed with Nonsense" (115). Chapbook literature is acceptable as a form of childish play as long as it is inoculated against with large doses of morality.

The Newbery formula makes it clear that what we mean when we speak of "children's literature" is a literature designed to appeal to both children and their bourgeois parents. This is hardly a surprising observation and Darton also insists that children's books are "essentially a middle-class product" (221), but it is important to keep this reality in mind. We know that prose fiction existed before the novel but we also agree that the novel first appeared in the eighteenth century and its difference from previous prose fiction is signaled by stylistic differences based upon the nature of its middle-class audience. In *The Origins of the English Novel, 1600–1740*, Michael McKeon argues that "'the novel' must be understood as what Marx calls 'a simple abstraction,' a deceptively monolithic category that encloses a complex historical process" (20). In attempting "to sophisticate and retrieve the familiar correlation between the rise of the novel and the rise of the middle class," McKeon argues that "like 'the novel,' 'the middle class' is one of those simple abstractions whose early modern origins mask a considerable preexistence" (22). "Children's literature" is also a simple abstraction with a considerable preexistence that solidifies out as a separate category at the same time as the novel. As the productions of Richardson and Fielding in the 1740's signal the appearance of the novel, so the productions of Thomas Boreman, Mary Cooper, and John Newbery in the same decade signal the appearance of "children's literature" as a separate category that reflects a middle-class social reality.

The social reality that pertains most closely to my thesis is certainly marked in all of Newbery's productions. Whether or not everyone in the eighteenth century thought of the child as a pre-reader, there is no doubt that Newbery did. *A Little Pretty Pocket Book* is essentially an extended alphabet book. The Author tells parents that if they "would have a Wise Son, teach him to reason early. Let him read and make him understand what he reads" (57–8). Jack the Giant-Killer steps out of the chapbooks to inform both Master Tommy and Miss Polly to "learn your book" (14, 18). "A little Boy, who learned his Book" so well that it "raised him from a mean State of Life to a Coach and Six" (71) prefigures the more famous Goody Two Shoes who also achieves fame and fortune through learning to read. Finally we are told that "all good Boys and Girls take care to learn their Lessons, and read in a pretty Manner; which makes every Body admire them" (75). The omnipresent concern with reading in all of Newbery's books is an expression the general concern of middle-class parents in the eighteenth century with the "problem" of their children's literacy.[8]

Finally, *A Little Pretty Pocket Book* makes explicit a basic truth about children's books: they are always addressed to a double audience. The author addresses a letter "to the Parents, Guardians and Nurses" filled with Lockean advice about child rearing followed by two identical letters to Master Tommy and Miss Polly, the latter written in a markedly different style suited to "good Boys and Girls." So explicit is this doubling of the audience that the technique seems crude to our taste since we expect this doubleness to be disguised by duplicity, by various rhetorical strategies designed to hide the parental presence.[9] This rhetorical duplicity can be achieved by simply merging the letters, so to speak, by creating a mixed style as in Perrault. Increasingly it becomes common to signal parental presence by its absence, by creating an illusion of childhood autonomy. Alternatively, in works of fantasy, one can transform all the adults into rather childish talking animals. For bourgeois parents since the eighteenth century the duplicity of children's books has been appreciated as a sign of the gap their children must bridge in becoming literate. For literary critics today the gap is the place to "play" and for them it is probably this element more than any other that defines what they term "children's literature."

Of course, this rhetorical duplicity, which is such an important part of children's literature after the eighteenth century, can appear sporadically prior to the eighteenth century. It is certainly present in Perrault and will exist in any work that assumes a gap between the mature reader and the pre-reader, a gap that a clever writer can exploit for rhetorical effect. Such an assumption is not present in chapbook literature and for this reason I suspect that *Guy of Warwick* does not make it unto the syllabi of many children's literature courses, despite the fact that it was a children's book for hundreds of years.[10] I also suspect that Adams is looking for this quality in the works that she is trying to locate in the Middle Ages, works that exist in the gap between the primer and the canon, between the child reader and the adult reader. The problem, however, is that there is not as compelling a reason to view children as pre-literate in a society in which, at best, 10 per cent of children will learn to read as part of their professional training and a society in which it is assumed that all children will learn to read. If I am correct and, in the case of England, the eighteenth century was the first period to generally recognize children as pre-readers, a cultural transformation signaled by the productions of Boreham, Cooper and Newbery in the 1740's, then this is certainly a development significant enough to be characterized as the rise of children's literature.

Just how significant one feels this development to be will depend upon how significant one feels literacy itself to be to the nature of human subjectivity but I think it could be argued that the discovery of the innocent child in the eighteenth century is, to some degree, nothing more than the discovery of the pre-literate child. Ariès himself distinguishes between two kinds of innocence. One, the assumption that children must be protected from immodesty, seems to me to have nothing to do with literacy[11] but "the association of childhood with primitivism and irrationalism or prelogicism" (119) most certainly does. The one thing that "primitive" people and children have in common is that they do not read and in the eighteenth century there develops an intense nostalgia for the pre-literate since as literacy becomes inevitable it is felt as a burden, indeed, as the burden of rationality itself.

The thesis that I have developed at such length has been suggested in passing by Peter Hunt who points out that before 1744 "most of the books used by children-educational texts, chap-books, tracts, and folk-tales-were used by adults as well. But, as the reading population increased, and the adult novel became established, those early texts were relegated to the nursery and formed the basis (either in spirit or in the solid fact that their woodcuts were reused) of eighteenth-century books for children" (28–29). Hunt also correctly observes that from the eighteenth-century on there develops a close relationship between children's books and the adult novel in that "the form and content of children's books lags behind the form and content of the adult book" (29) and as an example cites the adventure story that "was the staple of the eighteenth-century adult novel" (29) but by the nineteenth-century had largely been relegated to children. In *Children's Literature Comes of Age*, Maria Nikolajeva has produced a detailed analysis of the relationship of children's literature to adult literature but, because she subscribes to the Ariès thesis and believes that children's literature could not be invented until children were discovered in the seventeenth century and thus was late getting started, she is led into an interesting misunderstanding. She believes "that more and more children's books today are approaching the modern (or postmodern) adult novel. Children's literature, which emerged several thousand years later than mainstream literature, is now catching up with it" (10). In fact, children's literature and adult literature for a mass audience emerged at exactly the same time and there is little hope that one will "catch up" with the other since it is the "gap" that defines children's literature, that makes the very term intelligible.

Basically, we have all been reading the story backwards and it is to the nature of literacy itself that we should look for an understanding of the historical development of children's literature. When we factor in the appearance of print technology and the consequent rise in general literacy, we have the ingredients for a more accurate analysis of that development. Instead of looking to Ariès for the theory that would explain the rise of children's literature, we should look to Walter Ong whose works explore the consequences of literacy on the historical construction of modes of subjectivity. The close connection between the history of children's literature and the history of literacy and printing gives us a perspective from which to explore the intimate connection of that literature and some lost, "original" oral culture. In the end, we may return to the comfort of the familiar Ariès *via* the back door, in that I think it can be shown that at least some of the characteristics associated with the "innocent" child are simply derived from the general cultural assumption that children are pre-readers who must receive extended training in literacy. Instead of trying to understand how the "discovery" of the child in the seventeenth century gave rise to children's literature in the eighteenth century, we should investigate how the spread of literacy changed social institutions and led to the construction of the child as innocent, which is to say, as a pre-reader. Or, to put it simply, it is not the "child" that gives rise to children's literature but children's literature that gives rise to the "child."

Driven by the introduction of extended schooling in literacy, what develops at the end of the eighteenth century is a kind of bi-polar view of childhood. On one hand, the pre-literate child is endowed with a spiritual presence, an innocence that unfortunately must be abandoned, must be allowed to die so the adult can be born. On the other hand, the pre-literate child is a savage that must be trained, an uncivilized emptiness that must be supplemented with adult experience in the form of a constantly expanding series of steps or "grades." It is literacy itself that constructs this contradictory structure by imposing upon the biological and psychological development of the child a social structure that cannot be entirely accommodated to it. Oedipal childhood is unnaturally disassociated from the post-oedipal and tied to infancy on the idyllic side of the great divide and post-oedipal childhood becomes more closely linked to adolescence by sharing the common condition of being in school. In a sense Ariès got things backwards since what happened was not the appearance of the child but its disappearance as childhood was divided into two and entering school became a threshold of childhood of unprecedented significance. This way of thinking was already evident, at least among the literary elite, by the end of the eighteenth century and when we reach the twentieth century, with mandatory schooling to the age of sixteen, it has become a way of thinking so general and so natural as to make its historicity invisible. According to the OED, the first use of "preschool" as an adjective for children is found in 1924. It is not until 1954 that the term "preschooler" comes into use and it would be relevant to cite the text given: "Remember that preschoolers are people." Once rationality becomes synonymous with literacy, the pre-literate child is endowed with an alien otherness that is the object of both intense nostalgia and intense anxiety. When I try to disabuse my own students of the notion that children are innocent by prodding them to define their terms more precisely, they finally agree that children are innocent "only at a certain age" and what they invariably mean is that only preschoolers are innocent. The loss of innocence is the fall into literacy.

In *A History of Youth*, Michael Mitterauer observes that "schooling in its various forms has become the single factor which determines more than any other the shape of youth" (78). Extended schooling created a gap between the literacy of children and adults, a gap that children's literature was invented to fill and a gap that appears in the rhetoric of that literature. In a recent article in *Children's Literature*, Perry Nodelman has identified a rhetoric of binary oppositions that "resonate"(2) across the gap between the child and the adult, between the idyllic and the didactic and he applies this rhetoric to the astute analysis of a number of children's texts.[12] In order to understand the historical and social construction of this "gap" we must begin with an understanding of the universal, biological nature of childhood since this is one of the materials upon which the social operates. The social does not operate *ex nihilo*; it must work with material reality, including the material reality of the biological body.

The list of things that are universally true of all children at all times would probably not be very long or very interesting but it would form the foundation upon which to understand the social. In terms of child development, every human culture recognizes that childhood ends with puberty. All human cultures also recognize the beginning of childhood in the period that Freud called the anal stage. Given the reductionist nature of his theory it is not surprising that he emphasized toilet training as the crucial point of transition but the equally important sign of the end of infancy is weaning. Moreover, both constitute socialization through repression and the battle of the high chair can be just as tumultuous as the battle of the potty chair. In marked contrast, the other two points of transition into childhood, walking and talking, are biologically predetermined and require no adult intervention. Looked at this way, Freud's account of a child's socialization is somewhat one-sided in its emphasis upon parental repression. This kind of socialization could be seen as a kind of work that adults impose upon children but children also socialize themselves through a self-actualized process of play.

In *The Nurture Assumption*, Judith Rich Harris challenges the prevailing assumption among psychologists that parents are the socializers of children. She argues that children socialize themselves through a process of imitation and who they imitate are not adults but other children. Children are genetically predisposed to walk and to talk and to join play groups with other children in which they practice the social roles they will need as adults.[13] The family "self" is only one, and not the most important one, of many in a repertoire of "selves" that they develop through play. As she points out children — even preschoolers — are remarkably good at switching from one personality to another. Perhaps they can do this more easily than older people. Have you ever listened to a couple of four-year-olds playing House?

> STEPHIE (in her normal voice, to Caitlin): I'll be the mommy.
> STEPHIE (in her unctuous mommy voice): All right, Baby, drink your bottle and be a good little baby.
> STEPHIE (whispering): Pretend you don't like it.
> CAITLIN (in her baby voice): Don't want botta!
> STEPHIE (in her unctuous mommy voice): Drink it sweetheart. It's good for you!
>
> Stephie plays three parts here: author/producer, stage director, and the starring role of Mommy [58].

It is interesting to observe that this form of play is actually a play in a literary sense and thus children could be said to create their own literature before one is created for them. We usually assume that children are socialized by the literature we give them but I am going to reverse that assumption in order to consider to what degree the rhetoric of children's literature is influenced by the rhetoric of children's play. Harris' theory that "culture is transmitted by way of the children's peer group" (198) is a convincing and refreshing alternative to the Freudian account but it is also equally one-sided and I do not see how we can make do with a theory of socialization that does not include the reality of repression. Children are not weaned nor toilet trained by imitating their peers, nor can they learn to read and write in this manner.

Finally, there is another universally recognized aspect of childhood that actually splits childhood in two. All cultures recognize that at about the age of six or seven children become capable of a certain amount of independence and responsibility. As Harris puts it "the social and intellectual advances that occur around the age of seven are recognized all over the world. Parents in many societies believe that this is the age when kids 'get sense'" (176).[14] Thus, I distinguish between the oedipal and the post-oedipal child to describe this somatic development. Socially speaking, we could refer to the preschool child and the child in school and in relation to the thesis I am developing I am interested in this age as the age for entering school. In no culture is a child below the age of six expected to work except in the sense that the work we give them is the repression of instinctual pleasures. At the age of six children are capable of work in the sense that we can give them chores to do and they are also fully formed persons no longer in need of repressive discipline. It is at this time, then, that they are free to play and at the same time capable of work. What normally happens at this time is captured in the following anecdote quoted in *Play and Early Childhood Development*, in which Francis Wardle describes life in a village in Guatemala:

> While the boys were playing soccer on our highlands field, the girls were usually washing clothes in the stream. The girls seemed to make a game of it, though, by laughing and giggling, splashing each other, and throwing the soap. I have often observed children accompanying their parents in

1. The Fall into Literacy

work-related activities such as washing clothes, building fires for a barbecue, attending meetings, and caring for the corn and bean plants. In every instance, these children would develop a game to play while their parents worked: splashing the water, using sticks for swords, drawing in the sand, and playing with the leaves of the bean plants [134].

Before Ariès distorted our vision, this mixture of work and play is probably how most people would have imagined the nature of post-oedipal childhood.

The belief that children did not exist in the Middle Ages is constructed by pretending that they did not play. As was pointed out earlier, Ariès gives seven as the age at which a "tardy weaning" was completed and children entered "the great community of men" (411). He makes childhood disappear by unnaturally stretching infancy to encompass the oedipal child and by stretching adolescence to encompass the post-oedipal child. The result is a grotesque fantasy of a world in which children leave their mothers' breasts to go out and get jobs. Mitterauer provides us with a more realistic assessment of the nature of child labor. Citing J. Schlumbohm (84ff), Mitterauer summarizes "the hierarchy of farm service"(67) by age: "from 9 till 12, a boy must tend the cows; at 13 he becomes a stable boy, and looks after the horses until he is 16; ... from 17 to 20 he works as a junior farm-hand.... From the age of 21, the 'now strengthened and hardened youngster' can serve as a chief hand" (68). Mitterauer does not think that such "precise age brackets" correspond to "social reality" because there would be considerable variation by individual depending "on physical strength and skill" (68). He does, however, agree that "it is possible to identify a turning-point at about 12 or 13 years of age when children were regarded as able-bodied workers" (68). Similarly, "in trade and commerce" Mitterauer identifies "the beginning of an apprenticeship" as the significant transition point and observes that "in the eighteenth and nineteenth centuries this often happened between the ages of 12 and 15, most frequently at 14" (69). Alluding to Ariès, he admits that "in the Middle ages this may have been earlier, but certainly not often as early as 7 or 8" (69–70). In summary he finds that "in late medieval England, most children were still living in their parental home between the ages of 8 and 12. In fifteenth-century Cologne there were very few apprentices under the age of 12. And in sixteenth-century France 12 was the average age for beginning an apprenticeship" (70). Basically, whether they were potential farm laborers, artisans or merchants, children were not seriously expected to work much before the age of twelve. There is, however, one very important difference between the peasant child and the bourgeois child. While the peasant child was tending the cattle, an occupation that provides much opportunity for play, the bourgeois child was hard at work in school.

In *Orality and Literacy*, Walter Ong describes the consequences of literacy on human consciousness as follows:

> The interaction between the orality that all human beings are born into and the technology of writing, which no one was born into, touches the depths of the psyche. Ontogenetically and phylogenetically, it is the oral word that first illuminates consciousness with articulate language, that first divides subject and predicate and then relates them to one another, and ties human beings to one another in society. Writing introduces division and alienation, but a higher unity as well. It intensifies the sense of self and fosters more conscious interaction between persons. Writing is consciousness-raising [178–9].

One problem with this theory is that it encourages viewing the "primitive" mind as an alien Other to that of the rational, civilized mind but Ong is careful to resist this temptation. A more serious problem is that according to the experimental work of Scribner and Cole it is not true. In *The Psychology of Literacy* they describe their study of the Vai of West Africa, a study that discovered no such "consciousness-raising," except for a slight increase in the cognitive skills of those Vai that attended English school.

In *The Interface between the Written and the Oral*, Jack Goody has responded to Scribner and Cole to point out that we can only understand the cognitive effects of literacy as "*mediated* consequences" that are cultural rather than individual and which can only appear in the presence of a "written 'tradition,' the accumulated knowledge stored in documents as well as the mind" (222), a position that recognizes that literacy is primarily a technology of memory. Since the Vai use their vernacular syllabary almost solely to write letters to each other, they have no such tradition and can only get one by attending school and adopting the English tradition; whereupon, cognitive changes appear. Ong's own characterization of writing as "consciousness raising" is mis-

1. The Fall into Literacy

leading since it suggests that consciousness can exist apart from the material conditions that construct it. Literacy is only one of those conditions and elsewhere Ong correctly observes that its historical significance can only be understood in conjunction with "developments in food production, in trade, in political organization, in religious institutions, in technological skills, in educational practices, in means of transportation, in family organization" all of which "play their own distinctive roles" (175). Many of the characteristics of the bourgeois child have nothing to do with literacy but in order to understand how the bourgeois child was constructed as innocent one needs only understand two material facts about literacy: learning to read and write is hard work and, since the end of the eighteenth century, it is work that must be performed in the modern school.

The problem with an historical approach to childhood that is not grounded in material reality is demonstrated in Harry Hendrick's article "Constructions and Reconstructions of British Childhood: an Interpretative Survey, 1800 to the Present." As the title suggests, Hendrick wants to locate a series of different childhoods that historically replace each other, even though he elsewhere more accurately sees this process as an attempt "to *universalize*" what "historians refer to as the 'domestic ideal' among the nineteenth-century middle classes" (34). The "history" he describes begins in the seventeenth century with the Puritan child who because of his "original sin" must be severely disciplined. He is replaced by the Lockean child who is a *tabula rasa* and therefore needs encouragement rather than discipline. Next comes the Romantic child who, far from a blank slate, is a positivity of spiritual presence that must be cherished. According to Hendrick "the 'Romantic Child' was short-lived" (38) and in the early nineteenth century was replaced by the Evangelical child who is apparently a reversion to the Puritan child. By presenting this history as a series of costume changes one masks its coherency. One need only take a step back to see that we are describing one and only one childhood, that of the bourgeois child and especially of the male bourgeois child which is why I have so gendered him. The male bourgeois child is pre-eminently a Schoolboy and it is this paradigm which is extended to women and the working classes to create the modern conception of childhood.

Hendrick is mistaken in thinking the Evangelical child replaced the Romantic child; rather, the two coexist simultaneously in the mind of the bourgeois parent. It is possible that at all times parents have had mixed feelings about their children, both cherishing them for what they are and yet anxiously anticipating the adult they will become but, by the late eighteenth century, these mixed feelings had been exaggerated into a radical polarity of feeling that produced two entirely different views of the nature of child development. On one hand the child is a primitive savage who must be disciplined into adult rationality. The child is the site of a lack that must be supplemented by adult experience. On the other hand, the child is the site of a spiritual presence that must be sacrificed so that the adult can be born. The literature produced for the children of bourgeois parents demonstrates this same polarity and Nodelman has identified the resulting oscillation between the idyllic and the didactic as a defining quality of that literature.

The bourgeois child has been awarded an historically unprecedented degree of privacy and autonomy but has been made to pay for those qualities by being made the subject of an equally unprecedented degree of parental anxiety and training, which, as I argued earlier, is caused by concern over their literacy. Parental anxiety is also accompanied by increased stress among bourgeois children. Mitterauer explains this development as follows:

> As the old society began to decline, the educated middle class became the first group for whom the social position of an adult depended very much on personal achievement in youth. As a result, young people came under great pressure to fulfil their parents' expectations.... Here was a new source of conflict which had never existed in a society where status was decided primarily by birth [113].

More precisely, this complacency would be general with peasant children but in England, because of primogeniture, among aristocratic children it would be restricted to the eldest son. Younger sons would be much in the same position as bourgeois youth; indeed, their position would be worse since they would have been educated in "better" schools, schools designed to create gentlemen, and the prospect of slipping down the social scale would create greater anxiety.

In order to understand how schooling in literacy shaped the nature of bourgeois childhood, it might be more useful to compare their childhood to that of traditional, oral societies. Harris tells the story of how

1. The Fall into Literacy

"in the mid–1950s, a pair of American researchers were studying the child-rearing practices of the inhabitants of Khalapur, a rural village in a remote part of northern India. One day they asked a Khalapur mother what kind of man she hoped her young son would be when he grew up. The woman shrugged. 'It is his fate,' she said, 'no matter what I want'" (78). In traditional societies children are not the objects of anxiety that they are in bourgeois families and, indeed are generally ignored by adults from the time they are weaned to the time they are 6 or 7. As Harris points out "parents in traditional societies do not believe that babies have sense or that they understand what is said to them; therefore, they generally do not talk to them. Nor do they attempt to teach them to talk. Consequently, the child acquires very little language before the age of two and a half or three — much less than a North American child of that age" (91–92). Harris points out that children do not need to be taught how to speak. They simply learn to do so whether they are encouraged or not. Of course, the behavior of bourgeois parents who anxiously encourage their infants to speak and who go into raptures over their first word does result in earlier language acquisition but it is difficult to see what the advantage of that would be if it were not in anticipation of eventually teaching them to read and write.

Although it is possible to trace the increased anxiety of bourgeois parents to their concern that their children become literate, it is not as immediately clear what schooling in literacy has to do with the construction of the innocent child. That will be the burden of my subsequent argument. First, it might be useful to define what it is that we mean when we refer to childhood innocence. What appeared in the eighteenth century is an amalgam of various different meanings that can be assigned to what are real differences between children and adults. As I have said before, the social does not operate *ex nihilo* but must accommodate itself to material reality. In *Some Versions of Pastoral*, William Empson, in discussing Lewis Carroll's nostalgia, points out

> that there is always some doubt about the meaning of a man who says he wants to be like a child, because he may want to be like it in having fresh and vivid feelings and senses, in not knowing, expecting, or desiring evil, in not having an analytical mind, in having no sexual desires recognisable as such, or out of a desire to be mothered and evade responsibility [278].

There are actually four meanings of the term "innocence" described here. We all know that children are not sexually innocent but it is not unreasonable to think them so given the difference between their sexuality and that of adults. The belief in the sexual innocence of children is not so much an affirmation of their sexlessness as it is a fear that they will be harmed by any knowledge of adult sexuality. This fear certainly predates the eighteenth century and seems to have always been a part of bourgeois sensibility.[15] Of course, it is only possible to have such a belief if you are able to provide your children with private rooms but that does not explain where it comes from. We could perhaps evoke bourgeois Puritanism but I think it has earlier and deeper roots than that. The bourgeoisie are by definition people who live in towns and if one has read a description of what urban existence was like before the invention of plumbing, one would not be surprised if the bourgeoisie were unusually fastidious about cleanliness, a fastidiousness that could easily extend itself from the anal to the phallic. Also the prepubescent body is "cleaner" than the adult body, a fact that could evoke a belief in the sexual purity of children.

The moral innocence of children is supported by no less an authority than Christ himself, though it could be argued that he was more interested in the metaphor of rebirth than in actual children. People who have no children of their own might be excused for believing in their innocence but most twentieth-century parents are absolutely convinced that children are both morally innocent and deserving of punishment, a contradiction that causes them no difficulty and, indeed, which is one manifestation of that strange polarity which, since the eighteenth century, has characterized our view of childhood as a combination of innocence and savagery. It could be argued that children are more innocent than adults if only in the negative sense that they are, statistically speaking, less likely to cause harm; however, the assertion of the moral innocence of children, like the assertion of their sexual innocence, is more often not an assertion of their inherent goodness as an assertion of the need to protect them from evil. It is reasonable to want to protect children from evil but in the eighteenth century this desire manifests itself in the view that children, to paraphrase Empson, do not know, expect, or desire evil and, thus, what they must be protected from is knowledge of the vanity of human wishes. Thus in

1. The Fall into Literacy

his *Ode on a Distant Prospect of Eton College*, the melancholy Gray, from the vista of nostalgia, views the playing children and concludes that "ignorance is bliss." Children are people who believe that they can be anything they want to be when they grow up and who believe that when they become what they want to be then they will be happy. Again, I do not think it unreasonable to believe that children are more hopeful than adults providing, of course, they have a place to live, food to eat, and are not abused.

The third kind of innocence combines "not having an analytical mind" with "having fresh and vivid feelings and senses," since it is the acquiring of the former that leads to the loss of the latter. This theory of the cognitive innocence of children is an invention of the late eighteenth century though there are intimations of it in the late seventeenth century in the Cambridge platonists and the verse of Vaughan and Traherne. It is preeminently associated with William Wordsworth and the theory is most abstractly enunciated in *Ode: Intimations of Immortality from Recollections of Early Childhood*. As Wordsworth puts it, children see a "splendour in the grass" that is unavailable to adult perception. The notion that children feel and perceive more intensely has become so familiar that we tend to forget how strange an idea it is. It is necessary to be skeptical about any assertions about the difference in cognitive abilities of children and adults but most developmental psychologists assume that children lack abilities that they must acquire in order to become adults. One is inclined to attribute Wordsworth's reversal of this normal way of thinking to a peculiarity of his psyche but his strange idea is anticipated, to some degree, in Rousseau and Blake. It arises as literacy more and more becomes synonymous with rationality and, as a consequence, rationality is felt to be somehow unnatural. To understand how this happens, it is necessary to consider the fourth and final variety of innocence.

Empson places "a desire to be mothered and to escape responsibility" in the climactic position in his list of the motives for nostalgia and it does seem to be the most sensible and universal reason for wanting to return to childhood. In any culture, one could imagine a harried adult looking at the child at play and feeling a twinge of envy, which, if far from the full-blown nostalgia of a Wordsworth, is the seed of that feeling. More positively, if we understand the desire "to escape responsibility" as a desire to avoid work then we can translate it into the desire to play. This ludic innocence is the innocence of the children of William Blake, who sees in the desire to play the source of imaginative energy and spontaneous creativity which, by degrees, merge with Wordsworth's heightened sensibility. In the late eighteenth century, with the spread of literacy, there occurs a profound change in the economy of work and play among children with the result that there is an intense affirmation of the value of play. It is the desire to return to ludic innocence that is the force that drags all the other kinds of innocence behind it in the construction of what Peter Coveney calls "the Romantic child."

In his classic study, *The Image of Childhood*, Coveney locates the development of "the Romantic child" in "the half-century from Rousseau's *Emile* to Wordsworth's *Prelude*" and "in the whole movement of the late eighteenth century from Reason to Feeling" (37). He also suggests "that across the century Wordsworth's *Prelude* and Freud's Essay on Infantile sexuality may be said to join hands" (34). Similarly, Julia Kristeva has Rousseau and Freud join hands when she observes of them that "twice during the past few centuries Western reason perceived that its role of being a servant to meaning was imprisoning. Wishing to escape, it turned toward and became haunted by childhood" (271). Neither, however, is able to give a satisfactory account for this historical development. Coveney sees it simply as a history of ideas in which the pendulum swings from reason to feeling and "from the Christian doctrine of original sin to the cult of original virtue in the child" (33), but actually the notion of the child as a "savage" in need of civilizing persists even as the innocent child is evoked; indeed, they are merely opposite sides of the same coin, polarities that resonate, as Nodelman puts it, between the idyllic and the didactic. Kristeva understands this polarity as a matter of repression, as a psychological conflict between culture and nature, whereas I would like to consider it as a sociological conflict with an ancient history, the conflict between the civilized and the uncivilized.

Civilization has always had its discontents and one response to these has been to evoke the pastoral fiction, the fiction of a pre-literate, pre-urban existence of extreme felicity. Of course, at the dawn of civilization when it was less than certain that the civilized would triumph over the nomadic pastoralists, it might have been difficult to evoke the pastoral fiction. It is hard to imagine piping shepherds when the barbarian hordes are at the gates of the city. It is only with the consolidation of empire that the ruling classes can enjoy their Arcadian fantasies. At the height of Roman power under Augustus Caesar, when it might well have appeared as if the triumph over the Barbarian was secure, in his *Georgics* Virgil replaces the shepherd with the farmer and places the divide of otherness in class division. So, in *Windsor-Forest* when Pope wishes to recreate the Augustan age, he puts the British Empire firmly on the shoulders of his laboring swains. Similarly, in the age of exploration, the discovery of native peoples evoked the myth of the Noble Savage, again in support of Empire and the existent class structure. Then, at the end of the eighteenth century, for the first time, the child was placed in the space of the Other with strange and powerful results. First, what has always been a conservative device switches sides as the innocent child becomes a sign of revolution, of an imaginative energy that threatens to rewrite the old social codes. Second, a device based on sociological difference suddenly takes on a more profound psychological meaning. All the other Others were undeniably other, but the child is undeniably not. Once you place the child in this place you make yourself the Other, at which point psychoanalysis becomes possible and we can return to Kristeva's insight about this historical development, as, indeed, I will in my next chapter. In a very real sense, Rousseau's discovery of the innocent child was a precondition for Freud's own discovery of the savage child but the question that still remains is why did this development takes place at this particular moment in the history of civilization.

Even Coveney recognizes that the cult of the child arises from the need to resolve "the social, political, and, more especially, the intellectual problems arising from the French and Industrial Revolutions" and the particular problem he cites is "artistic alienation" (30). To some degree, alienation is simply a condition of civilization and as civilization becomes more technologically advanced alienation increases. By the end of the eighteenth century, Western civilization had reached an unprecedented degree of technological complexity but that in itself does not explain why the child became the focus of attempts to resolve the problem of alienation. Such an explanation needs to consider how the material condition of childhood was radically changed by the fact that for the first time in English history large numbers of children were in school. Of course the situation is complicated by questions of gender and class but by the end of the eighteenth century every middle-class, male child was a schoolboy and generally remained one until the age of fourteen. It is not until the end of the nineteenth century that this bourgeois paradigm is extended to everyone, regardless of gender or class, but even by the end of the eighteenth century it was schooling in literacy that was becoming the single most important factor in determining the shape of childhood.

In the analysis that follows I risk being accused of grammaphobia. Ong lumps together Greimas, Todorov, Barthes, Sollers, Derrida, Foucault, Lacan and Kristeva as a "group we may here call textualists" who "specialize in texts, and in fact in printed texts, and mostly in latter-day printed texts from the Age of Romanticism — a significant specialization when this age is recognized as marking a new state of consciousness associated with the definite interiorization of print and the atrophy of the ancient rhetorical tradition" (165–66). In other words, the final triumph of the literate over the oral in the late eighteenth century generates a compensatory logocentrism, or Romanticism, that is then deconstructed in the late twentieth century by a group of critics who are so immersed in text that they can conceive of it as operating outside of the spoken language. Ong believes Derrida did a useful job in pointing out that the spoken language is just as conventional as the written and neither has a "pipeline" to reality but he also points out that "the work of the deconstructionists and other textualists mentioned above derives its appeal in part from historically unreflective, uncritical literacy" and that, in fact "l'ecriture and orality are both 'privileged,' each in its own distinctive way" (169). Indeed, if one were to resurvey the Western philosophical tradition, I suspect that one could find as many examples of grammacentrism as logocentrism, the most famous example of which would be Locke's description of the mind as a *tabula rasa*.[16]

The simple fact of the matter is that the spoken language, both historically and developmentally, is prior to the written language. In *The Psychology of Reading*, Robeck and Wallace point out that "the human auditory analyzers apparently are phylogenetically prepared to

1. The Fall into Literacy

perceive speech, but no one has suggested that a similar visual mechanism is biologically inherited for the perception of print." Thus it is that "spoken language is fairly impervious to developmental disruption, whereas reading skills are elusive to many children and adults who speak fluently" (65). According to Robeck and Wallace most students of language believe that there is a "biological predisposition to language" (64), a belief that arises out of the fact that learning to talk is so effortless and natural when compared to learning to write that we must accept the fact that they are entirely different kinds of learning. If learning to talk occurs as naturally as learning to walk then, by analogy, learning to write is like learning to dance. One is all play and the other is work.

In his introduction to *The Acts of King Arthur and His Noble Knights*, John Steinbeck provides an eloquent description of his own initiation into reading:

> Some people there are who, being grown, forget the horrible task of learning to read. It is perhaps the greatest single effort that the human undertakes, and he must do it as a child. An adult is rarely successful in the undertaking—the reduction of experience to a set of symbols. For a thousand thousand years these humans have existed and they have only learned this trick—this magic—in the final ten thousand of the thousand thousand.
>
> I do not know how usual my experience is, but I have seen in my children the appalled agony of trying to learn to read. They, at least, have my experience.
>
> I remember that words—written or printed—were devils, and books, because they gave me pain, were my enemies....
>
> Books were printed demons—the tongs and thumbscrews of outrageous persecution. And then, one day, an aunt gave me a book and fatuously ignored my resentment. I stared at the black print with hatred, and then, gradually the pages opened and let me in. The magic happened. The Bible and Shakespeare and *Pilgrim's Progress* belonged to everyone. But this was mine–It was a cut version of the Caxton *Morte d'Arthur* of Thomas Malory [3–4].

Frankly, I do not recall my own experience of learning to read as painful and perhaps I am one of the fortunate few for whom it came rather naturally. There is clearly considerable variation of experience in different individuals and Robeck and Wallace begin their book with the sensible generalization that "reading can be learned almost as naturally as speech by a few children and is learned only minimally, if at all, by more than a few others who leave school virtually illiterate" (ix). The majority of children fall somewhere in between. Whether or not learning to read is the torture that Steinbeck describes, it is certainly work and like weaning and toilet training constitutes a discipline imposed upon children by adults. Since the end of the eighteenth century we have been demanding that our children, at the age of six, give up their play and enter school to be put to work. Of course, one could object to this thesis by pointing out that learning to read is only painful at first and once one has learned to do it, reading realigns itself with the pleasure of play as Steinbeck describes. Thus, it would be correct to understand children's literature to constitute the play of literate children. There are two answers to this objection.

First, learning table manners and learning to control one's feces are disciplines that also realign themselves on the side of pleasure but if we are to believe Freud they constitute acts of repression whose consequences persist in the unconscious and, in my next chapter, I intend to analyze those consequences in relation to the effect they have on the stylistic choices writers make when they write for children. In *Fairy Tales and the Art of Subversion*, Jack Zipes argues that in seventeenth-century France there was an increasing effort to train and control instincts "for their socio-political use value" and that "the supervised rearing of children was to lead to the *homme civilisé*" (23). This attempt to "civilize" children was accompanied by a general attempt to impose upper class modes of behavior upon the lower classes. Zipes lists such things as "the introduction of the knife and fork as instrumental and dignified tools for eating, sitting straight at the table, hierarchal forms of serving, maintaining a certain posture while speaking or moving in a prescribed way, repressing one's bodily functions, wearing special dress signifying one's social class" (23). I would simply add literacy to this list since, if one's goal is to create the "civilized man," then literacy is crucial since literacy has always been the foundation upon which civilization has been built. In England, in the eighteenth century, there was a similar attempt to impose the paradigm of the bourgeois child upon all children. The fact that Zipes does not include literacy in his list is not surprising since so successful was this imposition that literacy has become historically transparent and seems as natural as the air

1. The Fall into Literacy

we breathe. Also we are quite rightly less ambivalent about literacy than we are other forms of social behavior. It is always necessary for a Marxist to resist the temptation to succumb to a nostalgia for a prebourgeois past and especially in the case of literacy. Literacy is power and though we might be able to imagine, at least intellectually, a world in which the peasant is left free to eat with his fingers and to fart as he pleases, we would not be willing to deprive him of his right to be literate. As Ong points out "oral cultures today value their oral traditions and agonize over the loss of these traditions, but I have never encountered or heard of an oral culture that does not want to achieve literacy as soon as possible" (175).

The second reason why we must consider the acquisition of literacy to be work is that even after children can read with pleasure and for pleasure, they are still required to stay in school. The OED gives the first use of the term "schoolboy" to Shakespeare in 1588 and perhaps he coined the term. He uses it several times, usually in a pejorative sense. One defining characteristic of the schoolboy is his hatred of school. In *Romeo and Juliet*, Romeo asserts that "Love goes to love as schoolboys from their books/ But love from love, toward school with heavy looks" (II, ii, 56–57) In As *You Like It*, in his famous speech on the seven ages of man, Jacques equates childhood with being a schoolboy and places it between the infant and the adolescent "lover." The child is "the whining schoolboy, with his satchel/ And shining morning face, creeping like a snail/ Unwillingly to school" (II, vii, 145–47). So, in the late sixteenth century the "schoolboy" becomes the paradigm for childhood which is not surprising since, as Cressy observes, "the generation of school age in the 1560's and 1570's, to which generation Shakespeare belongs, experienced a significant upsurge in its ability to read to read and write" (9). It will not be for another two hundred years, in the late eighteenth century, that the term "schoolgirl" will make its appearance. Fanny Burney, who herself did not attend school, makes her character Evelina a "schoolgirl" (30). It will not be until the end of the nineteenth century that all children will be schoolchildren but this is not to say that only boys of the upper classes attended school. In 1599, in his *Travels in England*, Thomas Platter describes a hospital in London which "finds food and drink and clothes for several hundred young boys and girls, while reading and writing are taught in special schools in the same" (qtd. in Williams, 179). Many children, both male and female, received elementary schooling for one to four years between the ages of four and eight but such a level of literacy would have as little consequence as does the literacy of the Vai. It is extended schooling in literacy that has social consequences and so we must look to the schoolboy for the paradigm that constructs childhood as innocent.

Thus, it is not surprising that the cult of the child in the late eighteenth century seems largely restricted to males and it is quite clear that they are reacting to the experience of being a schoolboy. In *Emile*, Rousseau asserts that "reading is the plague of childhood and almost the only occupation we know how to give it" (116). Emile never goes to school, apparently teaches himself to read, though by 12 "he will hardly know what a book is" (116) and when he is finally allowed a book he is allowed only one, *Robinson Crusoe*. Blake makes his view clear in "The Schoolboy":

> I love to rise in a summer morn
> When the birds sing on every tree;
> The distant huntsman winds his horn,
> And the sky-lark sings to me.
> O! What sweet company.
>
> But to go to school in a summer morn,
> O! It drives all joy away;
> Under a cruel eye outworn,
> The little ones spend the day,
> In sighing and dismay.

Wordsworth's position is less explicit but in the first two books of *The Prelude*, although it is made clear that the young Wordsworth is in school, he never describes the experience. Presumably the classroom had nothing to do with forming his moral character. Childhood is that which happens outside of school.

One could find many examples of similar complaints stretching back to the Middle Ages though the medieval schoolboy is more likely to complain of the birch than the constraint on play. It is worth noting that Blake sees the pain of the schoolboy as rising not from corporal punishment but from lying under the monitoring "cruel eye" of the schoolmaster. The nature of the school changes in the eighteenth cen-

1. The Fall into Literacy

tury. The medieval school had no classes and consisted of boys of various ages receiving individual attention from the schoolmaster. Also, the rhetorical tradition would encourage more oral performance than would be found in the literate classroom where there would be a premium on silence. What we see happen in the eighteenth century, as the function of the school becomes the mass production of literacy, is a process whereby the school increasingly becomes like a factory. In *English Popular Education, 1780–1975,* David Wardle points out that at the end of the eighteenth century the first attempt to introduce mass education gave rise to the "monitorial system," which

> was the factory put into an educational setting. Every characteristic was there; minute division of labour; the assembly line, with children passed on from monitor to monitor until they issued complete from the top class; a complicated system of incentives to good work; an impersonal system of inspection; and finally an attention to cost-efficiency and the economic use of plant [87].

By the end of the nineteenth century this system had given way to the school as we know it but it is difficult to see how that school is any less of a factory with its rigid processing of children by cohorts taught in separate classrooms and moving through a series of grades according to a production plan called the curriculum. The school also institutes a series of breaks from work in imitation of factory breaks and it is only during recess and at lunch that children are allowed to play. Also, the modern school remains monitorial in its placement of teachers at desks in the front of the room watching their pupils arranged in rows facing front. Such a system is clearly designed to reduce illicit play in the classroom though children still manage to pass messages and throw spit balls from time to time. If the modern school is like the modern factory, it is also like that other invention of the eighteenth century, the penitentiary.

My argument has been premised upon the understanding that the normal condition of childhood is a state of play and that is why I evoked Mitterauer to refute the common notion begun by Ariès that children began to work at the age of seven. There is some difficulty, however, in applying this paradigm to late, eighteenth-century England. In *Childhood Transformed,* Eric Hopkins summarizes the report of the *Commission on the Employment of Women and Children in*

Agriculture (1843) and finds that "at the age of seven (sometimes earlier) boys were given simple jobs such as bird-scaring, watching poultry or cattle in the fields, couching (clearing weeds and roots), and stone picking. At nine or ten, they might help with reaping and threshing, corn-raking and stacking, and working generally in the hayfield. A strong ten-or eleven-year old might lead a horse at the plough, while at ten or after he could himself plough, mow, and ditch and hedge — all tasks requiring something like adult strength" (12). According to Hopkins much the same pattern can be found in workshop and factory labor and in all cases the large majority of child workers were over the age of ten; however, even if this pattern resists the notion that all children began working at seven, it certainly reveals a much more onerous condition of child labor than that described by Mitterauer. Unless we are to believe that the English worked their children harder than any other European country then we must accept that the condition of children in England in the early nineteenth century was an anomaly unprecedented in history. Nor is it difficult to understand the cause of this anomaly. The industrial revolution created a voracious demand for labor that sucked children into the workforce at an earlier age than ever before and which forced them to work harder. It also drew laborers to the city where they could make better wages thus forcing earlier and harder labor on rural children as well. Thus, the condition of working children in the early nineteenth century does not refute my thesis but rather complements it. Nor do we need to imagine any progress in enlightenment or humanitarian feeling to understand the general reaction against the condition of child labor in the early nineteenth century. People simply wished to return childhood to its normal condition. Hopkins gives an account of the various acts of legislation that addressed this problem throughout the nineteenth century but the main thrust of all such acts was to reduce the hours of labor and to return the age at which children began to work to twelve, which, according to Mitterauer, had always been the normal age.

Hopkins, on the whole, analyses what happened in the nineteenth century as an example of human progress because he assumes that children before that time suffered the same working conditions.[17] If Mitterauer is right then we might take a somewhat more cynical view of this development. When Parliament legislated working class children back into childhood, it did not legislate them back to a childhood of play; rather, it sent them to the bourgeois childhood of school. Looking back from today, mandatory schooling can be seen as a positive development that significantly improved the lives of the working class but understood from the perspective of the children that actually suffered this coercion one might take a less sanguine view of it. Hopkins himself points out that "it is difficult to assess the appeal of work in the [iron] industry to young children. For some, starting work must have been the beginning of growing up, a matter of joining adult society" (48). On top of that, unlike in school, you got paid for the work you did in the iron mill. He cites the example of one working boy who, when his father wanted to send him to school, "ran away because he liked cleaning the ash pit better than learning his letters" (48). Even as we recognize the futility of this rebellion, we can applaud it, just as we uneasily applaud the juvenile delinquent and street child, as signs of resistance to the ubiquity of bourgeois childhood.

Not surprisingly, since the invention of the modern school, the goal of educational theorists has been to conceive of ways of making school more fun. Peter Coveney quotes Lord Morley as referring to *Emile* as a book that "admitted floods of light and air into the tightly closed nurseries and schoolrooms" and observes that "Rousseau was indeed so seminal that if anyone now bewails the relaxation of discipline in the schools, he pays hostile, if unconscious tribute to the latter-day influence of his theories" (43). Considering that it took two hundred years for his theories to have any effect, we might more accurately attribute the liberalization of schools to the development of democratic institutions and concepts of human rights and to the professionalization of teaching. There is also some question as to how much "light and air" have been admitted. In *Play and Early Childhood Development*, the authors discuss the educational importance of play but when principals are surveyed it is discovered that "eighty-nine percent of the administrators believed that play should be an integral part of the preschool curriculum, whereas only 9 percent responded that play should have an important role in third-grade programs. The prevailing view is that while preschools are places to play, elementary schools should focus on 'real learning'" (Johnson, 333). Preschoolers can play but once you get to school you have to work and perhaps the principals are right. If we intend to maintain the democratic institutions and level of technological development that extended and universal schooling in literacy have brought us then we must resign ourselves to putting our children to work.

Clearly, the analysis I have given, in itself, has no political consequences. Revealing the historicity of the modern child does not magically deconstruct the social construct. Only a change in the material conditions of childhood could change our conception of the child. As long as the nuclear family persists and children continue to receive extended schooling in literacy, bourgeois parents will continue to protect them from adult sexuality and the evils of the world, will continue to intervene anxiously in the education of preschoolers, and will continue to cherish them for their alien otherness at the same time as they as they discipline them out of it. Perhaps by emphasizing the synchronic nature of modern childhood I have given too little weight to its diachronic development but that is in keeping with my insistence that the social construction of childhood is not infinitely flexible. Certainly, the eighteenth century saw the consolidation of the paradigm of bourgeois childhood and the beginning of attempts to impose it upon all children. Perhaps, in the twentieth century, the postwar baby boom generation has seen major modifications to the paradigm but, even if the concept of childhood innocence has become more problematic in the postmodern era, I cannot agree with Neil Postman that it is in any danger of disappearing.

Of course, at this point, it is almost mandatory, having analyzed where print has taken us, to speculate about where the new electronic media will take us in the future. Marshall McLuchan is perhaps the most famous of the prognosticators of the future of civilization and everyone is familiar with his vision of its demise as everyone huddles around their television sets in a new "global village" (31). The flower children of the time embraced this vision as a hopeful one though one could just as clearly see it as a warning. I see little evidence of a global village though alarming evidence of a global city is all around us. McLuhan's warning need not be taken seriously and, indeed, he could be seen as merely indulging himself in a favorite pastime of academics, complaining about the illiteracy of their students. In the past civilization has ended for two reasons, ecological disaster and barbarian

1. The Fall into Literacy

incursion. Never before in history has the possibility of ecological disaster been more with us but there are no more barbarians left except metaphorically speaking. Indeed, the effect of the rise of the bourgeois child has been to turn our own children into the new barbarians. Thus it is that we invest in them an imaginative energy in the hope that they will rewrite the old social codes and create a more humane civilization. Thus it is, also, that we anxiously fear that they will fail to master the difficult legacy of literacy we have left them. So it is that we look to our children in the hope and the fear that they will unwrite what we have so painfully written.

2

Children and Other Talking Animals

Having given a phylogenetic account of the spread of literacy and its role in developing the modern conception of childhood, I am now going to shift gears and give a purely ontogenetic account of the socialization process and its role in determining the choices writers make when they write for children. What follows is an exercise in psychoanalytical stylistics based upon the theory of Julia Kristeva and for those who believe that the materialism of the Marxist is irreconcilable with the materialism of the Freudian, this might seem a very great shift indeed. Indeed, I am not even going to try to reconcile the two except to make a few preliminary comments as to the shape that such a reconciliation might take. Clearly, as a number of my comments in the previous chapter make clear, I believe that psychoanalysis has a history but that is not to say that I think its insights can be merely reduced to that history.

Kristeva is one of the theorists that Ong calls texualists, theorists who talk about language without distinguishing between the spoken and the written language, though, implicitly, it is fairly clear that what they are interested in is text and specifically, nineteenth and twentieth-century texts, especially novels. Since I am interested in constructing a theory of the children's novel that is where I want to end up but for now I am simply going to follow Kristeva and talk about "language." This is a strategic choice designed to keep the argument simple but I would not want to entirely forget the history that I outlined in the previous chapter. It is possible to think of the written text as being more

2. Children and Other Talking Animals

material than the spoken word and this is the mistake that Derrida analyses in *Of Grammatology*. The written language seems more material because it consists of black marks that persist on the pages of an object that we can hold in our hands. Indeed, this persistence is precisely the special value of the technology of the book. One could expand on this initial mistake by seeing the black marks as excremental in contrast to the purity of the spoken word or by seeing the black marks as merely signs of some absent Author who speaks. But aside from these mistakes, there is a sense in which the written text is more material than the spoken language because it has been written on our own bodies by a repressive process of schooling. Psychoanalysis can give us insights into the consequences of this process. It is important to remember the history that leads up to Freud's theory but it would be an overstatement to assert that his theory only applies to literate, bourgeois males, as tempting as such a conclusion might be.

Kristeva simply talks about this process as the acquisition of "language," though she has perhaps been more honest than Freud in replacing his "talking cure" with a "writing cure." Still, she largely ignores the difference and for her child development is a process of repression that moves one from the semiotic, the language of the maternal body, to the symbolic, the language of the Father. This is presented as a universal process shared by all human subjects. What is ignored is the historical process that led to universal literacy and added a whole new level of repression to the socialization process. What really happens is that once one has left the oedipal stage and entered the oral Symbolic as a fully formed person, one is then subjected to a further repressive procedure of schooling which has the paradoxical effect of leading one back to the semiotic. The reason for this regression is that the written text seems more corporeal than the spoken language for the reasons given earlier but, more importantly, it *is* more corporeal since it has been written on the body in a way the spoken language has not.

In his short story, "The Penal Colony," Kafka invents a machine that bears some resemblance to a printing press but which actually executes people by writing their sentence upon their bodies in script. One cannot help but to see in this horrible amalgam of print and script, parchment and flesh and the Name of the Father that is Law, an image of the entire history of literacy and one remembers Steinbeck's characterization of learning to read as a form of torture. More particularly, one could begin where Derrida began, with Lévi-Strauss' description in *Tristes Tropiques* of the introduction of writing to the Nambikwara and his subsequent conclusion that "the primary function of written communication is to facilitate slavery" (335–6). This is certainly a one-sided and exaggerated version of the history of literacy but one does not write a chapter called "The Fall into Literacy" without seeing some merit in this view. Moreover, the thesis I am going to present in this chapter is that all writers for children suffer from grammaphobia and the stylistic choices they make are attempts to efface the materiality of the written text. So, I would keep in mind the historical reality described in the previous chapter as I proceed to follow Kristeva in talking about the acquisition of language because what I am really interested in is textuality and how the socialization process affects the choices that writers make when they write for children.

Everyone knows the difference between adult stories and children's stories; children's stories are "simpler" than adult stories. Everyone, however, does not include the majority of writers and critics of children's literature who are generally inclined to question or dismiss this difference that seems so obvious to common sense. As sympathetic as I am with those who would deny the difference I cannot help but think that the sophisticated denial is always an echo of an initial, naive affirmation. To explore this problem further, I shall compare a specific feature of C.S. Lewis's adult science-fiction trilogy to its counterpart in *The Chronicles of Narnia*. In the Narnia books, Lewis makes use of a device commonly associated with children's literature, the talking animal. Many people expect to find talking animals only in children's literature, although, as soon as one makes such a generalization, one thinks of exceptions such as *Gulliver's Travels* or *Animal Farm*. Invariably, generalizations about the nature of children's literature meet with such exceptions to the point where one becomes quite skeptical about this difference that is so obvious to everyone. While I share such skepticism, I cannot bring myself to deny the difference and so I am prepared to offer a theory of what it means to be "simple."

The problem with this task is that the term "children's literature" is something of an oxymoron and, as Peter Hunt has pointed out the contradictions inherent in the term has created opposing, critical

2. Children and Other Talking Animals

"camps" (6). Jacqueline Rose has defined one such "camp" in *The Case of Peter Pan: or the Impossibility of Children's Fiction*, in which she argues that the "simple" is a fiction or disguise that enables the adult to "colonize" the child. As her title suggests, Rose's strategy is to deny the difference and the result of this strategy is a powerful analysis of the complexity of a seemingly simple text; however, this strategy is based upon asserting what is clearly an analogy between socialization and colonization. Indeed, it is not so much an analogy as an inversion of the true situation, which is to say that colonization is a case of inappropriate socialization, a case of treating adults as if they were children. Her analogy is only meaningful because children *are* different from adults, a difference that is reflected in the nature of their literature. On the other hand, in *Poetics of Children's Literature*, Zohar Shavit begins by assuming that the "child" is an historical construction and then, somewhat inconsistently, ends up privileging the "simple" as that which really addresses the child. Unfortunately, the result of this strategy is to develop a definition of the "simple" that comes dangerously close to colonizing children as the "simple-minded." I intend to negotiate my way between these positions but in accepting the "risks" (Rose, 143) of asserting a poetics of children's literature, I have necessarily devised a definition of the simple that insists upon the existence of the child as something more than its cultural representation.

In his adult novel, *Out of the Silent Planet*, Lewis invents an alien race called the *hrossa*. The *hrossa* look like large seals and it would be interesting to consider the difference between talking animals and aliens, a difference that Lewis actually analyses early in his novel. When the hero of *Out of the Silent Planet*, Ransom, confronts an alien being whom he first mistakes for "a big, black animal," his initial fear turns to elation when he discovers that "the creature was *talking*. It had language" (55). Ransom is a philologist and is excited by the opportunity to study a new language; indeed, he speculates that "the very form of language itself, the principle behind all possible languages might fall into his hands" (56). The process that continues from this initial encounter consists of a language lesson in which Ransom and the *hross* exchange vocabulary items. During the course of this exchange, Ransom occasionally lapses back into the original state of fear he felt when he thought that the *hross* was an animal: "The huge, seal-like creature seated beside him became unbearably ominous. It seemed friendly; but it was very big, very black, and he knew nothing at all about it" (59). The chapter then ends with the following explanation for Ransom's emotional vacillation:

> It was only many days later that Ransom discovered how to deal with these sudden losses of confidence. They arose when the rationality of the *hross* tempted you to think of it as a man. Then it became abominable — a man seven feet high, with a snaky body, covered, face and all, with thick black animal hair, and whiskered like a cat. But starting from the other end you had an animal with everything an animal ought to have — glossy coat, liquid eye, sweet breath and whitest teeth — and added to all these, as though Paradise had never been lost and earliest dreams were true, the charm of speech and reason. Nothing could be more disgusting than the one impression; nothing more delightful than the other. It all depended on the point of view [59].

This is a provocative observation. The "difference" described could hardly be greater, the difference between Paradise and "snaky," "black" abomination, between the nadir of disgust and the acme of delight, but, in fact, there is really no difference at all. How would one tell the difference between a person who looks like an animal and an animal that talks like a person? To make the point clearer, we could refer to the disgusting alien as an animal talker, both to distinguish it from the delightful talking animal, and, at the same time to insist on the lack of any logical reason for the distinction. What is being asserted here is a difference that is not really a difference in the animal that talks but, as Lewis points out, a difference in "the point of view" of the observer.

As one might expect, this difference that is not a difference plays itself out in various ways through the course of the novel. For example, Ransom accompanies two *hrossa* on a hunting expedition against the ferocious *hnackra*, an animal that is basically a very large shark, a monster with a "great black pit" (85) of a mouth. They kill the *hnackra* which is then described as "wallowing on its side, bubbling out its black life. The water around him was dark and stank" (85). In their joy the three hunters embrace and Ransom has the following revelation:

> The breath of the *hrossa* which, though sweet, was not human breath, did not offend him. He was one with them. That difficulty which they, accustomed to more than one rational species, had perhaps never felt, was now

2. Children and Other Talking Animals

overcome. They were all *hnau*. They had stood shoulder to shoulder in the face of an enemy, and the shapes of their heads no longer mattered. And he, even Ransom, had come through it and not been disgraced. He had grown up [85].

What has happened above is fairly straightforward. The "not-different" option has been foregrounded. The difference has shifted to "animal as opposed to *hnau*" and all the "blackness" and disgust has shifted to the "otherness" of the animal *hnackra*. Animal talkers and talking animals are the same, a moral awakening that is presented as an initiation, a passage into adulthood. Presumably, it is "childish" to think that animal talkers and talking animals are different and adults know better, an interesting reversal of the conventional view in children's literature that only children can talk to the animals.[1]

The linguistic pattern I have been describing consists of two movements. On one hand, there is the "surface" play concerned with the purely logical question of the difference between an animal talker and a talking animal. Beneath this surface, almost as if cast like a shadow, is this profound ambivalence, this vacillation between disgust and delight. Strictly speaking, since there is no logical problem without the ambivalence, one might more properly speak of them existing side by side; however, the metaphor of surface and depth seems better to capture the "feel" of their presentation. Actually, Lewis himself likes to talk about "getting behind" language. Throughout the science-fiction trilogy, Ransom the philologist "longs" to discover "the principle behind all possible languages." Indeed, this quest defines the Christian argument of the trilogy. It is important to note that although the pattern of disgust/delight continues unabated in the Narnia series, the explicit references to language disappear. In Narnia disgust and delight are simply the different responses to evil *or* good and have no explicit connection to the "slippery" difference between animal talkers and talking animals that I have identified here. What is more or less explicit in the adult books is silenced in the children's . It is almost as if there is a secret about language that is too horrible for children to know, or, if not too horrible, certainly too "complex."

Of course, the point that I have been working up to is not one that would have escaped Lewis. He was too good a literary critic and too great a lover of stories not to appreciate the power of the Freudian story. At the end of *Out of the Silent Planet*, he specifically places a talisman to ward off black magicians like myself:

> [Ransom] was ill for several months, and when he recovered he found himself in considerable doubt as to whether what he remembered had really occurred. It looked very like a delusion produced by his illness, and most of his apparent adventures could, he saw, be explained psychoanalytically [165].

The "secret" that is revealed by the pattern of ambivalence that I have analysed is that there is a complicity between language and "bodies," a complicity that Lewis himself seems remarkably aware of in his exploration of the "otherness" of alien contact. The "language lesson" is described to be "like a courtship — like the meeting of the first man and the first woman in the world; it was like something beyond that; so natural is the contact of sexes, so limited the strangeness, so shallow the reticence, so mild the repugnance to be overcome, compared to the first tingling intercourse of two different, but rational species" (56–57). The difficulty of this contact is that for Ransom these "bullet heads and furry faces" are "meaningless" (66). Ransom complains that "its face seemed to him expressionless; it was only long after that he learned to read the Malacandrian face" (63). The body is something that one must learn to "read" as one learns a language.

As Ransom comes to know the language better, he becomes more comfortable with the *hrossa*. He observes that now he can tell "a male from a female *hross* at sight, and even individual differences were becoming plain" (67), but he cannot entirely escape from a sense of uneasiness among them except in one instance:

> The young of the species were different again. They were delightful. You could forget all about the rationality of *hrossa* in dealing with them. Too young to trouble him with the baffling enigma of reason in an inhuman form, they solaced his loneliness, as if he had been allowed to bring a few dogs with him from the Earth [67].

One could hardly wish for a better example of what Rose means by the adult colonization of the child but, if we consider this observation purely from a psychological perspective in the context of the ambivalence I have been describing, it provides us with a hint as to the nature of the stylistic principle that connects the "talking animal" to children and their literature. The young *hrossa* are "delightful" because

2. Children and Other Talking Animals

they are like dogs. Animals are "delightful" because they do not have language, do not trouble you "with the baffling enigma of reason in an inhuman form." Presumably, for some reason, we wish to be able to think that children have no language, although it may seem that what we wish to believe is that they have no bodies/sexuality. It would hardly be a very interesting, or very accurate, observation to suggest that the "supposition" about children that constructs their literature is that children do not have bodies/sexuality. However, it is interesting to observe that children's literature is constructed on the "pretence" that children have no body/language.

In her article "Place Names," Julia Kristeva addresses herself to the problem of children's language. In the first section of the article, subtitled "Childhood Language, Infantile Language," she observes that "twice during the past few centuries Western reason perceived that its role of being a servant to meaning was imprisoning. Wishing to escape, it turned toward and became haunted by childhood" (271). She is referring to Rousseau and Freud. Kristeva observes that reason "was forced ... to face reproduction of the species (the boundary between 'nature' and 'culture')" and "was thus transcended by a *heterogeneous element* (biology: life) and by a *third party* (I/you communication is displaced by *it*: the child). For if death is the Other, life is a third party; and as this signification, asserted by the child, is disquieting, it might well unsettle the speaker's paranoid enclosure" (271). Kristeva is describing what I would call the motive for pastoral, the desire to "unsettle the paranoid enclosure" of the castle which as children we thought was the end of our desire. From the point of view of Reason, or the Symbolic, the Other is death unless in that place can be placed "a third party," a third party who has traditionally been "simple" folk, women and children. Of course, the problem is that this place is "outside," "before," "behind," "at the heart of" language; in other words, the place is No place. Kristeva's answer is to give this place a language, to keep it within culture while yet bringing us to the threshold of nature, to "(the boundary between 'nature' and 'culture')." Kristeva takes us back "before puberty, before Oedipus, but also before the 'mirror stage'" (276), back to the discourse of the mother and infant, the discourse of the maternal body which she calls *le semiotique*.

John Lechte provides a succinct account of this theory, an account that has the added advantage of pointing to the poetic that is implicit in it:

> As drive energy is partially brought under the control of repression (that is, the symbolic), it assumes "*significance*": the voice as rhythm and timbre, the body as movement, gesture and rhythm; prosody, even word-play, and especially laughter fall within the ambit of the semiotic. Chronologically, the operations of the semiotic can be observed in children before the acquisition of language has been completed. The unarticulated sounds a baby makes thus have *significance* even if they have no specific — symbolic — meaning. The more complete the child's entry into the symbolic, the more repression constitutes an articulation of the spoken or written word. Not to have entered the symbolic at all, that is, not to have separated from the mother — as in extreme psychosis — is to be close to living death. On the other hand, not to be alerted to the material basis of the symbolic which the concept of the semiotic evokes, is to remain at the level of a static, fetishized version of language [27].

Lechte's emphasis on the synchronic relationship of the semiotic and the symbolic, on the way they can be seen as counter-prevailing tendencies in the making and breaking of discourse, leads to a theory of "the poetic." The tendency of the semiotic (rhythm, timbre, prosody, word-play, laughter) is to constantly seek to dissolve the sign back into the body and thus to alert us to "the material basis of the symbolic"; the symbolic counteracts to shore up the ruins. Actually the above way of putting it is most accurate in the case of literature, the form of discourse in which the semiotic is most privileged. In most other forms of discourse the symbolic is firmly in command. In other words, we can see a spectrum of discourse in which literature occupies one extreme (a privileging of the semiotic just short of schizophrenia) and scientific or mathematical discourse occupies the other where the symbolic is almost entirely successful in repressing the semiotic.

However, since my aim is to develop a poetic of children's literature, it will not do to forget that psychoanalysis is also a developmental theory and that, in those terms, the child can be seen as moving from the semiotic disposition towards the symbolic by a process of rejection of the maternal body and a consequent creation of the "abject." Elizabeth Grosz observes that "the abject defines a pre-oedipal space and self-conception: it is the space between subject and object, both repulsive and attractive, which threatens to draw the subject and its

2. Children and Other Talking Animals

objects towards it, a space of simultaneous pleasure and danger" (94). Here is the "space" of that extreme ambivalence that Lewis identifies in his depiction of Ransom's reaction to "other" talking bodies. This ambivalence is the necessary product of the movement into the symbolic, the movement of socialization. As Grosz observes, "Kristeva is fascinated by the ways in which 'proper' sociality and subjectivity are based on the expulsion or exclusion of the improper, the unclean, and the disorderly elements of its corporeal existence that must be separated from its 'clean and proper' self" (86). Grosz goes on to observe that "Kristeva's claim is not entirely new" but echoes Freud's claim "that civilization is founded on the sacrifice or expulsion of pre-oedipal polymorphous pleasures;" however, "what is new about Kristeva's position is her claim that what must be expelled from the subject's corporeal functioning can never be fully obliterated but hovers at the border of the subject's identity, threatening apparent unities and stabilities with disruption and possible dissolution" (86–87). One place that it "hovers" with a vengeance is in literature, the most subversive of all discourses.

This theory not only gives us a poetic but a poetic that can identify the difference between adult and children's literature. Children who have just entered into the symbolic and who thus still "have sight of that immortal sea" and can "hear the mighty waters rolling evermore" well may prefer the stability of the symbolic to the flux of the semiotic. Adult literature allows more free play to the semiotic, allows the text to cast shadows, to open up to depths, to achieve texture, in short, to reveal its "body." Most children's literature is more limited and conventional. One can almost taste this difference. For instance, what is striking about a folktale that has been adapted for children is its curious opacity, its smoothness, its resistance to penetration, its feeling of completeness that cannot be opened. As Lewis understands, the strategy that constructs children's literature is the "pretence" that they have no body/language, a pretence based upon our fear that they have too much.

The "feeling" that texts have bodies, that they are corporeal, is commonly evoked by the kind of visual metaphors that I have been using. Complex texts cast shadows, open up to depths, as opposed to the opacity or transparency (they come to the same thing) of simple texts. Another visual metaphor of "complexity" evokes the constant play of elements from foreground to background. But perhaps metaphors of touch or taste are more appropriate if we wish to evoke the corporeality/complexity of texts. Sight is too closely allied to the stabilities of the symbolic and what the semiotic does to the symbolic is cause "slippage," thus reminding it of its materiality. So we could speak of the "texture" of threads complexly plaited or interwoven in opposition to "smoothness," or of the complex "texture" of food in the mouth in opposition to "blandness." But whatever metaphor one prefers, what I am referring to is just as important a part of the "meaning" of a literary text as is the other kind of "sense" that belongs to the symbolic.

Not only do adult texts have more "texture" than children's texts but the text and the reader are in a kind of paradoxical mirror relationship to one another. Having arrived at what Lacan calls "the inexhaustible quadrature of the ego's verifications" (4), at the "fortress" (5) or castle that ends the story, the adult longs for the cottage. The child, who resides in the cottage that any wolf can huff and puff and blow down, longs for the castle. Although the normal way of talking is to see the adult as more "complex" than the child, it is possible, with a kind of psychoanalytic twist, to see the child as the one who is more "complex," if by "child" one means the semiotic disposition, the chaotic, fluid, unbounded body of the polymorphous perverse, in which to be polymorphic is to be multiform (the body having many shapes) but also, if I may be allowed some free play, to be polymorphic and polyphonic, to be blessed with many morphemes and phonemes. Looked at this way, the predominance of the semiotic in adult literature is an opening up to the greater complexity of the body; it is an escape from the "paranoid enclosures," the castles in the sky of narcissism, to the greater "texture" of life, to *jouissance*. Children, on the other hand, do not want to grow up because they think it will make life more complex; they want to grow up because they think it will make life simpler. They seek the "stable self" of the integrated ego. Theirs is a literature that aspires to the castle, to mastery, to the Name of the Father which is Law.

Having arrived at this generalization, I am inclined to take it back again and certainly it needs much qualification and clarification. My

2. Children and Other Talking Animals

argument is an attempt to theorize what is for me a phenomenological fact: children's literature tastes different than adult literature. Moreover, the reason that this is so is that adults who write for children assume that children have a different taste in literature, an assumption that may well reflect the reality of human socialization, the process by which a culture constructs a person as a talking animal. I am quite willing, however, to concede that much so-called children's literature is more complex than much so-called adult literature, a concession that implies that there are more factors at work in constructing this difference than the single one that I have isolated. For instance, one would have to take into account questions of genre. Clearly, in order for my taste test to work, it would be necessary to compare apples with apples. More importantly, one would have to take into account the specific cultural construction of the "child" in history. In my first chapter, I gave an account of the historical rise of literacy and what happens when the child must be constructed as a "reader." This purely phylogenetic account of the historical reality of the child as "reader" must be correlated with the purely ontogenetic account of the psychological reality of the child's construction as "talking animal." But, in the argument I have presented I am not talking about any particular children or adults at any particular time in history. I have ignored all sorts of significant questions about class, ethnicity, and gender. I have not even taken into consideration the factor of differences in age because, as my subsequent argument will make clearer, in the odd way that I am using the term "child," the child ceases to exist by the age of six, although the child never disappears any more than the adult fully appears. My distinction between the "child" and the "adult" is a distinction between psychological dispositions that exist in all persons by the very nature of the socialization process. Nor is the distinction a binary opposition since the two do not exclude one another any more than do the semiotic and the symbolic; rather, both must exist mutually in tension as polarities that define a spectrum of possibilities.

In the end, I cannot even claim that my generalization is very original. Chesterton makes much the same point when, commenting upon the disjunctive, good *or* evil, black *or* white, quality of ethical judgment in children's literature, he observes that "children are innocent and love justice; while most of us are wicked and naturally prefer mercy."[2] If I would wish to rewrite this to read that children, whose grasp of the symbolic is as yet tentative, prefer the language of mastery to the painful ambivalence of the semiotic, this rewriting in no way invalidates the original observation. Nor should it be surprising that writers, relying on their own personal histories and their own special understanding of language, should arrive at the same insights as psychoanalysis. Indeed, this is the reason that I have so carefully analysed Lewis's own text in order to demonstrate that he, if only half-consciously, understood the significance of the "talking animal" and the role of this device in the construction of texts for children. The device of the talking animal accommodates itself to the pretence that children have no body/language by both naming the abject and effacing it at the same time. There is a wide range of stylistic effect possible within this general strategy. A decision must be made about how "animal" and how "cultural" your talking animal is to be. For instance, one can decide to give one's animal clothes as well as language. It is also often the case that the talking animal is an adult who is curiously childish, a childishness evoked by its "flatness." Flat characterization is typical of many children's texts, and we may wish to understand this metaphor not only in its common visual sense but in a gustatory sense as well. This double obfuscation of "talking animal" and "adult child" is designed to make sure that, to use Lewis's words, we start "from the other end," that we start with the idea of an entirely "natural" or "innocent" body to which talking and adulthood are merely "added on." As Lewis suggests, this strategy resolves the ambivalence toward delight by affirming the basic integrity and stability of the body. If we start "from the other end," the alien, animal talker end, we create horror, which, on the lists of what is inappropriate for children, may well have the lead even over sex. Horror is evoked by the "monster" which is the "other end" of the "talking animal"—corpses that get up and walk, bodies sewn together, misshapen features, growths on the surface or within the body, and, ultimately, the blob.

Of course, the device of the talking animal works not by simply effacing the abject but by naming it, by giving it a certain amount of "play." Indeed, I would suggest the more "play" the better. This point can be best made by considering the talking animal as it is translated into the visual medium of the cartoon. It has been my experience that

2. Children and Other Talking Animals

if very young children (before the age of six) are given a choice between seeing a story enacted by cartoon characters or by "real" characters (in the sense that my children distinguished between the "cartoon" Ninja Turtles and the "real" Ninja Turtles that appeared in the movie) they will almost invariably choose the cartoon version. The appeal of the cartoon is that it is extremely "flat." However, good cartoons are also "funny" and they are funny only to the extent that they give play to the abject. Thus one has a pig who can talk but he also stutters; moreover, he wears a sports jacket but no pants. Of course, children are laughing *at* Porky and the hero, Bugs Bunny, is not allowed to suffer the same vicissitudes as the minor characters. The minor characters have their eyes bug out of their heads to the size of basketballs, their bodies flattened by heavy weights, or stretched to the thinness of an elastic band, or blown up into a thousand pieces and, always, the body springs back to shape. Parents who do not get the joke think this is violence, but the child who laughs understands that the cartoon is playing with dynamite. The cartoon flirts with the possibility of bodily danger but provides infinite assurance of the body's integrity.

The stylistic principle that I have isolated is a pretence designed to both hide and reveal the ambivalence that is at the heart of human socialization. This doubleness is necessary to all literary effect; there is no delight without hinting at the horror. I certainly would not want to suggest that the ambivalence I have been analysing entirely disappears in children's fiction. In fact, there are more monsters and odd half-human, half-animal characters in Narnia than there are talking animals. On the other hand, there is also a tendency to mute the ambivalence, to flip the coin so that the talking animal triumphs over the animal talker. Specifically, the animal talker/talking animal distinction reappears in *The Lion, the Witch and the Wardrobe* in the intriguing distinction between the *evil* "bull-headed men" (148) and the *good* "bull with the head of a man" (122). The ambivalence has been allegorized into a moral choice, into a symbolic assertion of the need for reason to bridle desire. In *A Preface to* Paradise Lost, Lewis refers to such symbolic constructions as "the expression of certain basic elements in a man's spiritual existence, ... the words of a language which speaks the else unspeakable" (56). Although Lewis and I would disagree about the meaning of the term "unspeakable," the phrase "a language which speaks the else unspeakable" is an excellent definition of the semiotic.

The "talking animal" has been highlighted in my analysis because it is the most logical entry into Kristeva's theory and from this particular device we can generalize about how writers for children go about flattening the abject. Indeed, Carroll provides us with the basic formula in the first sentence of *Alice in Wonderland*: "once or twice she had peeped into the book her sister was reading, but it had no pictures or conversations in it, 'and what is the use of a book,' thought Alice, 'without pictures or conversations?'" The talking animal is a picture, or a cartoon, with a voice, a speaking voice that is oral rather than literate. An emphasis on the pictorial and oral serves to efface the abject that exists in the materiality of the written word. The writer for children pretends to deny the literariness of the text by providing "pictures" and "conversations."

Lewis himself creates Narnia out of the same thematic material present in his adult fiction not only by turning his aliens into talking animals but by refusing to talk about talking. When Lewis explains where his texts come from, he claims "I see pictures. Some of these pictures have a common flavour, almost a common smell.... A whole set might join themselves so consistently that there you had a complete story without doing anything yourself.... Images always come first" (41). I suspect that Lewis is ingenuously confusing the cause of his texts with their effect and it is interesting how he acknowledges the semiotic part of the process by suggesting that his pictures can "have a common flavour." He is consistent in insisting that the entire Narnia series arose from a "picture of a Faun carrying an umbrella and parcels in a snowy wood" (53) and this assertion does accurately reflect his stylistic technique.

At the same time as Ransom, the philologist, becomes Aslan, the talking animal, Ransom's moral dilemma in the face of "other" talking bodies is translated into landscapes, into scenic icons. This technique of "flattening" ambivalence by iconizing it is typical of many children's texts. Aslan tells the children: "Here on the mountain I have spoken to you clearly; I will not often do so down in Narnia. Here on the mountain the air is clear and your mind is clear; as you drop down into Narnia, the air will thicken. Take great care that it does not confuse your mind" (*The Silver Chair* 27). The abject has become a direction — down into the fog. The "talking animal" itself partakes of this pictorial quality. Lewis describes the device as "an admirable hieroglyphic which conveys psychology, types of character, more briefly than novelistic presentation and to readers whom novelistic presentation could not yet reach" (36). The connection of the "talking animal" with the "hieroglyphic" exactly evokes how the device exists half way between the "naturalness" of a picture and the conventionality of language/culture. My only disagreement with Lewis is that it is not so much that "novelistic presentation" could not reach children as that children are reaching in another direction.

The direction of the adult novel is toward more and more ambivalence, towards an increasingly ironic presentation. Perhaps third on the list of things thought to be inappropriate for children, after horror and sex, would be irony. I imagine that most people would argue that this is so because children do not understand irony, do not get the point. I, on the other hand, would argue that irony is considered inappropriate precisely because they *do* "get the point" and it hurts. There is perhaps no literary device as conducive to producing "depth" or "texture" in a literary text as irony. Even in its simplest forms it involves "duplicity"; there is always someone "behind" the mask. In its more complex forms irony creates depths within depths that make reading an extremely ironic text like walking a tightrope over an abyss. Nothing more radically challenges our illusion that we have a stable body/ego. Irony rubs our noses in the abject. Irony is a barb. It punctures the skin; indeed, it tears the skin right off and children are too "thin-skinned" for that sort of treatment. In describing the difference between writing for children and for adults, Isaac Bashevis-Singer argues that children are too "sensitive" for unhappy endings (which is to say ironic endings) and "if I have to torture someone, I would rather torture an adult than a child" (12).

It would be useful, however, to determine at what point the "torture" begins since I suspect that most adults overestimate the child's sensitivity. Shavit points out that even Lewis Carroll removed "all the elements of satire or parody" when adapting *Alice in Wonderland* to the form of *The Nursery Alice* and, not surprisingly, at the same time adopted a "condescending authoritative tone." She points out that "this tone has nothing whatsoever to do with Alice Liddell, as is often suggested, who was thirty-seven when *The Nursery Alice* was published." She seems to think that this was a sensible adaptation because "the satirical poems, which mainly contributed to the parody level, were left functionless in a version meant for children only" (87). In other words, the change to an authoritative tone and a version with no parody is the result of Carroll's decision to address "the child" rather than "the adult." However, when I look at exactly the same facts, I arrive at precisely the opposite conclusion. The *specific* child who was the addressee of the original *Alice in Wonderland* is now an adult of thirty-seven. Alice Liddell at ten had no trouble understanding parody, but, having lost her, Carroll creates *The Nursery Alice*, a work addressed, not to "the child," but to adult preconceptions, specifically the preconceptions that children are so simple-minded that they do not understand parody and so simple-minded that they must be condescended to. To see how mistaken these preconceptions are, one need only look at the empirical evidence provided by the Opies in *The Lore and Language of School Children*.

The Opies point out that by "seven or eight years old" children "establish their independence by parodying the rhymes their parents taught them" (90). They provide a number of examples, of which I would like to quote two of my favorites:

> Mary had a little lamb,
> She fed it castor oil,
> And everywhere the lamb would go
> It fertilized the soil.
>
> Mary had a little lamb,
> Her father shot it dead,
> And now it goes to school with her
> Between two chunks of bread [90].

Lest it seem that I am undercutting my thesis that irony hurts, it should be pointed out that this is very simple irony and the children are in command of it. Moreover, the children are of school age, and the Opies also point out that younger children consider "the words of the verses ... inviolable; and a way of teasing them, when four or five years old, was to make deliberate mistakes: 'There came a big spider who drank all the cider and so the poor doggie had none.' A misrecitation like this used to infuriate them" (90).[3] It has been my experience that children of this age respond to this and other forms of teasing not only with fury but, more specifically, by tensing their bodies, growling at you or giving you the "raspberry," or shaking their fist at you, all of which would suggest that they feel irony as a physical attack upon the inviolability of their own bodies as well as upon the inviolability of the text.

My own experience is supported by the observations of Martha Wolfenstein in her book *Children's Humor: A Psychological Analysis*. After describing an incident of word-play between two four-year-old children in which the subject of verbal attack responds with "great distress" (78), she concludes that

> word-play, associated in its beginnings with sex- and name-changes, has originally the force of a sexual and hostile attack, regardless of the meaning of the words involved. To accept it as harmless, we must overcome the tendency to react to it as dangerous. We are then able to laugh through an economy of emotion, as the threat of the transformed meaning ceases to effect us with its original force [79].

By the time children are six years old and have turned the corner into the symbolic, they respond to teasing much as adults do, which is to say, if they do not get angry, then they respond with a smile and a comeback, the typical parry and riposte of verbal irony. Of course, writers must rely on their own instincts in judging how far to go in adapting their style to their audience but, on the whole, it would seem that adult judgment on this matter is far removed from the norm of playground culture and tends to err in the direction of excessive simplicity. *Alice and Wonderland*, on the other hand, for many people would seem to be the most obvious choice of a work that goes well beyond those norms and errs in the direction of excessive complexity. It would be useful to consider this matter further.

In "The Schizophrenic and Language: Surface and Depth in Lewis Carroll and Antonin Artaud," Gilles Deleuze has noted the "superficial resemblances" that exist between the "esoteric words and portmanteau words" found "in the rhyming chants of little girls, in poetry, and in the language of madness," but has insisted upon the need to "note the different functions and depths of *non-sense*" (277). He compares the work of Lewis Carroll to that of Antonin Artaud in order to demonstrate just how great is this difference. He quotes Artaud as follows:

> I did not do a translation of "Jabberwocky." I tried to translate a fragment of it, but it bored me. I never liked the poem, which always seemed to me to smack of affected infantilism.... *I do not like surface poems or languages* which smell of happy leisure moments and intellectual triumphs [279].

Deleuze then goes on to analyze just how "superficial" the Alice books are, which, although they begin "in deeply dug wells and rabbit holes, as well as in the mixture of bodies which penetrate each other and co-exist" (285), they quickly give way to nothing but "surface games." Deleuze agrees with Artaud in asserting that Carroll is merely "a minor pervert, who limits himself to the creation of a surface language and does not sense the true problem of language in its depth — the schizophrenic problem of suffering, of death, and of life" (280). Finally, Deleuze concludes that Carroll awaits the child

> ... at the moment at which the child leaves the depths of the maternal body without yet having discovered the depths of her own body, that brief moment of surface when the little girl breaks the surface of the water, like Alice in the pool of her own tears. Carroll and Artaud are worlds apart. We may believe that the surface had its monsters (the Snark and the Jabberwock) its terrors and its cruelties which, though not from the depths, nevertheless have claws and can snatch laterally, or even pull us back into the depths whose dangers we thought we had averted. Carroll and Artaud are nonetheless different; at no point do their worlds co-incide. Only the commentator can move from one dimension to the other, and that is his great weakness, the sign that he himself inhabits neither. We would not give one page of Antonin Artaud for all of Carroll; Artaud is the only person to have discovered a "vital" body and its prodigious language (through suffering as he says) [294–5].

Intemperate judgments of this kind may well explain why so many writers for children are so intent upon denying the difference that I am attempting to assert.[4] But surely all good writers for children must wait for the child "at the moment at which the child leaves the depths of the maternal body"; indeed, this is as far as children's literature can go and still remain children's literature. Most children's literature seldom even gets near to this point. Anyone who has taught the Alice books as children's literature has heard the complaint that these books give children nightmares. The only possible response to this complaint is that children have nightmares more terrible than anything *Alice in Wonderland* can hope to be. Still, if one agrees with Bashevis-Singer

2. Children and Other Talking Animals

that if we are going to torture anyone we would prefer to torture adults, then it is difficult to conceive of a children's literature that is not "simpler" than adult literature and it is difficult to conceive of a children's literature much more "complex" than *Alice in Wonderland*.

The problem of placing *Alice in Wonderland* as children's literature points to the difficulties inherent in trying to locate a fixed boundary when dealing with concepts such as simple/complex, child/adult, or semiotic/symbolic. There is no moment when one clearly passes from one to the other. On the other hand, it is possible to locate the stylistic changes that occur when one moves from one polarity to the other. I have provided some examples of the nature of this transformation in the work of C. S. Lewis. A close analysis of the changes that occur when one adapts *Gulliver's Travels* for children would be another test case for anyone interested in questions of body/language and irony in children's literature. The Alice books are clearly another arena for contention and Deleuze's comments are a salutary antidote to critics like Shavit who argue that *Alice in Wonderland* is too complex for children. In her book, Shavit shows us clearly and in some detail how one must adapt *Alice in Wonderland* in order to make it acceptable to the "children's system." One must leave out all those elements that are obscure or ambiguous. One must interpret everything, demonstrate complete mastery of the text:

> In the original *Alice in Wonderland*, Carroll intentionally made it impossible to determine whether things happen in a dream or in reality.... The transfer into children's literature resulted in a simplified presentation that insisted on a clear distinction between reality and fantasy. For instance, one adaptation opens in the following way: "Once upon a time there was a little girl called Alice, *who had a very curious dream*" (Modern Productions, my italics). Another adaptation ends in a phrase which leaves no doubt that it was anything but a dream: "'I am glad to be back where things are really what they seem,' said Alice, as she woke up from her strange Wonderful dream" (Disney) [125–26; parenthetical references are Shavit's].

It is just a dream; there are no monsters; it is just a story. After you take everything else away you take the story too. You interpret, you simplify, you limit, until the text achieves utter opacity, utter superficiality, until there is nothing left to get your teeth into. When there is nothing left to chew then the text is palatable enough for children. To be fair to Shavit, she does not say that she approves of this procedure; she has deliberately "avoided traditional evaluative questions" (xi). But one point I have wished to make in this chapter is that without evaluation there is no interpretation. In his article, "On Three Ways of Writing for Children," C.S. Lewis begins with the assumption that he knows what makes a children's story "good." All the many writers for children who deny the difference do so because the question of evaluation inevitably arises. I would suggest that the real point of this denial is to assert that when a children's story is good its difference from an adult story is insignificant in the face of the great difference between literature and non-literature. Fortunately, there are writers for children who understand this truth and who resist the inevitability of mastery by putting the abject in play. These are the writers who understand what all good writers understand, that all of us, child and adult alike, are just talking animals.

3

Playing with Books

In the first chapter, I provided a phylogenetic account of the rise of children's literature and the concept of modern childhood based upon the historical consequences of the spread of literacy. The spread of literacy constructs the pre-literate child as the Other and in doing so makes psychoanalysis possible. In the second chapter, I provided an ontogenetic account, based upon psychoanalytical theories of child development, of how writers find a language with which to speak to children. By emphasizing the oral and the pictorial, writers for children attempt to find a language that flattens irony and effaces the abject. In this chapter, I will construct a rhetoric of the children's novel based upon a study of the nature of their play. The curtailing of play that is the result of the spread of literacy resulted in a compensatory valuing of play that is the foundation for the construction of childhood innocence. Specifically, the children's novel was invented in an attempt to translate the phantasmagoric play of pre-literate children into the literate form of the novel, a translation that most clearly takes place in the Alice books. Lewis Carroll, because he knew how to play like a child, was able to invent the children's novel and in doing so provided the rhetorical model for all subsequent children's novelists, a rhetoric based upon a tension between the idyllic and the didactic. But before we can understand the nature of that rhetoric we must understand the nature of children's play.

The argument that follows was inspired by the philosophy of Gilles Deleuze, and most specifically by *The Logic of Sense* which is founded upon an analysis of the works of Lewis Carroll. I do not pretend to explain Deleuze and my use of him is very selective. If one wishes to understand Deleuze one would do well to read Brian Massumi's *A User's Guide to Capitalism and Schizophrenia* which is not so much an attempt to explain Deleuze as to translate him into other terms or, as Massumi says "to play *Capitalism and Schizophrenia* the way its authors suggest" (9). I also intend to translate Deleuze into other terms by making use of the work of Gregory Bateson, an American social scientist who developed a theory of play that also led to a theory of schizophrenia. I have also found useful *Gilles Deleuze: An Apprenticeship in Philosophy*, in which Michael Hardt explains how Deleuze constructed his anti–Hegelian materialism through a selective reading of Bergson, Nietzsche, and Spinoza. For Deleuze "difference" is not negation but "the principle of the positive *movement* of being," defined "by a notion of efficient causality" that avoids both the final cause of Platonic idealism and the material cause of mechanism. As Hardt puts it "opposition, Deleuze claims, is too crude a notion to capture the nuances that mark real differences; it hangs loosely on reality like baggy clothes" (113). Since I have always thought the dialectic to be mystical nonsense, I naturally find this an appealing philosophy. Also appealing is that this is a materialism that admits of the possibility of free will, though that is perhaps too grand a term; rather it admits of the possibility of novelty, of chance, of the lucky throw of the dice.

The "Sense" that is referred to in *The Logic of Sense* is a term with more than one meaning. On the most basic level, it could simply be translated as "meaning" and the library quite sensibly categorizes Deleuze's book as a work of semantics but it is much more than that. "Sense" could also be translated as "sensation" and his work provides a very convincing account of how bodies acquire minds, though, as Mussoni points out, this account has "nothing to do with the phenomenological concept of originary experience" (161). Finally, "Sense" could be understood to refer to the various codes immanent in material reality which envelop the political Subject, what Bourdieu calls *habitus*, and what I would be inclined to call "common sense," though that is always a term of abuse in Deleuze. Frankly, I cannot be as fervent an enemy of common sense as Deleuze is but I am not primarily interested in his politics and so will return to his semantics. Deleuze develops a theory of meaning by positing an interesting ontological entity called the "event." One common theory of how language means is to

3. Playing with Books

assert that propositions correspond to facts. Deleuze tries to solve the many problems associated with this theory by simply replacing the duality of the proposition/fact with the monism of the event. If I may use an analogy, the event is like the soap molecule which works because half of it dissolves in water and the other half in oil. The event subsists in both the material state of affairs and in language. Events always exist on the flat surface where the depths of the body meet the heights of the mind. The event is an act of becoming; it is always in play.[1]

In *The Logic of Sense*, Gilles Deleuze devotes his "Tenth Series of the Ideal Game" to an analysis of the Caucus-race from *Alice in Wonderland*, which he describes as the "ideal game" that produces "events" in opposition to the usual game that produces only winners and losers. I would reinterpret this distinction as the distinction between the play of children and adults. The fundamental difference between children and adults is that whereas children play, adults play games. In order to understand what Deleuze is saying about the caucus race, it might be useful to turn to Bateson's article, "A Theory of Play and Fantasy."[2] He begins where Deleuze begins, with the philosophical attempt of Whitehead and Russell to resolve certain paradoxes that have plagued philosophers for centuries, such as the paradox of the Cretan Epimenides: All Cretans are liars. Bateson's hypothesis is that statements of this kind are basically of the same type as the message "this is play." He begins by pointing out that "human verbal communication can operate and always does operate at many contrasting levels of abstraction" (119). There is a meta-discourse whose subject is language itself (meta-linguistic) and the relationship between speakers (meta-communicative). One example of the latter would be the message "this is play." Bateson observes that "if we speculate about the evolution of communication, it is evident that a very important stage in this evolution occurs when the organism gradually ceases to respond quite 'automatically' to the mood-signs of another and becomes able to recognize the sign as a signal: that is, to recognize that the other individual's and its own signals are only signals which can be trusted, distrusted, falsified, denied, amplified, corrected and so forth" (119). What he is describing is the evolution of what Deleuze calls Sense, and both agree that this step, both phylogenetically and ontogenetically, is the step of play. One only arrives at Sense by passing through Nonsense.

Bateson arrived at his theory from watching two young monkeys playing at a zoo. He saw that they were "engaged in an interactive sequence of which unit actions or signals were similar to but not the same as those of combat. It was evident, even to the human observer, that the sequence as a whole was not combat, and evident to the human observer that to the participant monkeys this was 'not combat'" (120). In his "examination of the message 'this is play'" he came to "the realization that this message contains those elements which necessarily generate a paradox of the Russellian or Epimenides type—a negative statement containing an implicit negative meta-statement," a statement that would sound like this: "These actions, in which we now engage, do not denote what would be denoted by those actions which these actions denote," or, more specifically, "The playful nip denotes the bite, but it does not denote what would be denoted by the bite" (121). He concludes:

> According to the Theory of Logical Types such a message is of course inadmissible, because the word "denote" is being used in two degrees of abstraction, and these two uses are treated as synonymous. But all that we learn from such a criticism is that it would be bad natural history to expect the mental processes and communicative habits of mammals to conform to the logician's ideal. Indeed, if human thought and communication always conformed to the logician's ideal, Russell would not—in fact could not—have formulated the ideal [121].

To restate Bateson's insight more simply, if with less logical precision, when we play, we do not mean what we mean or, to put it even more simply, we pretend. But in simplifying the concept of play we must not forget what a strange and paradoxical thing it is and how important an evolutionary development it was. As Bateson points out it is "characteristic of unconscious or 'primary process' thinking that the thinker is unable to discriminate between 'some' and 'all,' and unable to discriminate between 'not all' and 'none'" (124). Play is the framing device that allows us to step from that pre-logical state into Sense because "the discrimination between 'play' and 'not play,' like the discrimination between fantasy and non-fantasy, is certainly a function of secondary processes, or 'ego.' Within the dream the dreamer is usually unaware that he is dreaming, and within 'play' he must often be reminded that 'this is play'" (124–5). Bateson concludes

3. Playing with Books

that the play frame as here used as an explanatory principle implies a special combination of primary and secondary processes. This, however, is related to what was said earlier, when it was argued that play marks a step forward in the evolution of communication — the crucial step in the discovery of map-territory relations. In primary process, map and territory are equated; in secondary process, they can be discriminated. In play, they are both equated and discriminated [125].

In regard to this observation one cannot help but to think of that marvelous joke in *Sylvie and Bruno* in which the ideal map is created by making the distance between points in the territory exactly correspond to the distance between points on the map. Unfortunately the map can never be consulted for fear of blocking the sun. Carroll, that master of nonsense and victim of nostalgia, is pointing out that once one has taken the "step" into Sense, Sense wants to step back, to reintegrate what has been divided and to achieve an original oneness that has been lost. Play plays both ways and recognition of that fact is necessary to understand how play constructs a rhetoric for the children's novel but first we must say more about the nature of play and its paradoxes.

In *The Ambiguity of Play*, Brian Sutton-Smith gives an overview of the remarkable diversity of forms of play and of the diversity of theories about it, which he calls "rhetorics" to distinguish them from scientific theories. His book is also a critique of what is probably the dominant rhetoric among social scientists, what he calls the "progressive" rhetoric, associated with Piaget and others, who think play is a stage in child development that is discarded upon becoming an adult. So skeptical is Sutton-Smith of this theory that there are times when he comes close to asserting that there is no difference between the play of children and the play of adults. To some degree I share this scepticism but I cannot agree that there is no difference between the play of children and adults and indeed, this difference is essential to my theory of the difference between the adult novel and the children's novel. But we need not think of the adult as being simply the negation of childish play but, rather, merely one end of a spectrum of various different forms of play, moreover a spectrum that can be traversed in both directions. Thus, though it is certainly true that when children play they are in the process of becoming adult, it is also true that when adults play they are in the process of becoming child. Play plays both ways.

In his article "On the Uses and Abuses of Literature for Life," Gregg Lambert asks the question "Why does Deleuze seem to love children and writers so much? Or rather, why are writers so often described in the process of 'becoming-child'?" The answer is "because the child knows how to play (that is, to experiment), and the writer in the process of 'becoming-child' does not imitate children but repeats a block of childhood and allows it to pass through language" (145). Lambert points out that this is "Freud's original intuition" in his "Creative Writers and Day-Dreaming" in which

> Freud noticed that the child, contrary to the adult, plays in the full light of day, plays openly, and even causes his or her creations to transform the external world of perception. In contrast, adults can only play in secret and often actively hide their creative activities — even from themselves! The "unconscious" is a kind of hidden or secret form of play, a game that goes on in the darkness and randomly chooses its own players. Adults are, first and foremost, guilty; they have lost the innocence of play, have repressed it, meaning also that they aggressively prohibit all "public displays" of such activity by transforming the nature of play itself into an unconscious source of pleasure. Freud used this distinction primarily to distinguish the play of child from the fantasy life of the adult in order to show that the origin of the phantasm itself has this sense of "hiding," a guilty source of satisfaction for the adult who can only play in secret (and alone). At the same time, even Freud noticed that the artist constitutes the exceptional case to this internalisation and continues to play out in the open [145–46].

What Freud is alluding to is the empirical fact that what pre-oedipal children are doing when they participate in phantasmagoric play is essentially daydreaming out loud. His point could be extended more generally to assert that all healthy adults are ones who, like writers, know how to play like a child. Moreover, though what he says is true of daydreaming, it is not true that adults are unable to play openly.[3] The real difference is that when adults play openly they, unlike young children, tend to do so within the strictures of a rule-based game. I will return to this point but first I would like to return to Bateson's theory. One problem with his theory is that it would seem to restrict the category of play to activities involving more than one person since meta-communicative discourse, by definition, always involves the framing of a relationship between at least two persons. But this only appears to be a problem and actually leads us to insist upon yet another paradoxical element of play: play always doubles the subject. Within the play frame there is always a person who plays and a person who is played. This fact is most obvious in the case of sophisticated singular play such as daydreaming but it also true in even the most simple of singular physical play. The child who whirls about in order to become dizzy is not the child who is whirled; indeed, that would seem to be the very point of the game, the becoming other to oneself. Thus, just as in play one does not mean what one means, so also one is not who one is. Of course, in play groups the situation becomes somewhat more complex and in pre-school pretend play the players must not only be players playing roles but also their own audience. The more popular and skillful players will also take on the roles of author and director. The result is an intricate improvisation involving a complex interplay between context and text that begins to verge upon the kind of performance that takes place when a child reads a book, with the advantage that it is there before our eyes to read.

Bateson extends his analysis of play as paradoxical meta-discourse to other activities such as threat, histrionics, spectatorship, ritual, psychotherapy and art. Indeed, play may simply be the principle of all creative activity, including the activity of constructing a theory of play. Also, as I indicated above, it is necessary to distinguish between play and a game. "This is play" is not a message that precedes a text; rather it is a "context" that "frames" a text. Context and text are simultaneously and constantly in play together. Helen Schwartzman, in describing Bateson's theory, emphasizes this distinction:

> In games, the paradoxical reference system of play is embodied in a codified system of rules that organize the use of objects, space, and time, as well as player activities. Here it is not necessary for metacommunication to occur continually to define or "frame" the player's actions, as this is achieved by the game's explicit rule structure. In games, the ambiguity and paradox inherent in play, which necessitates constant metacommunication for maintenance of the event, has been "ruled" out [219].

This distinction seems very similar to Deleuze's if we understand "the ideal game" of the caucus-race to be what Schwartzman calls play. Moreover, he calls the caucus-race "a game of innocence" and though he claims "it would amuse no one" (60), in fact, it is precisely the kind of game that amuses writers and children. Actually, I do not think that the distinction between play and a game is an absolute one, but rather a matter of degree that defines a spectrum. Even the most rigid game is clearly not work, but rather, as Deleuze correctly observes, a "caricature" (59) of work.

The distinction between play and a game is one that should be of special interest to literary critics. The question we might ask is whether reading a book is more like playing or like playing a game. I suspect that the predominant answer has been the latter and I will give one example of its articulation. In *The Elements of Poetry*, Robert Scholes asserts that "poetry is essentially a game, with artificial rules, and it takes two — a writer and reader — to play it" (1). I have no problem with such a view of literature but it does have certain consequences. Reading tends to become agonistic as literary critics wrestle with authors to wrest their meaning from them. They then turn on each other in an endless, and enjoyable, game of one-upmanship. Also such a view of literature tends to the view that the book produces a representation whose relationship to the world is that of map to territory. A game can be described abstractly by listing its rules, delineating good moves and defining a range of possible outcomes. Games can be categorized into different kinds or genres. Play is not without rules but they are often implicit and immanent in the actual performance. Play is more provisional and experimental. Of course, unlike the play of pre-schoolers, a book is clearly a thing created by someone other than yourself and having a certain fixed form, but Deleuze has invited us to think of this thing, not as an authorized map, but as an "assemblage" or "machine" designed to create chains of percepts and affects. The writer constructs this machine and invites the reader to play with it. This is a view particularly appealing to the critic of children's literature because ever since the eighteenth century we have increasingly been providing our children with manufactured objects to play with. These fall into three categories: toys, games, and books. It is natural for the literary critic to privilege the last but it might be more interesting to think of the book as just another toy. As a consequence, we would cease to ask what this book is about but, rather, what does it do and what do children do with it. An understanding of how children play with their books will lead us to a rhetoric of the children's novel.

One danger in taking play as one's subject is the inclination to

3. Playing with Books

idealize it, to imagine that children live in some state of ludic nirvana.[4] I have perhaps already taken the first step in that direction in my original aphorism that asserts that whereas children play, adults play games but I have qualified that assertion by stating that this is not an absolute division but a matter of degree. Moreover, I have resisted any idealization of play by locating it in the material reality of our evolutionary history. It is difficult to idealize play when you remember that it is something that all higher animals do. Finally, the idyllic is always counter balanced by the didactic, which is the recognition that play is dangerous. Play is dangerous because it often involves the assertion of an illusory competence, as any parents know who have watched their children in the playground and wisely repressed the desire to intervene. Play is also dangerous because it involves all the cruelty of social interaction unmasked by the routines of adult civility, the complex negotiation whereby children enter and participate in play groups. Again it would be wise for parents not to intervene. Play is also dangerous because it constitutes a perversion of the "good sense" and "common sense" that constitute adult reality.[5] But, ultimately, play is dangerous because it is not work, understanding work to constitute that which we must do to survive. Thus play must always come to an end, though the highest imaginable human felicity would be to imagine a social reality in which work and play were indistinguishable.

Following from its role in our evolutionary history, we would also wish to locate play in the ontogenetic development of the biological body. Freud, of course, had a theory of play and one which, as we saw above, distinguishes between children and adults. Freud's most famous analysis of play occurs in *Beyond the Pleasure Principle*, in his analysis of the *fort/da* game played by his eighteen month grandson as a way of dealing with the tensions arising from separation anxiety. We could, however, go back even further to find the primal scene of play. Instead of crying the infant sticks its thumb into its mouth. Here we have the basic logic of play.[6] The action certainly does not denote the action that would be denoted by the action that the action denotes. The playful thumb denotes the nipple, but it does not denote what would be denoted by the nipple. One could perhaps object that this is not really play because it lacks the doubling effect and, indeed, that doubling must wait for the mirror stage; however, there is already an inkling here of what is to come. The thumb is not the nipple but merely a substitution for what I lack. But the nipple does not come when I demand it; it is not *mine*; it belongs to some *other*. The thumb is *mine*; it comes when I demand it; I am its master. This action, then, is one of the first of the many throws of the dice that make up the game of life. It is the first step is a series of steps that leads one out of the body through Nonsense into Sense.

The Freudian theory of play leads to a theory of reading. One submerges oneself in a text in order to "play out" certain tensions; one plays out in fantasy what is lacking in realty or one vicariously plays out emotional trauma to the end of purging it. This is a powerful theory of reading but it is not entirely satisfactory because it neglects the social aspect of play, the sense that when children play they are "playing at" the various roles that their culture provides them. The notion that play is part of the socialization process and that the pretend play of children is a practicing of the roles they will need as adults seems to appeal to common sense and is probably the most widely held view of the nature of play, especially among sociologists and anthropologists. When considered as a theory of reading, the social constructionist view is certainly the favorite among literary critics who seem endlessly satisfied with analysing children's books as pernicious prescriptions of racism, sexism and class superiority. Apparently the didacticism that is a vice in writers of children's books is a virtue in the critics of them. In fact, an analysis of children's play does reveal what seems to be an alarming degree of conservatism. Thus Judith Rich Harris tells the story of the girl playing doctor who insisted the doctor had to be male and the nurse female despite the fact that her own mother was a doctor and, as she points out, when children play house they recreate Ozzie and Harriet (71).[7] There is, however, an alternative explanation of this phenomenon and one which resists the social constructionist theory of play and reading by insisting upon the nonsensical nature of play. Play is not only paradoxical but also profoundly parodic.

Biologists have always found play perplexing since, at first sight, it appears counter-adaptive. As Robert Fagan points out, the play of animals

> includes repeated re-structuring of functioning behavioural procedures, behaviour which appears to maximize inefficiency and instability, pro-

longed fights in which attack engenders attack though the chance of injury is small, and puzzling variations of hunting, fighting, and escape routines which could never serve to capture prey, to injure or drive off a rival, or to flee from a predator [97].

In other words, play is not practice; it does not imitate adult behaviour but parodies it. If you actually tried to hunt in the way you play at hunting, you would starve to death. The conclusion that Fagan, and other biologists, have arrived at is that play is "innovative potential" (98). If Fagan is right then the adaptive value of play is that it is the behaviour that enables mammals, and especially human beings, to change their behaviour in response to a changing environment or to change their environment through the invention of technologies. Play is so odd because it plays both ways simultaneously. It deconstructs Sense, that is, destroys and constructs at the same time. It is the principle of all creative thinking and if adults want to think creatively they must become like children.

The pretend play of children between the ages of three and six has the same parodic elements as the play of animals described above. Children do not imitate adult behaviour; rather they exaggerate, repeat and recombine elements of it. If we return to Harris's description of pre-oedipal phantasmagoric play that I quoted in the first chapter, we are now prepared to see the parodic elements in it. She writes:

> children — even preschoolers — are remarkably good at switching from one personality to another. Perhaps they can do this more easily than older people. Have you ever listened to a couple of four-year-olds playing House?
>
> STEPHIE *(in her normal voice, to Caitlin)*: I'll be the mommy.
> STEPHIE *(in her unctuous mommy voice)*: All right, Baby, drink your bottle and be a good little baby.
> STEPHIE *(whispering)*: Pretend you don't like it.
> CAITLIN *(in her baby voice)*: Don't want botta!
> STEPHIE *(in her unctuous mommy voice)*: Drink it sweetheart. It's good for you!
>
> Stephie plays three parts here: author/producer, stage director, and the starring role of Mommy [58].

Harris reads this scene sociologically as role playing and, like most sociologists, assumes that the older or more dominant child would assume the superior "Mommy" role. But, even though Baby only gets to repeat one line, there is clearly a great deal of rebellious and regressive fun to be had in adopting this position and Mommy is the victim of vicious parody.[8] The scene does not correspond to reality since real mothers do not need to force bottles upon babies nor do real babies deny them. Nor could a real baby articulate that denial. The scene exaggerates, repeats, and recombines elements of real behavior. It is parodic. It also demonstrates the same rhetoric that Nodelman identifies as the rhetoric of the children's book, the setting up of a resonating tension between the adult and child subject positions. Thus it is not surprising that this scene of pre-literate play can be directly translated into the play of the book in chapter six of *Alice in Wonderland*, in which we see the Duchess nursing her baby in a manner likely to kill it until she flings it at Alice who is thus forced into the Mommy position until she can escape when Baby turns into a pig. The genius of Lewis Carroll is that he knew how to play like a four-year-old girl.

In *Pretend Play as Improvisation*, R. Keith Sawyer provides a rigorous empirical study of the phantasmagoric play of pre-school children based upon a year of observation and audio taping of that play in a day-care center. Unfortunately, Sawyer decided to concentrate on indoor play because in the case of the outdoor play of children "their rapid movement made it hard to acquire audiotapes" (60–61). This decision is unfortunate since outdoor play is the kind most likely to be represented in the children's novel and I suspect it is likely to be more dangerous and perverse than indoor play, though I have no empirical evidence to support that suspicion, only my own experience and common sense. In any case, I do not think the difference to be of great importance and I shall ignore it. The one advantage of indoor play is that the children "tended to engage in more verbal play interactions" (61) and so it is possible to imagine that this verbal play would directly translate into the textual play of the children's novel. Indeed, Sawyer identifies three "performance styles" that bear a remarkable similarity to three of the major genres of the children's novel that developed in the nineteenth century: the girl's domestic novel, animal fantasy, and the boy's adventure story.

Corresponding to the girl's domestic novel is what Sawyer calls "direct style" in which "the child acts out a play role that is different from the roles of his interlocutors" (83). This is a theatrical style with the children playing different domestic roles and it is the preferred play style of girls though boys will occasionally be invited to participate as "visitors," subject to the sufferance of the girls. In Sawyer's study this play was always realistic and "*fantasy role enactment*" (84) only appeared in the other two play styles. Corresponding to animal fantasy is the "indirect style" in which "the child enacts the play role through the medium of a toy figure such as a zoo animal or a dinosaur" (84). The child plays the figure and gives it a voice. This style does not appear to be gender specific. Corresponding to the boy's adventure story is the "collective style" in which "a group of children collectively perform a single play role" (85). This is the preferred play style of boys and there is already here a hint of what Eve Sedgwick calls the "homosocial" as the boys form a corporate entity to construct a narrative of heroic adventure. In the example Sawyer gives, three boys are preparing an epic journey into space. They are each building their own rocket ship and the dynamics of their interaction is revealed in the passage that follows, a passage whose ethical significance hardly requires further commentary:

> EDDY: I am making a rocket like ...
> ARTIE: That's not even a rocket, that's a small rocket. Mine is bigger than yours
> EDDY: Mine is even bigger, ... [85].

Even at the age of five, boys will be boys.[9]

The connection between these play styles and the realm of the novel is explicitly evoked by Sawyer:

> In Bakhtin's terminology, each of these styles could be referred to as a way of *voicing* a character. In the same way that a novelist writing dialogue has to "voice" as the fictional character, a child performing a dramatic pretend role voices as that play character. Like the novelist, this provides the child with opportunities for double-voicing, or *dialogism*; the child can blend an out-of-play voice with the play character's voice, and use this as a strategy for metapragmatic negotiation [86].

Sawyer also points out that "children never switched from one style to another during a group episode," a fact that suggests the inherent conservatism of oral play. This generic rigidity is not to be found in the children's novel which quite happily crosses these boundaries but this is to be expected since the translation from the orality of play to the textuality of the children's novel encourages an erosion of generic boundaries. The Alice books contain all three possibilities since they contain domestic scenes, tea parties and croquet matches, talking animals and Alice's adventures. The Alice books capture the pure essence of play and contain all the generic possibilities of the children's novel *in potentia*.

If the study of the pretend play of pre-schoolers can point the way to how children play with books, it would be useful to gather other and more direct empirical evidence. Unfortunately the only evidence of that kind I have is the statement of a mother who told me she was reading *Alice in Wonderland* to her five-year-old son who was enjoying the experience. Apparently what he liked was how rude the adults were to Alice. Since this critical comment is considerably more profound that what I typically get from my students, I can only conclude that he, unlike my students, knew how to play the *Alice in Wonderland* game and the reason he knew is because it is like his own pretend play. He clearly recognizes the existence of a tension between child and adult but more than that he recognizes that the double has been redoubled, that the adults are childish and the child is wise. Proponents of both psychological and sociological views of reading tend to agree that the pleasure of reading lies in identifying with the protagonist, that the book is a kind of second-hand daydream, but such a view cannot explain the pleasure of our five-year-old. No child wants to be the victim of teasing. He plays the wise Alice. And more than that the pleasure of reading does not lie in being fixed in one position but in the constant play of various subject positions and the basic double of child/adult is constantly being transformed by the play of other doubles such as animal/human, large/small, and, according to Deleuze, most centrally to both this book and to the human condition, the doubling of things to be eaten with words to be spoken.

What I am proposing, then, is a theory of reading that is neither sociological nor psychological, that does not understand reading as either socialization or therapy. The theory of play that I am proposing is one that allows us to understand reading as an intellectual activity in its own right. Deleuze has invited literary critics to cease to play their usual games and, by becoming child, to recapture the pure pleasure of reading because the transformative power of the book lies in its

3. Playing with Books

existence as an object of play. The task that remains is to describe the nature of that play.

If Nodelman is right and the defining characteristic of the children's book is a tension between the idyllic and the didactic then the fundamental subject of every children's novel, no matter what else it might be about, is play itself. The idyllic is nothing but the assertion of the value of play; the didactic is nothing but a warning about the dangers of play. The adult's nostalgic desire to return to a state of play generates the idyllic; the child's will to power, the desire to master the rules of the game, generates the didactic. The reader of a children's book is caught in the middle, is simultaneously an adult who knows how to play and a child who knows that play must end. The writer of a good book for children is someone who achieves a certain poise in balancing these contrary tendencies. Shifting the balance toward the idyllic generates a sentimental pathos; shifting toward the didactic generates a neurotic anxiety. At either extreme the children's novel approaches but never reaches the tragic. The ideal writer for children is one poised in the middle, a humorist. If the characteristic tonality of the adult novel is irony, that of the children's novel is humor. This is not to say that all children's novels are funny but that at their core they all contain a kernel of humor and this is the reason that the Alice books set the basic formula for the children's novel. They are fundamentally about nothing but play and to extent they are not nightmares, they are humorous.

It is no accident that Gilles Deleuze chose the Alice books as the ground upon which to build *The Logic of Sense*. In order to understand Sense one must understand Nonsense or play. He dedicates chapter nineteen to the subject of humor and ends that chapter with a statement that might make clearer what I mean by asserting humor to be fundamental to the children's novel:

> Nonsense and sense have done away with their relation of dynamic opposition in order to enter into the co-presence of a static genesis — as the nonsense of the surface and the sense which hovers over it. The tragic and the ironic give way to a new value, that of humor. For if irony is the co-extensiveness of being with the individual, or of the I with representation, humor is the co-extensiveness of sense and non-sense. Humor is the art of the surfaces and of the doubles, of nomadic singularities and of the always displaced aleatory point; it is the art of the static genesis, the savoire-faire of the pure event, and the "fourth person singular" — with every

> signification, denotation, and manifestation suspended, all height and depth abolished [141]..

To translate what he is saying here would probably require a chapter of its own so I am only going to extract what I need, the assertion that "humor is the art of the surfaces and of the doubles." Humor is created when nonsense and sense collaborate, "enter into the co-presence of a static generator," which, in the case of the children's novel, is an idyllic/didactic machine. Nodelman provides a list of the doubles that are typically evoked in the children's book all of which are part of the general tension between the idyllic and the didactic. The first double he mentions is human and animal and more specifically this can be evoked by the double that particularly fascinates both Carroll and Deleuze, speaking and eating, the question of whether you are going to be presented to the mutton or eat the mutton. Food jokes of this kind have become a mainstay of the children's novel, just as essential to Nesbit and Dahl as they were to Carroll. The point of the joke is that the human animal, to the extent that it speaks, reaches up and, to the extent that it eats, reaches down.

The movement to the heights is the movement toward the mind, God or platonic ideas, a movement that Deleuze refers to as a "Platonic conversion." The movement to the depths is the movement into the body, referred to as a "pre-Socratic subversion." The Stoic, who is a humorist like the Zen master, plays on the surface, a "philosophical operation" that Deleuze playfully refers to as "perversion," and one which "implies an extraordinary art of surfaces" (133). Irony reaches up and down. In the ironic adult novel the reader aspires to the magisterial heights of the Austen narrator and, in the process, constructs the "individual," a rich, complex, three-dimensional subjectivity that looks down upon others. At the same time, however, this structure cannot be maintained because it is grounded in the body and its inevitable failures; it must collapse into the chaos of abjection that it is founded upon and this is a truth that the novel also conveys. Thus the adult novel both converts and subverts at the same time. The children's novel, on the other hand, perverts, as it always operates on the surface, that flat plane of Nonsense where language and matter meet, where the mouth that speaks is not afraid to be a mouth that eats.

It might be useful at this point to digress for a moment from this argument in order to provide a parallel analysis of the difference between irony and humor, and one that is historically more specific. Deleuze, as a philosopher, tends to take a wide view of human history, one that takes us back beyond the dawn of civilization, but one can see similar ideas in the more specific historical context that Bakhtin explores in *Rabelais and his World*, the history of Western Europe in its transition from the medieval to the modern. Through his study of Rabelais, Bakhtin attempts to recreate a vital folk culture which manifested itself through various forms of "carnival" that express the humor of "the grotesque body," concepts that clearly have some affinity to "play" and "perversion." Humor is the immanent laughter of the body and as such is seen as "low" and "superficial" in contrast to irony, the "high" and "deep" laughter of the transcendent mind, but it is really humor that is the creative principle. As Bakhtin puts it "the grotesque liberates man from all the forms of inhuman necessity" because

> historically the idea of necessity is relative and variable. The principle of laughter and the carnival spirit on which the grotesque is based destroys this limited seriousness and all pretense of an extratemporal meaning and unconditioned value of necessity. It frees human consciousness, thought, and imagination for new potentialities [49].

In terms of the history of Western culture, the construction of the bourgeois individual results in an overdetermined socialization in which the individual is alienated both from her body and the larger, grotesque body of the people. The grotesque body of carnival which generates humor is replaced by the individual body which generates irony. Irony is simply the manifestation of this alienation and over the last four hundred years has been canonized as superior to the mere coarse, vulgar humor of the once vital folk culture. Of course, the grotesque body cannot be entirely eradicated since it is the real body of the species and thus continues to be rediscovered. Bakhtin analyses Romanticism as such a moment of rediscovery, but always subsumed to the triumphant individual, which is why Romanticism must always fail. The child is "discovered" at the same historical moment and this discovery gives rise to the children's novel, which, in its purest form, is always a celebration of the grotesque body but in a very attenuated form. The children's novel represents a brief moment of free play before its inevitable loss in the triumph of the didactic.

To return to the terms used by Deleuze, the writer for children must be a pervert, which is not too surprising since children are perverts themselves. I am not merely evoking this term in a Freudian sense though it is true that pre-oedipal children are polymorphous perverse and in the few cultures that do not repress their sexuality they will quite freely play with themselves and each other as freely as they play at anything else.[10] I am more centrally evoking a sociological idea of perversion that is closer to the first definition that my dictionary gives to the term "perverse": "willfully determined or disposed to go counter to what is expected or desired; contrary." It is from the Latin *perversus*, meaning "turned the wrong way." Children are perverse in the sense that they are turned the wrong way, which is to say turned away from the adult. This sense of the perversion of children is perhaps best captured in the following passage from the prologue of Kenneth Grahame's *The Golden Age*:

> These elders, our betters by a trick of chance, commanded no respect, but only a certain blend of envy — of their good luck — and pity — for their inability to make use of it. Indeed, it was one of the most hopeless features in their character (when we troubled ourselves to waste a thought on them: which wasn't often) that, having absolute licence to indulge in the pleasures of life, they could get no good of it. They might dabble in the pond all day, hunt the chickens, climb trees in the most uncompromising Sunday clothes; they were free to issue forth and buy gunpowder in the full eye of the sun — free to fire cannons and explode mines on the lawn: yet they never did any one of those things [2].

The Golden Age is not a children's novel but it does describe a childhood that is a more realistic, if still somewhat exaggerated, version of what Carroll presents and which becomes, in a softer, more sentimental form, the standard version for the first half of the twentieth century. This is the childhood of Nesbit, Potter, Montgomery, Ransome, Blyton, Milne, Seuss and Estes, to mention some of the better-known names. It is sentimentalized by some more than others but basically the child is treated humorously as a pervert totally dedicated to a play that is transgressive and anarchic and though the representation is playfully exaggerated it is not too much different from the actual play of children.[11]

In the children's novel the idyllic is evoked by the contrariness of children at play. At times in *The Golden Age* the nostalgia is Wordsworthian but most often it is simply a paean to children's play and a satirical comment of the inability of adults to enter that world. Of course, the joke plays both ways equally and the children are equally mocked for their perversity. The rejection of Wordsworthian nostalgia is made quite explicit in *Dream Days* at the beginning of "The Reluctant Dragon." The children find footprints in the snow which they think belong to a dragon and Grahame prefaces the story with the comment that such are "unfailing provokers of sentiment," alludes to a poem by Wordsworth on the subject which the children "didn't think very highly" of, and ends with the observation that "footsteps in the sand, now, were quite another matter, and we grasped Crusoe's attitude of mind much more easily than Wordsworth's. Excitement and mystery, curiosity and suspense-these were the only sentiments that tracks, whether in sand or snow, were able to arouse in us" (106–7). The children's novel has no use for the idealized child, only for the child who knows how to play dangerously because that is how all children actually play.

Of course, it could be argued that I am being naive and that this representation is merely an arbitrary fiction serving some ideological function, not an accurate description of the real play of children. I have offered empirical evidence to support the contention that children's play is perverse and to that I can add the evidence of my own childhood and that of my children. The childhood that Grahame describes at the end of the nineteenth century is not much different from the childhood that I experienced at the middle of the twentieth century. I walked the trestle of an abandoned railway bridge, risking a fall that would probably have killed me. I lit fires in the woods surrounding our suburb, thus threatening its very existence. I used my chemistry set to try to make nitroglycerin but fortunately failed. I joined a gang of boys who endlessly built forts. One of them was an elaborate, camouflaged underground fort. One boy told his father about this construction, presumably because he was proud of it, whereupon his father destroyed it, claiming it was too dangerous. Needless to say, that boy was expelled from our group for violating the cardinal rule of childhood: never tell your secrets to the "natives." By the end of the twentieth century not much has seemed to change. My two boys joined a male horde that roved the fields and woods while I, now a native myself, prudently turned a blind eye. Now that they are adolescents they can tell me what they did and what they did was build fires and forts and play endless war games. I recognize, of course, that this is a privileged childhood. Not all children were like me in enjoying access to woods and fields and creeks or in being in walking distance of a vast lake that could only be reached by climbing down dangerous clay bluffs, but that fact is irrelevant to the point that I am making. No matter what their socioeconomic circumstances, no matter how bleak is their environment, unless they are abused or abandoned, children must and will play and that play, by its very nature, will be paradoxical, parodic and perverse.[12]

I am not claiming that Grahame's childhood has no ideological function. Clearly, he is describing bourgeois childhood but that fact is not very interesting. To state that children's novels inculcate bourgeois values is merely to state the obvious. What is more interesting to observe is that while the children's novel is in play what it presents is a parody and perversion of bourgeois values. The children are all properly dressed in clothes indicative of their class which they promptly dirty and tear. They are constantly scrounging money from anxious uncles which they promptly spend on candy and gunpowder. They rampage through the neighborhood trespassing upon and attempting to destroy the property of others. Of course, in the end, the didactic will triumph. Play will be seen as dangerous and it will come to an end. The girls will all be transformed into Florence Nightingales or Angels of the household and the boys into Capitalist entrepreneurs or managers of Empire but what the children's novel reveals is just how much processing is involved in that transformation and in doing so the children's novel, in its existence as an object of play, offers the hope that what has been done can be undone and redone because play is that which deconstructs Sense.

I would not want, however, to overstate this position. The children's novel is no Deleuzian "war-machine" but then again neither are many adult novels.[13] The children's novel is a toy. It is more conservative than revolutionary. The idyllic is always hedged about and encircled by the didactic and this is as it should be since the novels are written *for* children. Children do not want to change the world; they want to enter it. But then what is the moral status of the adult who reads children's novels? This might not seem a very important question since the class is probably limited to students of the genre but a case could be made for encouraging adults to read children's novels. We have all become alert to the dangers of nostalgia to the point that we forget its value. I find the children's novel to be a bracing tonic, a way of refreshing the mind by allowing oneself to remember what it was like to play freely, out in the open, and, frankly, I can think of a good many adults who would be much improved by the prescription of a large dose of such reading. I would much rather be an adult who knows how to play like a child than a puritanical fanatic, or, in Deleuzian terms, anarchy-schizophrenia is always preferable to fascism-paranoia.

It is for this reason that I assert that play plays both ways and agree with Sutton-Smith in his critique of progressive theories of play. In his book *Pretend Play as Improvisation*, Keith Sawyer also points out the weakness of progressive theories of play. Piaget and Vygotsky are often seen as having contrasting play theories largely because Piaget emphasized intellectual development and Vygotsky emphasized social development. One follows Freud and the other follows Marx. But as Sawyer points out "in contrast to script theories, which propose that play is structured by a cognitive representation of a temporal ordering of events, Vygotsky argued that play is structured by a cognitive representation of role-appropriate behavior. Both approaches fail to account for the creative, improvisational aspects of children's play" (12). In other words, both see play as moving in the direction of the final game. Play only plays one way and that is toward the triumph of rules. They both emphasize the didactic to the point of denying the idyllic.

Sawyer goes on to point out that "rather than exploring the improvisational, contingent nature of interaction, most research has focused on structuralizing models of scripts, frames, discourse grammars, or routines.... These models are structuralizing because they assume that the structure of the interaction existed prior to the interaction. From an improvisational perspective, interactional structure is always potentially novel, varying from any preexisting structure" (32). Sawyer quotes from George Herbert Mead's *The Philosophy of the Present* that

> "it is the task of the philosophy of today to bring into congruence with each other this universality of determination which is the text of modern

science, and the emergence of the novel" (14). The difficulty, Mead continued, is that once an emergent appears, the analyst attempts to rationalize it, showing (incorrectly) that it can be found "in the past that lay behind it (14)" [32].

This insight is similar to what Deleuze is attempting to convey in his concept of the "pure event," and lies behind his attempt to promote a new way of reading. Structuralist literary critics make the same mistake as structuralist social scientists. They read the novel as if it were a game that has already been played rather than as an improvisation that is being played out in the process of reading. They emphasize Sense at the expense of Nonsense because as Deleuze puts it "Good sense affirms that in all things there is a determinable sense or direction (*sens*); but paradox is the affirmation of both senses or directions at the same time" (1).

Sawyer concludes his book with the following observation:

> The script model of development has one of the same weaknesses as the play theories of Piaget, Vygotsky, and Freud. All of them saw the randomness and chaos of social play, and argued that it occurred because children hadn't yet achieved the competence level of some later stage.... These models miss the unique positive importance of play in development. The focus on play as improvisation suggests that its wandering, chaotic nature is what makes it so valuable for children. Play is important because improvisation, fundamental to everyday social interaction, continues on in adult life. Adult conversations, although constrained in many ways by social and cultural factors, are also creative improvisations [169].

Sawyer has the right idea but he cannot quite escape from the rhetoric of progress, the notion that child play is a preparation for adult conversation. By ignoring the paradoxical, parodic and perverse elements of the play he analyses, he misses its true importance. Then again perhaps the problem is that "adult conversation" is an inadequate formulation of what Sawyer really means. If he really means what Deleuze means by Sense then I have no problem with his theory but, as a social scientist, perhaps he would be more comfortable with the term used by a sociologist that he actually cites, Bourdieu's term *habitus*.

In *The Logic of Practice* Bourdieu writes that "the *habitus* represents the 'real logic of action,'" a logic "which is observed in the intentionless invention of regulated improvisation" (57), a phrase that could be used to describe the play of children. Elsewhere he calls this logic

3. Playing with Books

"practical sense" which "is a quasi-bodily involvement in the world which presupposes no representation of either of the body or of the world, still less of their relationship. It is an immanence in the world through which the world imposes its immanence, things to be done or said, which directly govern speech and action. It orients 'choices' which, though not deliberative, are no less systematic, and which, without being ordered and organized in relation to an end, are none the less charged with a kind of retrospective finality" (66). In other words, practical sense requires no map. As an example of this practical sense he refers to 'the feel for the game' which makes sense of the game. He writes:

> Because native membership in a field implies a feel for the game in the sense of a capacity for practical anticipation of the 'upcoming' future contained in the present, everything that takes place in it seems *sensible*: full of sense and objectively directed in a judicious direction. Indeed, one only has to suspend the commitment to the game that is implied in the feel for the game in order to reduce the world, and the actions performed in it, to absurdity, and to bring up questions about the meaning of the world and existence which people never ask when they are caught up in the game — the questions of an aesthete trapped in the instant, or an idle spectator [66–67].

Bourdieu does not make the distinction between the games of adults and the play of children that is so important to my thesis but such a distinction does not contradict his argument. If what Sawyer means by "adult conversation" is the same thing that Bourdieu means by *habitus*, then I have no problem with understanding that conversation to be grounded in the improvisational play of young children. Sense *is* grounded in nonsense but it must not be forgotten that play plays both ways.

The reason for my dissatisfaction is actually expressed by William Corsaro in his foreword to Sawyer's book:

> I would argue that we should not be so quick to equate fully the skills of improvisational pretend play to metapragmatic skills in everyday conversation. Sawyer may indeed be correct that the former contribute to the development of the latter. But the specific types and the range of skills necessary to participate competently and effectively in improvisational pretend play (and for that matter in adult improvisational comedy or jazz) may wither away without use and practice. Here we may have a case where

the improvisational skills of pre-school children actually surpass those of most older children and adults, but most children lose this improvisational edge as they become part of and participate in the social worlds of older children and adults where opportunities to routinely use and sharpen these skills are severely limited [xiv].

It is for this reason that I insist upon my aphorism: play plays both ways.[14] The adult who forgets how to play like a child is emotionally and morally flawed, a fact which is the moral of every children's novel. I have argued previously that the historical development of universal schooling created just such a "social world" that would contribute to such a loss. In response, the children's novel was invented to keep the play of children alive in a literate form. But beyond that historical fact, our task as literary critics is to learn how to continue to play with books like a child. By understanding reading to be a form of play we can assert a revitalized humanism, one grounded firmly in the material reality of our evolutionary history and one that does not forget that reading, like writing, is a creative activity. I do not need to invent such a theory since it already exists in the extensive writings that fall under the rubric of reader-response criticism. So I will proceed to practise what I preach and, in what follows, provide a history and rhetoric of the children's novel by studying how those novels have been put into play.

4

The Children's Novel

In the next three chapters, I am going to discuss the narrative techniques of a number of novels to the end of differentiating the techniques of the children's novel from those of the adult novel. I shall begin with some broad generalizations before narrowing in on particular examples. In *Transparent Minds: Narrative Modes for Presenting Consciousness*, Dorrit Cohn argues that the defining characteristic of the formal realism of the novel is its ability to render consciousness. After summarizing the work of Käte Hamburger, she concludes that *The Logic of Literature* "gives a stringently argued theoretical grounding to the interdependence of narrative realism and the mimesis of consciousness" (8). She quotes Schopenhauer to the effect that "the more *inner* and the less *outer* life a novel presents, the higher and nobler will be its purpose" (*Sämtliche Werke*, ed. Arthur Hübscher [Wiesbaden, 1947], VI/2, pages 468–469). Although, to some degree, I am in agreement with this assertion, it does create a problem in relation to the children's novel, which, of course, Cohn does not consider and which, given this assumption, must be considered "lower" and "baser" in its purpose since it strongly resists the rendering of consciousness. Of course, to the extent that the children's novel is a novel, it will represent consciousness but it is far more interested in the representation of play. Just as in the previous chapter, I followed Deleuze and Bahktin in resisting the knee-jerk assumption of literary critics that irony is superior to humor, I will now resist the exactly parallel assumption that the representation of consciousness is superior to the representation of play. To the extent that the children's novel represents play, it will represent children as playing perverts who have no minds at all much less transparent ones.

Cohn isolates six possible narrative techniques for rendering consciousness, three first- person and three third-person techniques. The first-person techniques are autonomous monologue, autobiographical monologue and memory monologue. In *The Rhetoric of Character in Children's Literature*, Maria Nikolejeva finds "the distinction too subtle to be of practical interest" (250) and I would agree, if what one is interested in is the difference between children's novels and adult novels. One might be tempted to associate autobiographical monologue with children's novels because so many boy's adventure stories use that narrative technique but then they are only imitating the use of the same technique in the adult novel *Robinson Crusoe*. Also one might be tempted to suggest that it is the logical technique to use in the children's novel because it would help to establish the gap between adult narrator and child protagonist, but there are other ways of doing that and it is not at all clear that is how the technique is actually used. In *Treasure Island*, there is a difference between the adult who is telling the story and the child who is its hero but it is a difference that is not strongly marked and one could quite happily read the novel without noting it.

Cohn also distinguishes between three kinds of third-person narration: psycho-narration, quoted monologue and narrated monologue. Nikolejeva refers to quoted monologue as "the most primitive" of narrative techniques and seems to associate it particularly with the children's novel (244) whereas narrated monologue "is more complicated and ambiguous" and "allows for irony and satire" (256). In fact, quoted monologue and psycho-narration are both used in both adult and children's novels of the eighteenth and nineteenth centuries with narrated monologue becoming more and more common as we approach the twentieth century. It would be nice to generalize that children's novels use quoted monologue and adult novels use the more sophisticated narrated monologue but such a generalization does not hold up. Jane Austen is generally given credit for inventing narrated monologue but it is not clear that she is aware that she is using it and she does not use it often. Narrated monologue occurs quite often in twentieth- century children's novels and Nikolejeva gives examples from *Mary Poppins* and *Anne of Green Gables* so it is difficult to necessarily think of it as the more sophisticated technique. This is especially true when one considers that Enid Blyton uses it to render the consciousness of the dog:

4. The Children's Novel

Timmy was hoisted up to the black hole, and disappeared into it with delight. Rabbits? Rats? What were the children after? This was a fine game! [*Five Go Down to the Sea*, 122].

Also Cohn uses the term "quoted monologue" to refer to a spectrum of effect from soliloquy to stream of consciousness which would imply that both *Alice in Wonderland* and *Ullyses* share the same narrative technique. Here we have a perhaps more useful generalization: when the technique used is quoted monologue, the children's novel is more likely to use soliloquy or "talking to oneself" whereas the adult novel inclines toward stream of consciousness. In the children's novel consciousness is often represented as "talking to oneself," a representation that accurately reflects the fact that, when pre-oedipal children play, they are essentially daydreaming out loud. Thus it is, that until they learn to internalize their vocalizations, they can be thought of as pre-conscious. Also, it is possible that the age of six has been chosen as the logical age to start teaching a child to read and write because it is necessary that this internalization take place in order to create the inner space that will become what David Bolter calls a "writing space," or, as Locke put it, the *tabula rasa*. Also Cohn has pointed out that Vygotsky demonstrated that the egocentric speech of young children is formally very much like Joyce's stream of consciousness (97). Again we have a kind of reversal of the real situation. Children in the children's novel speak to themselves with a simplicity and coherency that is not found in the language that they actually speak, whereas adults in the adult novel speak to themselves with a complexity and incoherency not found in the language they speak out loud but in the language they internalized as children.

The above example suggests that the difference between the adult novel and the children's novel lies not so much in what techniques are used but in how they are used and to what extent. To pursue this possibility further I am going to consider a much simpler and more familiar concept, that of point of view, conceived of as consisting of two related aspects, "voice" and "focus." In *The Narrator's Voice*, Barbara Wall has done a good job of giving us a history of the children's novel based upon an analysis of "voice," a history that I am largely in agreement with. Like her I think *Alice in Wonderland* is the first successful children's novel in which the narrator finds a voice with which to address the child narratee and like her I am willing to give Nesbit the credit for continuing this practice and influencing all subsequent writers for children. My problem with her analysis is that it concentrates too exclusively on the voice of the narrator and thus neglects the other equally important aspect of point of view, the narrative focus or camera angle, the position the narrator adopts in relation to the child protagonist. It is relatively unimportant whether the narration is first or third-person and I do not think it is very much more important whether or not the narrator speaks in an intrusive, avuncular voice or in an unintrusive, matter-of-fact voice, though the latter is the preferred mode for most writers of the twentieth century. What is most important is the focus of the narration because that is what produces a certain vision of childhood that is the defining characteristic of the children's novel. To make my point clearer I will briefly summarize Wall's theory.

Basically, she insists "that the narrator-narratee relationship, rather than that of implied author and implied reader, is the distinctive marker of a children's book, and that this relationship has changed markedly in the last one hundred and fifty years" (9). To simplify her argument she sees an historical process whereby writers of the early nineteenth century were too embarrassed to be seen as only speaking to children so adopted a technique of "*double address*," which is to say they address both children and adults in two different voices, as we have already noted in Newbery's *A Little Pretty Pocket Book* (1744). By the beginning of the twentieth century writers became more comfortable with talking to children and so adopted "*single address*" (9). I find this account less than convincing for a number of reasons not the least of which is that it does seem to lead to a theory of the history of the children's novel that sees the culmination of that history in the works of Judy Blume. Actually I find her notion of a "*dual address*," a voice that addresses both children and adults simultaneously, a much more useful concept, both rhetorically and historically. One sees the point at which her thesis goes awry at the moment she concludes that "dual address, which might be found at any time, is rare and difficult, presupposing as it does that a child narratee is addressed and an adult reader simultaneously satisfied" (36). I agree that dual address is difficult but I do not see that it is rare; rather, it is the distinguishing characteristic of the children's novel.

4. The Children's Novel

Wall sees in the Alice books a prime example of what she calls dual address and attempts to diminish their historical significance by suggesting that they were "the result of the happiest of happy accidents" (97). The accident, of course, was the biographical fact that Dodgson actually told some version of this story to a real child with the result that he "was able to talk to Alice Liddell, his friend, not his subordinate, without condescension, and to invite her involvement in his language jokes and his sense of fun. Narrator-Carroll could share with ten-year-old narratee-Alice delight in the adventures of seven-year-old Character-Alice, warm sympathy for her perplexities and affectionate amusement at her inability to see the mistakes she was making" (100). Wall's analysis is exactly right but let us not dismiss it as an accidental rarity but see it as a possibility that was already inherent in the historical development of a gap between literate adults and pre-literate children, a gap, moreover, that Carroll could bridge because he knew how to play like a child. Wall also misses the opportunity to generalize from this particular case. Once discovered, the accident becomes a rule and Carroll could easily repeat it again in *Through the Looking-Glass* without the need of an actual child. Let us assert this discovery as a simple rule of the children's novel: the narratee is always older than the protagonist or implied child. By corollary, the narrator is always younger than the implied author, an effect achieved by the stylistic devices described in the second chapter. Thus it is that in the children's novel, the adult and the child always meet in the middle in a Janus-like construction that looks both ways simultaneously.

Wall's contention that the narrator views the protagonist with "warm sympathy" and "affectionate amusement" is exactly right and again the same thing is true of every children's novel, or at least every one that is humorous and this effect is created by the narrative focus.[1] Wall observes:

> Walter de la Mare ... wrote of Alice's "pellucid consciousness": "Apart, too, from an occasional Carrollian comment, the sole medium of the stories in *her* pellucid consciousness: an ideal preached by Henry James himself, and practised — in how different a setting — in *What Maisie Knew*" [1932, 55]. In fact, however, it is not quite Alice's consciousness that we are given. Maisie's consciousness, her dim struggles to understand, "the child's confused and obscure notation," of the events in which she is enmeshed, certainly dominates *What Maisie Knew*. Alice, however, is portrayed not so

much by what the narrator shows going on inside her head as by what Alice herself tells us. She is a great conversationalist [101].

Wall has put her finger on the essential difference between the adult novel and the children's novel. Whether narrated in the first or third-person, the one thing that the children's novel has little use for is interior monologue and it does everything possible to avoid the preferred narrative mode of the canonical adult novel, third-person centered consciousness. The children's novel is not interested in "consciousness" but in play, and the best way to bring play to an end is by becoming self-conscious about it.

The children's novel always prefers to tell the story through dialogue, or conversations, and description of events, or pictures. As I pointed out earlier, Carroll provides us with the formula in the first sentence of his novel: "once or twice she had peeped into the book her sister was reading, but it had no pictures or conversations in it, 'and what is the use of a book,' thought Alice, 'without pictures or conversations?'" Wall goes on to point out that

> Dodgson was able to break up his narrative and to satisfy Alice-as-reader by constantly externalising Alice's consciousness into direct speech. This of course contributes to the "pellucid" quality of Alice's mind which so pleased de la Mare. But it also keeps the narrator outside Alice's mind, and both narrator and narratee at a discreet distance, just far enough away to overhear with ease, and be entertained. In partnership they witness and understand Alice's plight.... The narrator asserts his detachment from Alice-as-character, and invites his narratee to share it [102].

Again this analysis is exactly right but clearly we are dealing with a matter of focus rather than voice, and again we can generalize from Carroll's practice to that of all writers of humorous novels for children. For instance, it is the practice of Nesbit and Ransome as I will demonstrate shortly. Perhaps we could refer to the humorous children's novel as the pure children's novel both for the sake of brevity and to indicate that it is purely about play. The pure children's novel always views the child from "a discreet distance," or, as I would put it, from a middle distance that avoids the heights and depths of irony. As Wall puts it "Dodgson shows us a child who feels, but is armoured against depth or persistence of feeling by the constant stream of happenings" (102). In Deleuzian terms, the pure children's novel places us in a world of

4. The Children's Novel

pure events, the world of play. In the process the child is constructed as the Other in the perversity of its play, although in the case of *Alice in Wonderland* there is yet another twist on this basic formula.

Wall does not talk about play in her analysis, perhaps because the subject has already been covered by Kathleen Blake in *Play, Games, and Sport: The Literary Works of Lewis Carroll*. Obviously, I agree that Blake had the right idea when she analysed *Alice in Wonderland* in terms of play but because she is following Freud and Piaget in her theory of play she overemphasizes the importance of rule-based games at the expense of improvisational play, the didactic at the expense of the idyllic. She is correct when she points out that "Alice has a game attitude, with which goes a great concern for the terms and rules of play. She is on the lookout to learn these so as to fit in and even master the peculiar universe she has entered" (109). Indeed, as Blake points out, many critics have observed that she is a bit of a prig. But I think Blake is wrong when she asserts that "in most cases the narrator's attitude is close to [Alice's] own" (109). I think that it is clear that whenever Alice is so represented she is being teased, and the novel must be understood as, among other things, a satiric attack upon the rules of adult reality and, even more specifically, upon the rules of Victorian society. If we remember that play plays both ways, we can better understand the perfect poise of the idyllic/didactic machine that Carroll has constructed. The nostalgic Carroll thrusts his protagonist into the dream of childhood, the realm of phantasmagoric play, and the child just as sturdily resists as she demands to grow up, to understand the rules of the game. The implied author and the protagonist do not agree and the narrator and narratee are caught in the middle of what could be thought of as an ongoing debate about the merits of remaining a child or growing up, a debate that Carroll is well aware he is going to lose.

Actually Blake is disagreeing with a number of critics who have asserted a view closer to my own, especially Roger Henkle who, in "The Mad Hatter's World," asserts, according to Blake, the existence of "an idyll of 'free play,' supposedly to be the original condition presented in *Wonderland*, where each creature determines his life solely by whim and self-indulgence. The action of both novels involves the fall from this condition" (116). Failure to read the novels this way is the result of following Piaget on the subject of play. The fantasy formula that Carroll creates is one in which the adults play like pre-school children and the child is presented as prematurely wise, or, to put it in the terms I have been using, the adults are all perverts and the child is a prig. This pure reversal of the real situation is only possible in fantasy and, in the realistic portrayal of childhood that Grahame presents, the real situation must be asserted but still the basic formula remains the same and is used by Nesbit, Ransome, Seuss, and Dahl, all of whom recognize that the pervert is essential to the children's novel and always create a character to represent the adult who knows how to play like a child. Thus, we have Albert-next-door's uncle (Albert being the child prig), Uncle Jim, the Cat in the Hat, and the Big Friendly Giant, all of whom are ultimately based upon the Dodo and the White Knight.

Roald Dahl is a particularly interesting writer since he is one of the few postwar novelists to keep alive the spirit of the children's novel as originally invented by Carroll. In *The BFG* he actually characterizes himself as a writer in the title character who creates wonderful dreams for children and is the epitome of the pervert, especially when he releases "whizzpoppers" in the presence of the queen. Dahl is often faulted for his lack of subtlety but it is surely no accident that his protagonist is a wise child named "Sophie" and that the back jacket cover of my edition has a photograph of Dahl looking very much like the BFG who turns out to be the author of the book we have just read. Even more specifically, in *Matilda*, he has the protagonist articulate my theory of the children's novel in the following scene:

> "I liked *The Lion, the Witch and the Wardrobe*, " Matilda said. "I think Mr C. S. Lewis is a very good writer. But he has one failing. There are no funny bits in his books."
> "You are right there," Miss Honey said.
> "There aren't many funny bits in Mr Tolkien either," Matilda said.
> "Do you think that all children's books ought to have funny bits in them?" Miss Honey asked.
> "I do," Matilda said. "Children are not so serious as grown-ups and they love to laugh" [80–81].

It could be observed, in defence of Lewis, that, although he is not known for his "funny bits," the adventures of the children in *The Lion, the Witch and the Wardrobe* begin with a game of hide-and-seek and the Resurrection and the state of grace it brings is represented by a

4. The Children's Novel

romp. Moreover, he is capable of amusing word play as when Mr Tumnus (whose own name is a Latin joke) describes Lucy as being from "the far land of Spare Oom where eternal summer reigns about the bright city of War Drobe" (13). Admittedly, Lewis is more dour than Dahl but considerably less so than a number of postwar writers for children. Also, Lewis clearly knew what a children's novel was and knew exactly what he meant when he claimed that one of the ways of writing for children "consists in writing a children's story because a children's story is the best art-form for something you have to say" (32).

Of course, it could be argued that the theory of the children's novel that I have presented does not apply to all children's novels and I agree that we would need to consider other genres but I also think that the fact of children's play always comes into play in the children's novel. I shall consider the two other major genres, aside from the pure children's novel, that developed in the nineteenth century, the boy's adventure story and the girl's domestic novel. One might wish for finer distinctions, the moral tale, the school story, historical romance, the animal story, but the three broad categories I have delineated cover most of the possibilities of the children's novel.[2] Previously I agreed with Hunt's assertion that children's books lag behind the adult novel but that generalization needs to be qualified when we think specifically of the development of the pure children's novel. I agree with the many critics who would see *Alice in Wonderland* as the first successful children's novel and so the long period between the appearance of *A Little Pretty Pocket Book* in 1744 and 1865 must be seen as a period of failed experiments. Of course, in the case of the particular example that Hunt gives, the adventure story, the case is somewhat different since from the beginning *Robinson Crusoe* was adapted for chapbook distribution and thus the successful formula for children was established and so the lag time is considerably shorter and Marryat, Ballantyne, and Kingsley all precede Carroll, though the genre was not perfected until *Treasure Island* (1883). In any case, the boy's adventure story is a special category that must be dealt with separately from the children's novel as invented by Carroll.

Of course, if you are of the opinion that the adult novel also had to undergo its own development and only reached its perfection in Jane

Austen then one can view things differently. In that case, if we agree that the first successful attempt to create the child's version of the adult domestic novel, as exemplified by *Pride and Prejudice* (1813), occurs in 1868 in *Little Women* then we are marking the same boundary since Alcott's book appeared four years after Carroll's. A comparison of Austen's novel with Alcott's is crucial to an understanding of the difference between the adult novel and the children's novel since, although they are both about the courtship of a group of female siblings, they are radically different in their narrative technique. What Austen did was perfect the narrative technique of omniscient, third-person centered consciousness, thus inaugurating what Leavis called the Great Tradition. One of the reasons that the children's novel is not a part of that tradition and is considered an inferior sub-group is that, with some exceptions, it never adopts that narrative technique until after the Second World War, a lag time of 150 years. As far as I know, no one except Lois Kuznets has noticed that fact yet it is crucial to an understanding of the development of the children's novel. Thus the history of the children's novel can be divided into three periods, the period from Newbery to Carroll, 1744–1865, often referred to as the didactic age, the period from Carroll to Boston (I take *The Children of Green Knowe* as the boundary marker), 1865–1954, a period often called the Golden Age, and the period after 1954, a period we might call the age of the adolescent novel, or, if one wants to be clever, the neo-didactic age, since that novel is often referred to as the "problem novel."

To some extent, *Alice in Wonderland* was a lucky accident. Everyone knows the story of the famous boat trip and probably what Carroll thought he was doing as he told his story to Alice was telling a fairy tale. The fairy tale was already a well-established children's genre, dating back to Perrault and other French writers of the late seventeenth century. But *Alice in Wonderland* is not a fairy tale; it is a novel with a very real Alice, having a very real dream in a very real Victorian context. Of course, this is a very different realism from that of the domestic novel but clearly the fantasy novel is still a novel. If the subject of the children's novel is play then that subject can be treated in a mix of fantasy and realism as in Nesbit, or entirely realistically as in Ransome. The important thing that Carroll taught all the writers of the Golden Age that follow him is that the subject of the children's novel is play and that the novel must exist as an object of play. Thus, we can understand that the importance of *Alice in Wonderland* to the development of the children's novel lies in the fact that in this case the children's novel did not lag behind the adult novel but preceded it. In *Alice to the Lighthouse*, Juliet Dusinberre talks about how important Carroll was, not only to writers for children, but for writers of adult novels such as Virginia Woolf, and how, by teaching them how to play, helped usher in the age of modernism. The influence is more general than particular since Woolf still wrote in the tradition of the adult domestic novel. If David Lodge is right and *Alice in Wonderland* is "the first great surrealist novel" (175) then we have to wait for the 1920's for the adult novel to catch up. He discusses Leonora Carrington's *The Hearing Trumpet* (1976) as an example of a surrealist novel and suggests Carrington's "work is now perceived as pioneering a good deal of postmodernist experimentation, especially by women artists and writers such as Angela Carter and Jeanette Winterson, who use surrealist effects to subvert patriarchal cultural assumptions" (175). It might be argued that the whole direction of the post-modern novel can be understood as nothing more than an attempt to create an adult version of *Alice in Wonderland*.

Indeed, this argument has been made, sarcastically, by Raymond Tallis in his *In Defence of Realism*:

> The trouble is ... the criteria that place ... Bartheleme on the side of the angels will also put A. A. Milne, the Rev. W. Awdrey and a host of other writers of children's books in the forefront of the *avant garde*. Once you start reading anti-realist theory into the practice, you can find it everywhere and in children's literature most of all [132].

Hunt quotes this passage as "a warning to those of us in the field of children's literature who are inclined to look for allies in the realms of literary theory" (135). I am sympathetic to aspects of Tallis' argument that counter certain excesses of post-modern theorizing, but his sarcasm only works if one assumes that the children's novel is inferior to the adult novel. Without that assumption one can see an element of truth in his assertion and not only in the case of the surrealist novel. In chapter 25 of *The Art of Fiction*, "Staying on the Surface," Lodge analyses Malcolm Bradbury's novel *The History Man* (1975) in a way that suggests how the post-modern novel imitates the children's novel by "staying on the surface" and rejecting the representation of individual consciousness. As Lodge points out "the novel consists of description and dialogue" (118), as does the children's novel, but it goes further in rejecting past tense narration and thus any narrative authority. The result is certainly humorous but in a way quite different from the children's novel because the effect is not created by putting the idyllic/didactic machine into play. There are no playing children in this world as Bradbury intentionally flattens the adult novel in order to explore the philosophical position of his protagonist who believes "that the self is an outmoded bourgeois concept" (118). The result, as Lodge notes, is "at once comic and chilling" (119) because the protagonist, who is a sociologist, likes playing games with other people's lives, games that he always wins.

But if *Alice in Wonderland* can be understood as preceding the adult novel, the two other genres clearly lag behind, but both alter the narrative techniques of the adult novels that they are imitating in a way that indicates that the writers in these genres are as much aware of the nature of children's play as was Carroll. The boy's adventure story is neither humorous nor is its subject the play of children but it is certainly the script for the play of children as Ransome demonstrated in *Swallows and Amazons*. Generic boundaries are always porous and Ransome stepped across to translate boy's adventure into the play of a group of realistic siblings. Then Enid Blyton stepped back by translating the play of a group of realistic siblings into real adventures. It is useless to speculate which comes first, the script or the play, but both are of ancient origin and it is possible that boys have always played games of heroic conflict as they do today. The only thing that has changed is the nature of the good guys and bad guys.

At this point it might be useful to point out that the pure children's novel is not rigidly defined by gender, as are the two other genres, though it is theoretically possible to make a boy the protagonist of the domestic novel as Burnett did in *Little Lord Fauntleroy*, or to make girls the protagonists of adventure stories as in the works of Bessie Marchant. But *Alice in Wonderland* is not a girl's story despite the gender of its protagonist and both Nesbit and Ransome mix the genders of their protagonists who share equally in the adventure of play. In her essay "Explorers," in which Gwyneth Jones describes her own adventur-

4. The Children's Novel

ous play as a child, she correctly observes that "in the golden age, between two world wars, misogyny was not a big feature in children's fiction. Nobody ever called Captain Nancy Blackett maladjusted, because she liked to wear shorts and was the captain of her own ship. Nobody in the books ever cheeked Mate Susan either: or showed anything but respect for her domestic arts and steely control over the commissariat" (18). It is perhaps for this reason that feminist writers like Carter and Winterspoon turn to the children's novel for inspiration. The gender equality of the children's novel is all the more startling in that it is clearly a rhetorical device, an assertion of an ideal that is not found in the real world where boys and girls do, for the most part, segregate themselves by gender in separate play groups. In Sawyer's study of pre-school play "61% of the group episodes were all-boy or all-girl groups" (91). He also discovered that boys commonly discuss "good guys" and "bad guys" but he did not discover a single instance of girls assigning such roles (65). Of course, just because these children are pre-readers does not mean that these differences are not culturally constructed but it does indicate how deeply ingrained the dichotomy is and how extraordinary the children's novel is in allowing girls entry to boy's adventure. It is Titty who is the main protagonist of *Swallows and Amazons* and the most bloodthirsty of all the players, although, admittedly, that fact itself is part of the humor.

The other major genre, the domestic novel as exemplified by *Little Women*, owes more to Dickens than it does to Austen, despite the similarity of subject matter in the female writers. Dickens is the ultimate master of tears and laughter. More specifically the origins of *Little Women* can be traced to Susan Warner's *The Wide, Wide World* (1850) and to Charlotte Yonge's *The Daisy Chain* (1856). In *What Katy Read*, a feminist study of the girl's domestic novel, Foster and Simons point out that *The Wide, Wide World* "is one of the earliest and best examples of what was to become probably the most popular nineteenth-century fictional genre in America — the sentimental/domestic novel" (37). They correctly begin their study with Warner and Yonge before moving on to Alcott and Coolidge's *What Katy Did* (1872). Wall never mentions either of the two earlier novels, presumably because they are not addressed to children, but I think is necessary to consider them in order to understand what Alcott and Coolidge did later. In doing so,

Foster and Simon actually confirm Wall's theory. They compare a passage from Warner's novel to a passage from Coolidge and a passage from Yonge to a passage from *The Secret Garden* and conclude that the earlier novels make "no concession to a juvenile audience." Moreover, they recognize that this change is not merely a change of voice but also of focus since, in the later novels, though "the speaking voice is obviously adult, the engagement is with an implied young reader who is invited to adopt a position of close identification with the protagonist" (11–12).

Foster and Simon are right in that the girl's domestic novel, like the boy's adventure story, encourages more identification with the protagonist than does the pure children's novel. This is also why they are potentially more insidious in inculcating gender roles. But never can this identification be complete. Always the narrator and narratee meet in the middle because if they did not there would be no humor and if we follow the trajectory that Foster and Simon map, Warner to Yonge, to Alcott to Coolidge to Nesbit to Montgomery, the one thing that is clear is that the novels are becoming increasingly humourous. I will speak of this in more detail later but a brief overview will make the point. *The Wide, Wide World* is all tears. Ellen is seen playing on three occasions, all with unhappy results. The novel also confirms that, at least in America, children in Evangelical families were not allowed to play on Sundays. British Evangelicalism appears less strict in *The Daisy Chain* since the young children are often seen playing and the novel is often humorous, though for every laugh you have to pay with a dozen tears. Alcott pretty much balances out the laughs and tears. *What Katy Did* is an odd case since the first half is all laughter and the second all tears. The first half is Nesbit but then Coolidge reverts to Warner. By the time you reach Montgomery laughter has prevailed and with *The Railway Children*, the only domestic novel that Nesbit wrote, you are right on the generic boundary. In the same way, if we map the trajectory of the boy's adventure story, from Defoe to Marryat, from Ballantyne to Twain, you reach the generic boundary with *Bevis, the Story of a Boy*, before you cross over into the realm of pure play with Ransome. In both genres there is an increasing tolerance for the perversity of play and a finer balancing of the idyllic with the didactic, a process that will be the subject of more precise analysis in the next chapter. For the

4. The Children's Novel

remainder of this chapter, I will discuss the characteristics of what I have called the pure children's novel in the work of Carroll, Nesbit and Ransome.

Alice in Wonderland begins with the example of quoted monologue already quoted when she speculates about the use of a book "'without pictures or conversations'" and it would be convenient if this were the only narrative technique Carroll uses and we could follow Wall in asserting that Alice is "a great conversationalist" (101), whose consciousness is always rendered as talking to oneself, but this is not the case.[3] In the next four paragraphs her consciousness is rendered through psycho-narration before returning to quoted monologue in paragraph six and paragraph seven actually begins with a bit of narrated monologue: "Down, down, down. Would the fall *never* come to an end?" (10). In the first chapter I count twelve examples of quoted monologue and eight of psycho-narration but such counts are not definitive because one cannot just count paragraphs because in the same paragraph she will switch from one to the other and many of the cases are ambiguous but it does support my contention that it is not what technique is used but how it is used that is important.

For example, after the bit of narrated monologue quoted above, the next sentence is "'I wonder how many miles I've fallen by this time?' she said aloud" (10). This is still quoted monologue since she is alone but the effect of making her talk to herself out loud is to make her seem younger than she is and she continues to do so through the next two paragraphs. In paragraph thirteen she returns to thinking to herself but in paragraph fifteen her bit of internal monologue is "said" (13) and continues to be "said" to the end of the chapter, making unclear whether or not she is still thinking out loud. Again it would be convenient if only protagonists in children's novels talked to themselves out loud but Elizabeth Bennet seems to do the same thing after she has read Darcy's letter. When adult protagonists talk to themselves out loud, it is invariably a sign of emotional turmoil but it has no such connotation in the children's novel. After all, an adult who talks to herself out loud is considered insane but young children, who do it all the time, are considered cute. The technique is used to evoke a humorous childishness.

There is also some ambiguity in the use of psycho-narration in the children's novel since it is not always clear whether we are dealing with interior monologue or merely description. The first chapter of *Alice in Wonderland* is not a good place to look for this ambiguity since, for the most part, Alice is thinking and feeling about what is happening to her but there is one clear example of what I mean. We are told that "soon her eye fell on a little glass box that was lying under the table" (15). This is a very common technique in the children's novel, one that we might call descriptive psycho-narration, in that we are allowed access to children's minds in order to see and hear what they are seeing and hearing but not what they are thinking or feeling. A further variation on the same technique is a kind of negative psycho-narration:

> In another moment down went Alice after it, *never once considering* how in the world she was to get out again.
> The rabbit-hole went straight on like a tunnel for some way, and then dipped suddenly down, so suddenly that Alice *had not a moment to think* about stopping herself [10; italics added].

In this technique the child's mind is characterized by what it does not think, as being essentially unthinking. All these techniques, talking to oneself out loud, descriptive and negative psycho-narration, are designed to create a distance between the narrator/narratee and the child protagonist whose perverse otherness is the source of humor but equally as important is the use of narrative asides.

What follows is the second paragraph of *Alice in Wonderland*:

> So she was considering, in her own mind (as well she could, for the hot day made her feel very sleepy and stupid), whether the pleasure of making a daisy-chain would be worth the trouble of getting up and picking daisies, when suddenly a White Rabbit with pink eyes ran close by her.

This is psycho-narration in which we have access to what Alice is "considering" although in the end we merely see what she sees. It might be possible to read the part in brackets as further psycho-narration about what she is feeling but I think that it is clear that this is the narrator speaking to the ten-year-old narratee about how "stupid" the seven-year-old protagonist is. There are ten of these bracketed asides in the first chapter, some of which are less ambiguous than this one, such as "She generally gave herself very good advice (though she very seldom

4. The Children's Novel

followed it)" (15) and some of which are merely informational: "(Dinah was the cat)" (11) but all of which are designed to signal a narrative voice at a comic distance from the protagonist. Again it would be convenient if Carroll always put such comments in brackets but sometimes the brackets are merely implied as in the statement "For, you see, so many out-of-the-way things had happened lately, that Alice had begun to think that very few things indeed were really impossible" (13). Sometimes distance is signaled more subtly as in what is probably the most commented upon passage of the first chapter:

> It was all very well to say "Drink me," but the wise little Alice was not going to do *that* in a hurry. "No, I'll look first," she said, "and see whether it's marked '*poison*' or not"; for she had read several nice little stories about children who had got burnt, and eaten up by wild beasts, and other unpleasant things, all because they *would* not remember the simple rules their friends had taught them: such as, that a red-hot poker will burn you if you hold it too long; and that, if you cut your finger *very* deeply with a knife, it usually bleeds; and she had never forgotten that, if you drink much from a bottle marked "poison" it is almost certain to disagree with you, sooner or later [13–14].

Distance is signaled by the phrases "wise little Alice," "nice little stories," "other unpleasant things," "the simple rules" and this is probably a much commented upon passage because it is here that the tone approaches the kind of irony that we associate with the adult novel.

The techniques that Carroll devised in his first chapter to distance the narrator/narratee from the child protagonist will be repeated by subsequent writers of children's novels. Also these techniques are unusually dense in the first chapter precisely because Alice is alone and thus we are asked to spend an unusual amount of time in her consciousness. Once she has other characters to interact with and someone to talk to other than herself, dialogue will play a much larger role and the formula that prefers "pictures and conversations" to interior monologue will be more accurately realized. For example, in the chapter of the caucus race there are six brief, one line moments of psycho-narration culminating in her "idea"of the mouse's "tale" (28). The chapter then ends with a bit of ambiguous quoted monologue: "'I wish I had our Dinah here, I know I do!' said Alice aloud, addressing no one in particular" (29). The joke is on her as her inability to prevent herself from thinking out loud loses her all her new friends. The chapter ends with a full paragraph of quoted monologue and psycho-narration as she finds herself alone again. This kind of analysis could go on endlessly so I will conclude by observing that the point of these techniques is always to characterize the protagonist as an unthinking pervert subject to the amused but affectionate gaze of the narrator/narratee. All are designed to create a collusion between an adult narrator and a child narratee but when a first-person narrator is used there is a slightly different twist on the rhetorical trick.

In most of her novels, Nesbit adopts a third-person narrative voice that could be characterized as intrusive. This designation is always a matter of degree and although I have noted Carroll's extensive use of narrative asides no one would characterize his narrative voice as intrusive when compared to Nesbit's but, if I might make a generalization that I will not support until my next chapter, the narrative voice in the children's novel is always more intrusive than that in the canonical adult novel. Wall characterizes Nesbit's voice as follows:

> More even than Dodgson, Nesbit deliberately made the relationship between the adult narrator and child narratee a dominant element in her books. Although superficially her narrative manner seems light-hearted and playful, her address to her narratee casual and familiar, in reality she treated child readers with a new seriousness, for she placed them first, and in doing so gave the act of communicating with children, of writing *to* them, a new significance [148].

While I am largely in agreement with this characterization, Wall does tend to overstate the novelty of Nesbit's narrative manner, especially in the next paragraph when she claims that this narrator is "unlike any which had come before." The narrator of *Little Women* is also intrusive though admittedly less so than Nesbit's but the narrator of *What Katy Did* is just as intrusive and in the same way as Nesbit's and this novel constitutes the missing link that connects *Little Women* with the novels of Nesbit. Wall's failure to even consider *What Katy Did* constitutes a serious flaw in her analysis of the history of the children's novel. Nesbit's third-person narration is very much indebted to that history as, indeed, is her use of first-person narration.

In *The Treasure Seekers* and the subsequent novels in the series, Nesbit uses a first- person narration to create much the same effect that Carroll does, that is to create a focus that puts the narratee at an

4. The Children's Novel

"amused but affectionate" distance from the protagonists. The task is made somewhat more difficult by the lack of an adult narrator with whom the narratee can collude in laughing at the protagonist but that narrator is simply replaced by the implied author. As Wall puts it, the child reader shares "the implied author's ironic detachment" (153), and though her subsequent analysis expresses some concern about a child's ability to understand some of the irony, I think she overestimates the difficulties. Of course, one consequence of adopting this narrative technique is that the narrator also becomes an object of humor, or, to generalize, in the pure children's novel a first-person narrator is always unreliable.

Wall locates the antecedents of this narrative technique in Dicken's *Holiday Romance*, Ewing's *A Great Emergency*, and, most importantly, Grahame's *The Golden Age*. Nesbit herself acknowledges her indebtedness in *The Would-be-goods* when Alice is given *The Golden Age* for her birthday and it is described as "A1 except where it gets mixed with grown-up nonsense" (75). Of course, Wall emphasizes the difference between the two since the first-person narrator of *The Golden Age* is an adult whereas the narrator of *The Treasure Seekers* is a twelve-year-old boy. This is indeed an important and significant difference but Wall tends to overemphasize its importance with the result that she misreads *The Golden Age*. She asserts that Grahame "is always asking his adult reader to join him in laughing at the absurdities of children. His point of view hovers between that of the child he was and that of the adult he is now, regarding with cynicism or self-pity the child he was then" (135). Actually, there is just as much nostalgic regret for the child he was as there is cynicism and adults are equally the victims of his satire. Wall's statement is a good example of the problem of emphasizing voice at the expense of focus and the only thing she gets right is her comment on his "point of view." His voice is indeed that of an adult but his focus is much like that of *Alice in Wonderland*, hovering as it does between the child and the adult. Nesbit learned to do what she does from *The Golden Age* and the focus, and thus the humor, of *The Treasure Seekers* is identical to that of the earlier work.

Also there is more to Nesbit's narrative technique than just the first-person narrator. There are three important elements, all of which are present in the opening sentence of the novel:

> This is the story of the different ways we looked for treasure, and I think when you have read it you will see that we were not lazy about the looking [11].

Aside from the "I" speaking with the voice of a child, we also have a collective "we" as protagonist and a "you" who is the reader, and, at times, quite specifically a child. Given her theory, Wall makes much of the last technique and sees it as being intimately connected to the success of "I" in addressing children but it is probably the least important of the three and Nesbit cannot be given credit for inventing the technique since both Alcott and Carroll do the same thing though, admittedly, less frequently and pointedly. The technique persists in the twentieth century in writers such as Lewis and Dahl who are strongly influenced by the Golden Age novelists but most, like Ransome, forgo it. A number of my students, perhaps reflecting a modern prejudice, find it irritating, though I suspect that the ones who do are the ones who are the least playful.

The collective protagonist is a more interesting technique and Nikolajeva, who coined the term, quite rightly sees it as unique to the children's novel. I was originally going to refer to this technique as the use of multiple protagonists but Nikolajeva's term is preferable since this character is an extra character that actually appears in the narrative as "we" in first-person narration or as "they" in third-person narration. Moreover, this character does not merely act collectively but it is also represented as thinking and feeling collectively, which is not very realistic but then the children's novel is not interested in the formal realism associated with the adult novel, a realism evoked by its technique of centered consciousness, a technique that the collective character so markedly repudiates. Nikolajeva has dedicated a whole chapter of *The Rhetoric of Character in Children's Literature* to an analysis of the collective character and its use in *Five Children and It* and there is no point in repeating what has been done. I do, however, have a few additional points to make. It must be strongly emphasized that the collective character is an extra character and all the members of the collective also appear as unique individuals with their own personalities and stories. Moreover, one member of the collective is almost invariably singled out as the main protagonist. Also Nikolejeva asserts that Nesbit was "the first to make the collective character her primary aesthetic principle" (68) but surely Alcott must be given the credit and, indeed, she goes on to analyse Alcott's use of the technique (73–76). Also, Alcott herself was probably imitating its use in *The Daisy Chain*. Finally, Nikolajeva never really articulates a theory explaining why this technique is used in the children's novel and there are at least two reasons I can think of.

First, the collective character is simply a representation of the actual nature of a child's play group, and especially of the corporate entity that boys form in their adventurous play, which is the kind of dangerous play that is most likely to be represented in the children's novel. Second, and most importantly, as indicated above, the collective character is a repudiation of the centered consciousness of the canonical adult novel. Actually, Nikolajeva hints at this explanation when she observes that "individual characters allow a deeper penetration into their psyche," a statement that would imply that the collective character is designed to avoid such penetration. Also, in the same paragraph, she rightly points out that even the single protagonists in the children's novel "are rarely complex psychological existents" (68). In children's novels with a single protagonist, writers avoid the rendering of consciousness by the use of techniques of objectification. In the next chapter, I will be examining the use of objectification in the girl's domestic novel but it would be useful to say a few words about it here since it throws some light on the rhetorical techniques used in *The Treasure Seekers*.

Objectification is the rendering of the child protagonist as the object of the adult gaze, either that of the narrator or of adult characters. This technique can be used to generate either humor or pathos and it is used to do both by Alcott who learned how to do it from Dickens. The most consistent and coherent use of the technique can be found in *Anne of Green Gables* in which our knowledge of Anne is mediated through the consciousness of Marilla and other adult characters. For obvious reasons Nesbit cannot use this technique in *The Treasure Seekers* but she still manages to achieve much the same effect. What I am referring to is the fact that every time the children meet a sympathetic adult the narratee knows exactly what that adult is thinking and feeling about the children even though the children are completely oblivious and the adult consciousness cannot be rendered because of the first-person narrator who is also completely oblivious. This technique is the source of what Wall calls "Nesbit's ironies" (153) which she worries might cause difficulties for the child reader so it would be useful to analyse how Nesbit pulls off this trick.

The novel consists of a series of what could be understood to be play episodes but the joke is that the children are represented as not being able to tell the difference between play and reality, or, to put it more accurately, they are represented as pretending not to be pretending. The latter way of stating the matter captures the essential ambiguity of Nesbit's technique. For example, in chapter two, "Digging for Treasure," the narratee knows that one cannot find treasure by digging in one's backyard and so is laughing at the children but also, at the same time, the narratee is laughing with them in understanding the moral significance of the episode, the fact that Albert-next-door deserves to be buried up to his neck because he is a prig. The situation is exactly captured by the following observation and comment of the narrator:

> Albert-next-door only sniggered and said, "What silly nonsense!" He cannot play properly at all. It is very strange, because he has a very nice uncle. You see, Albert-next-door doesn't care for reading, and he has not read nearly so many books as we have, so he is very foolish and ignorant, but it cannot be helped, and you just have to put up with it when you want him to do anything. Besides, it is wrong to be angry with people for not being so clever as you are yourself. It is not always their faults [20–21].

There are a number of things going on here. First, and most importantly, the viewpoint of the implied author and narratee is not that of either Albert-next-door nor Oswald but hovers in between, between the idyllic and didactic. We are perhaps slightly more sympathetic with Oswald in this case since, here, at least, he seems to be aware that the children are just playing. We are also laughing at him because of his egocentricity, the fact that he is, as Wall puts it, "a compulsive, if engaging, braggart" (152). His unreliable egocentricity is one of the ongoing jokes of the novel, balanced always by the fact that he is also clever, honorable and brave. His identification of reading as a source of play is significant because it recognizes the historical process that created the children's novel and incorporated it into the play of literate children. Finally, the introduction of Albert's "very nice uncle" foreshadows his very important appearance later in the scene.

4. The Children's Novel

Albert's uncle is a representation of the adult pervert, the adult who knows how to play like a child, but more than that he also serves an important rhetorical function in the novel in that, to some degree, he replaces the missing adult narrator. His viewpoint is identical to that of the implied author and narratee and though that viewpoint can never be represented it can be easily deduced from what he says and does. For example, as he is digging out his nephew, he makes the following observation:

> I confess that I am not absolutely insensible to the dramatic interest of the situation. My curiosity is excited. I own that I should like to know how my nephew happened to be buried. But don't tell me if you'd rather not. I suppose no force was used? [23–24].

He is clearly amused by what has happened to his nephew and entirely sympathetic with the Bastable children and their dangerous play but at the same time wants to be sure that no cruelty was involved and is as relieved as we are that Albert-next-door was digging with his feet and not his hands. Later when he pulls his handkerchief trick and rewards the children with a coin, the child reader knows exactly what is going on and is laughing at the silly gullibility of the children at the same time as she is admiring them for their moral superiority as they insist that Albert-next-door get his share. Albert's uncle, who after all is an adult, thinks he is giving them five pence each and must add another coin when he is made aware of the solidarity of the play group. The moral lesson is perfectly available to any child reader even though the child narrator is completely oblivious to it. Indeed, the humorous discrepancy between the viewpoint of Albert's uncle, the implied author and the narratee and that of Oswald is made even more explicit in the next chapter. When Albert's uncle comes to the rescue of the unconscious Oswald, the narrator retrospectively asserts that "Dicky thinks he heard Albert's uncle say, 'Confound those kids!' which would not have been kind or polite, so I hope he did not say it"(35).

The above analysis depends, in part, upon the child reader knowing that the first person narrator is Oswald and the above passage is one of many rather explicit clues since only Dicky and Oswald were present at the scene of the rescue. Wall observes that "while some of the ironies may be beyond the young reader of *The Story of the Treasure Seekers*, every child who works out that the narrator is Oswald has learnt to share the implied author's ironic detachment and to comprehend how irony works" (153). I have no problem with this generalization except it would seem to imply that some children would have difficulty in arriving at this knowledge whereas, in fact, no careful reader, child or adult, could arrive at the end of the first chapter without knowing that the narrator is Oswald. The evidence is both implicit and explicit. The narrator throws down the gauntlet on the first page:

> It is one of us that tells this story—but I shall not tell you which: only at the very end perhaps I will. While the story is going on you may be trying to guess, only I bet you don't.
> It was Oswald who first thought of looking for treasure. Oswald often thinks of very interesting things [11].

This immediate and glowing characterization of Oswald is quite a strong clue that he is the narrator and three pages later he refers to "we boys" (13), thus ruling out Dora and Alice. H.O., who is too young anyway, is ruled out when the narrator says "he told me" (14). Then on the next page, after Oswald has described his plan to become robbers, we have the following scene:

> Dora screwed up her nose the way she always does when she is going to talk like the good elder sister in books, and said, "That would be very wrong: it is like pickpocketing or taking pennies out of Father's greatcoat when it is hanging in the hall."
> I must say I don't think she need have said that, especially before the little ones—for it was when I was only four [15].

If the reader somehow misses this clue, the fact that everyone except Oswald, Dicky and Noel have been explicitly ruled out and the narrator always describes Oswald positively whereas Dicky is characterized as a pragmatic dullard and Noel as a milksop would constitute fairly strong implicit evidence. In any case, at the end of chapter three, when Oswald visits the lady next door, he explicitly lets his disguise drop when he says "she kissed me, and I did not mind" (36–37) and he does so three more times in chapter four. His inability to keep his disguise in place is just another joke at his expense and by the time you reach chapter thirteen, "The Robber and the Burglar," there is not even an attempt to pretend that "I" is not Oswald.

First person narration, used humorously as Nesbit does, may present difficulties for the child reader but I think they have been exaggerated. It is true, however, that it has not been a popular narrative technique in the children's novel except in the boy's adventure story which requires a completely different analysis. I would like to consider two more contemporary examples of the use of the technique which will reveal its positive and negative possibilities. In *Jacob Have I Loved*, the protagonist, Sarah Louise, is a first-person narrator despite the fact that the author, Katherine Paterson, is on record as having said "I have always sworn that I would never write a book in the first person. It is too limiting, too egotistical. And yet, the book refused any voice but Louise's" (239). Paterson has no use for the humorous egocentricity of an Oswald and modifies Nesbit's technique by beginning the novel with the voice of an adult "I" who is retrospectively recounting the events, thus clearly differentiating the woman Sarah Louise will become from the girl who tells the story. Paterson then introduces her thirteen-year-old narrator with a voice that includes slang and malapropisms, techniques also used by Nesbit. But Paterson's central intention is not to create humor but to present the reader with a moral challenge that is in keeping with her Christian intentions. She needs an unreliable narrator so that readers can extricate themselves from Sarah Louise's point of view and realize that her anger against her sister is completely unjustified. Caroline is guilty of nothing, unless one considers it a sin to be talented, charming and beautiful. It is Sarah Louise who is guilty of the sin of envy, a sin that threatens to drag all the other deadly sins along with it unless she can find the grace to extricate herself from her own egocentricity. This could be understood to be a more sophisticated use of first-person narration than that of Nesbit, which is why this is considered a novel for young adults and is the subject of much critical acclaim.

One can, however, move in the opposite direction. At the beginning of this chapter, I objected to Wall's overemphasis of the narrative voice because it leads to a theory that would see Judy Blume as the culmination of the history of the children's novel. In *Are You There God? It's Me, Margaret*, Blume, much to the legitimate chagrin of her critics, developed a first-person narrative voice that threatens to be truly single, to eliminate the distance between the narrator and the implied author. However, despite the fact that Blume tries to collapse the distinction between the narrator/protagonist and narratee, she does not really because she still manages to create humor out of the naivete of her protagonist but the humor is bland rather than exuberant. Her children are perverse and her adults are ridiculous only in the mildest of manners. The effect of her narrative technique is to turn the idyllic into a kind mean-spirited solipsism and the didactic into a rage for conformity, a desperate need to be normal, to be like everyone else. When my students, most of whom loved her as children, wish to defend her from this critique, they argue that this is realism, that children are really like that. It is impossible to simply deny this charge except to point out that it is a charge and one that is hardly consistent with their equally fervent belief that children are innocent. Yes children are often like that but so much the worse for children and for the children's novel.

I cannot leave Nesbit without saying something about her fantasy series but there would be little point in analysing a third-person narrative technique that arises out of the nineteenth-century domestic novel that is the subject of the next chapter. I will return to her in that context with an analysis of *The Railway Children*. It would be worth pointing out, however, that her use of fantasy solves some of the problems that confront her in her realistic novels since the children no longer have to pretend to be not pretending since now all their wishes come true. Also, the effect is somewhat different from that of Carroll since her realistic protagonists continue to live in a real home in a real London with real servants. This realism allows her to construct such recurring jokes as the fact that no matter how far they soar in idyllic adventure it is always threatened by the mundane reality of the need to return home for dinner.

Of the three fantasy novels, *The Phoenix and the Carpet* is clearly the best though this judgement might be prejudice on my part since I clearly remember that this was my favorite novel as a child. The first in the series, *Five Children and It*, suffers from a slightly too heavy hand on the didactic side of the formula as the children's wishes are always represented as stupidly wrong-headed. A better balance is achieved in the second novel and the phoenix must be one of the most delightful perverts to grace the children's novel, though, of course, once he has almost burnt down the theater, the children must reluctantly decide to get rid of him. *The Story of the Amulet* starts out well as the

4. The Children's Novel

children begin to have more successful adventures and the novel is less episodic in that it is goal-directed like an adventure story. They must complete the amulet in order to get their parents home. Unfortunately, Nesbit decided to take a higher tone in this novel so that when the amulet is evoked we are informed that "this was not like the things that had happened in the country when the Psammead had given them their wishes. That had been funny somehow, and this was not. It was something like Arabian Nights magic, and something like being in church" (51). At the same time, she unfortunately discovers that the children's novel can be used allegorically to promote her socialist values, and this higher tone combined with allegory is presumably what gave the hint to C. S. Lewis. Admittedly the Queen of Babylon episode is hilariously funny, if one can hold one's nose at the anti–Semitism, but the description of the Egyptian working class is silly and patronizing and the "dream" of "The Little Black Girl" is mawkishly sentimental. Most unfortunate of all is the final vision of a future utopian London. There is some wit in naming the expelled boy "Wells" but her utopia is boringly dreary and violates the central principle of the children's novel by creating a world in which children consider it a punishment not to be allowed to attend school. That Nesbit is allowing her socialism to detract from her strengths as a children's writer is seen when the normally compassionate Anthea, the main protagonist of the series, uncharacteristically and rather sadistically, drags the mother back to contemporary London to rub her nose in its horrors. Unfortunately, Nesbit, in her subsequent works of fantasy, never manages to avoid this higher "seriousness" and I, for one, much prefer her pre–*Amulet* novels.

    I end this chapter with Arthur Ransome because he presents an interesting development in the history of the pure children's novel. In *Swallows and Amazons,* he follows Nesbit in making use of a collective protagonist but departs from her in abandoning the intrusive narrator. Except for a few occasions, he completely foregoes the I/you relationship between narrator and narratee that is characteristic of both Nesbit's first and third-person narration. Wall is equally laudatory of both Nesbit's and Ransome's voices even though they are entirely different. Both are seen as examples of single address despite the fact that Nesbit is constantly reminding her narratee that she is a child being addressed by an adult. Wall also has a problem with the fact that Ransome insisted that he was not writing *for* children and accuses him of being "disingenuous" (29) but all he meant was that he was writing *for* a narratee who is both child and adult, who hovers between the idyllic and didactic. The point of view of *Swallows and Amazons* is just as dual as that of *Alice in Wonderland* and *The Treasure Seekers*.

The whole novel is an elaborate evocation of the pretend play of four siblings, which, although unrealistic in its length and intensity, is quite accurate in its understanding of how children enter and leave the play context, particularly in the exciting description of how the Swallows enter into a "treaty" with the Amazons, in chapter ten:

> "Let's be allies," said Peggy. "Really we wanted to be allies as soon as we saw your smoke on the island yesterday. We are sick of natives. And we wanted to be allies at once, if only we hadn't promised to be home for lunch. That was why we just sailed round the island and defied you with our flag. There wasn't time for anything else. Then we went home" [109].

This passage is representative of the entire chapter in its mixture of play and reality and in the way that the children swiftly negotiate a merging of their separate plays, a feat that requires considerable imaginative flexibility when one considers that the Swallows are "explorers" and the Amazons "pirates." Also one sees that the Amazons have the same problem with lunch that Nesbit's children had with dinner. The narratee is clearly poised in the middle between the view of the protagonists, intent on their play, and the view of the adult "natives" who insist that they be home for lunch, that is, poised between the idyllic and the didactic. Indeed, if the child reader were not in that position it would be impossible to play with the book in the way it asks to be played. Wall's contention that Ransome "simply put himself in the place of the children" and that "he has no viewpoint apart from theirs" (30) misrepresents his practice.

The narrator in *Swallows and Amazons* is clearly an adult but the kind of adult that is actually represented in the novel in the characters of the two middle-class mothers and in the more eccentric Uncle Jim, that is, an adult who knows how to play. The middle-class bias of the book has been much commented on but there is nothing unusual about that. In the terms of the book, all adults are "natives," including the mother but the mother, being middle-class unlike the other natives we

4. The Children's Novel

meet (the nurse, the farmers and the policeman), knows that she is a native, which is to say she knows how to play the game, largely because she has read the right books, *Treasure Island* and *Robinson Crusoe*. She tactfully only visits the island three times and on the third occasion finds her younger daughter has been left alone. In a touching evocation of the book's framing device, she responds to Titty's greeting of "Hullo, Man Friday" as follows:

> "Hullo, Robinson Crusoe," said mother. That was the best of mother. She was different from other natives. You could always count on her to know things like that.
> Robinson Crusoe and Man Friday then kissed each other as if they were pretending to be Titty and mother [189].

Under the circumstances the mother naturally invites Titty to come home and she bravely resists the temptation three times, although on the third occasion she wavers and calls out to her mother as she is rowing away:

> But in that moment Titty remembered again that she was not merely Robinson Crusoe, who had a right to be rescued by a passing ship, but also Able-seaman Titty, who had to hoist the lantern on the big tree behind her, so that the others could find the island in the dark, and then to light the leading lights so that they could bring their prize into the harbour [193].

She chooses to stay on the island but the choice to continue to play is a painful, therefore a moral, choice as she does her duty to her brothers and sisters.

Clearly the reader is not simply being asked to identify with Titty in this scene even though we are allowed considerable access to her consciousness; rather, we are hovering somewhere between the mother and child's perspective. This view is supported by the way the scene ends:

> "Goodbye," called Titty. She lay down on the look-out point, and watched mother through the telescope. Suddenly she found that she could not see her. She blinked, pulled out her handkerchief, and wiped first the telescope glass and then her eye.
> "Duffer," she said. "That's with looking too hard. Try the other eye" [193].

The narratee, whether child or adult, is looking at Titty from above, from that middle position so characteristic of the children's novel.

When Ransome denied that he wrote for children he was simply trying to convey the fact that in a good children's novel the adult narrator and the child narratee occupy much the same position; indeed, they are merely opposite sides of the same coin, caught as they are in the tension between the idyllic and didactic. If the narrator of a children's novel is an adult who knows how to play then the narratee is a child who knows that play must end.

The delicate balance between the idyllic and the didactic so characteristic of the children's novel is everywhere maintained in *Swallows and Amazons*. The extremely intense and satisfactory incident of the night raid is balanced by John leaving the island and his play behind to talk what Titty calls "native talk" (245) with his mother, at which time he confesses and agrees with her that their behavior was "very nearly like being duffers" (246). Meanwhile Susan, the least adventurous of the foursome, and seemingly the inspiration for C.S. Lewis's Susan, "was in a very native mood that day, as Able-Seaman Titty observed. Perhaps the adventures of the night were heavier on her conscience than on those of the other Swallows" (243). Titty, the main protagonist, is appropriately the most adventurous and imaginative, the one with the most dangerous and blood-thirsty suggestions, but her play, precisely for that reason is the most restrained by the didactic as one can see in the scene analysed above. The basic principle is summed up in the observation that "natives were like that, useful in a way, but sometimes a bother. They all held together, a huge network of gossip and scouting, through the meshes of which it was difficult for explorers and pirates to slip" (242). In the end, of course, after the storm, all the natives rush to the island and all play comes to an end as it always does in the children's novel.

The story unfolds for the most part through "pictures and conversations," that is narrative summary and dialogue and when we do enter the consciousness of the protagonists it is, in many cases, through what I have called descriptive psycho-narration. The novel begins with an "amused but affectionate" description of the seven-year-old Roger as he tacks against the wind to his mother. The focus is at a middle distance that remains fairly constant throughout the novel. In the second paragraph we briefly pan in as we see his mother through his eyes and hear his thoughts concerning the first moral dilemma the novel

4. The Children's Novel

evokes, the question of whether he is old enough to participate in the dangerous play of his siblings. Theoretically, it would have been possible to tell the whole story centered on Roger as Carroll did with his seven-year-old but this is realism not fantasy and so, realistically, he is represented as the least competent and most timid of the siblings, and we never enter his consciousness again except for some brief moments of descriptive psycho-narration. The fact that he is allowed to join his siblings might well alarm some bourgeois mothers but such alarm is somewhat allayed by the use of the collective protagonist that is anchored on the other end by John. We are never told John's age and this is probably a good strategy since he must necessarily be an ambiguous character, both old enough to be responsible for his siblings and yet young enough to participate in their play. The idyllic/didactic machine is largely constructed on the contrast between Susan and Titty, the latter being the child pervert and the main source of humor.

The collective protagonist is also given a collective consciousness as we are told that "on the lake they had seen the island. All four of them had been filled at once with the same idea. It was not just an island. It was *the* island, waiting for them. It was their island" (17). The collective is then precipitated out, according to age, as four fixed types who do not change in the course of the novel, much in the manner of Alcott with her four siblings:

> John was thinking of the sailing, wondering whether he really remembered all that he had learnt last year. Susan was thinking of the stores and the cooking. Titty was thinking of the island itself, of coral, treasure and footprints in the sand. Roger was thinking of the fact that he was not to be left behind [19].

This collective consciousness persists sporadically throughout the novel mainly in the form of descriptive psycho-narration: "they could see into the bay no longer" (36) and "four pairs of eyes searched every little jetty" (90). This collective consciousness can be more fully rendered at times, as in the long paragraph when they are giving names to the various places they have discovered but cannot agree on a name for their island because they "were bothered by the thought of the fireplace which they had found there" (82). In such cases there is often some ambiguity about whether or not we are dealing with a collective consciousness or not. For example, on her second visit, the mother makes a potentially critical comment about the Amazons with the following result:

> There was silence. It was all right to talk to mother about their own affairs. Mother was a friendly native. But nothing could be said about the affairs of the Amazons. Mother noticed the silence, and at once began to talk of something else. She was really the very best of natives [172].

There could be some debate about whether this is narrative summary or narrated monologue but in either case the result is the same. As always, the narratee is caught in the middle, balanced equally between admiration of the children's reticence and admiration of the mother's tactful repression of her legitimate concerns.

Of course, one of the collective must be selected as the main protagonist and Ransome is quite subtle in this matter. It would seem reasonable to expect that the main protagonist would be the one whose consciousness we enter most often and, on these grounds alone, Roger and Susan are ruled out. We only briefly enter Susan's consciousness four times in the novel and on all occasions it is to confirm her role as the didactic voice, the one least committed to dangerous play. The first occasion is when she is worried about being hit by a jibing sail and remembers a previous occasion when it happened (36). The second occasion is when the other children are joyfully "galumphing" down the hill and miss the signs they left of their blazed trail:

> Susan, however, saw it. She had begun looking out for it as soon as she was in the path through the trees, and on that account her galumphing could hardly be called galumphing at all [146].

This technique could be characterized as reluctant psycho-narration, when the narrator allows you entry to a character's consciousness but then draws back to a middle distance with an ironic comment, in this case a comment on Susan's lack of commitment to dangerous play. The third occasion is very subtle. She "looked down" on John swimming and sees that "He was moving very slowly," whereupon she suggests that he come ashore, a suggestion quickly countered by Titty shouting "You're nearly round" (166). Again, the effect is to create a perfect balance between a didactic and an idyllic perception of the same scene. The fourth occasion repeats this pattern as we are told that Susan "did not like thinking of Titty alone on the island for so long" (221).

4. The Children's Novel

At the beginning of the novel it would seem that John has the best claim to the role of main protagonist. *Swallows and Amazons* arises from the tradition of the boy's adventure story and John embodies the stereotypical hero from that tradition, a brave, competent leader of men who swims around the island, conducts a daring night raid and worries about his honor when Uncle Jim accuses him of being a liar. Narrative technique would seem to support this conclusion since, in the first half of the novel we spend the most time in his consciousness. In the course of the novel we enter John's consciousness on nineteen occasions for a total of twenty-three paragraphs of interior monologue. Of those, three are cases of descriptive psycho-narration; six involve purely practical concerns about sailing the ship and understanding the harbour markings and the remaining fourteen paragraphs constitute moral anxiety about his relationship with Captain Flint and the propriety of sailing the ship at night. The climactic moment of his moral dilemma comes in chapter 15, when his solitary confrontation with Captain Flint and the accusation that he is a liar is preceded by three paragraphs of interior monologue. This problem is resolved eventually by a manly handshake as we enter John's consciousness for the last time except as part of the collective:

> There was a most unpleasant lump in Captain John's throat. He found that it was almost more upsetting to have things put right than it had been when they went wrong. Then at least he could be angry, and that was a help. This was worse. He swallowed twice, and bit the inside of his lip pretty hard. He held out his hand. Captain Flint took it, and shook it firmly. John felt suddenly better [274].

This is effectively the end of John's story and by this point the reader is well aware that it is Titty, not John, who is the protagonist of the novel.

It would be interesting to speculate when the reader first becomes aware that Titty is the main protagonist of the story. In the course of the novel we enter her consciousness fifteen times for a total of sixty-six paragraphs of interior monologue but these numbers are misleading since only two of the occasions are in the first half of the novel.[4] The first time we enter her consciousness is in a moment of descriptive psycho-narration when she awakens to their first day on the island:

> The next day was a busy one. It began early. Sunshine in a tent is even

> more waking than sunshine in a room. Titty woke first and lay awake looking at patches of sunlight and shadow playing on the white walls of the tent as the sun came through the waving tops of the trees. Then she crawled to the door of the tent and put her head out, sniffing the damp morning air and listening to the rustling of the leaves and the noise of ripples on the island shore [62].

The very fact that we are introduced to the island through what Titty sees, smells and hears is a strong clue that she is to be a major player. In the next chapter she is established as the most imaginative of the siblings when, in three paragraphs of interior monologue, she unsuccessfully plays at "being a cormorant"(74) until it transmogrifies into "pearl-divers" (75). This is a significant moment since it foreshadows the fact that when we enter her consciousness, as we do quite often in the second half of the novel, what she is mostly thinking about is the nature of the script and how she is to perform it. In other words, what she typically thinks about is play itself. Of course, there are other clues at the beginning of the novel that Titty is the main protagonist. She is comically represented as the one most fanatically dedicated to complete adherence to the script and the others defer to her judgment in this matter. Also her passionate obsession with dangerous play is one of the main sources of humor as in her oft repeated assertion that "we ought to sink the houseboat" (164).

The turning point comes when the decision is made to leave her on the island alone and we are told that she "longed to have Wild Cat Island all to herself, to be a lonely lighthouse keeper, to be Robinson Crusoe, and to feel just what a really desert island was like. A blanket would do for a goatskin" (177). This is followed in chapter eighteen by twelve paragraphs of interior monologue consisting of psycho-narration, quoted monologue and narrated monologue followed by her meeting with her mother in the scene analysed above. It is at this point that we are strongly asked to identify with Titty though some comic distance is maintained by the fact that the island is somewhat recalcitrant in accepting the Robinson Crusoe script, that she is distracted by yet another bird and that she is working with two scripts at once, that she is supposed to be both Robinson Crusoe and Jim Hawkins. Our identification with Titty becomes almost complete in chapter 20 which consists almost entirely of interior monologue as we watch her revise

4. The Children's Novel

the script so as to snatch victory from defeat and win the war single-handedly. This is the most exciting moment in the novel and our identification with Titty becomes close to that which we feel for the first-person narrator of a boy's adventure story, though some comic distance is maintained by the incongruity of the fact that Jim Hawkins is a ten-year-old girl and by the fact that this is, after all, just play. Also, the narrator intrudes with two narrative asides. When Titty thinks the story is over the narrator informs us that "she was wrong. It is never safe to say that nothing more can happen" (211). And, when the story does end somewhat anticlimactically with Titty thinking that she is going to fall asleep, the narrator informs us "she was right" (213). After this chapter, the novel returns to its more typical comic middle distance, and though Titty is to triumph again in discovering buried treasure, that triumph is somewhat attenuated by the fact that it is completely by accident.

Titty's position as protagonist is recognized by two moments of collective consciousness at the end of the novel. As the six children huddle in their tent during the storm, we enter all their minds except Roger's. In comic contrast to the somewhat prosaic reactions of the older children, we end with Titty, who, still splendidly intrepid, "with sparkling eyes, was thinking of typhoons" (330). The adventure ends as it begins as we enter all the minds of the siblings as they look back on the island as they are leaving it. There is a significant reordering of their positions as Titty takes the climactic position she has earned:

> John, looking at it, remembered the harbour and the leading lights and his swim all around it, and climbing the great tree. For Roger it would always be the place where he had swum for the first time. For Susan it was the camp and housekeeping and cooking for a large family. Titty thought of it as Robinson Crusoe's island. It was her island more than anyone's because she had been alone on it [350].

The revelation that Titty is the protagonist and not John is evoked by a very sophisticated and subtle use of third-person narration and Ransome does not often get the critical attention he deserves, probably because, like Nesbit at her best, his novel is not about anything but play. Wall's contention that his narration is "single address" fails to capture the nature of his accomplishment and I fail to see why the adult reader would have any difficulty in taking the position of narratee. The adult who is unwilling to play *Swallows and Amazons* would have to be a complete prig, which is pretty much the point, and pretty much the only point, that the novel makes.

Of course, the pure children's novel has its antecedents in the nineteenth century and in the next chapter I shall analyse that history. *Alice in Wonderland*, was, to some degree, a lucky accident but one that is firmly grounded in the material reality of the historical consequences of the rise of literacy. The importance of the Alice books to subsequent writers of children's novels is attested to by the fact that almost all those writers include some allusion to the Alice books in their own novels. Nesbit's novels are clearly indebted to the tradition of the girl's domestic novel and she began her career as a writer for children by parodying that tradition. Similarly, Ransome's novels are clearly indebted to the tradition of boy's adventure and in both cases it is possible to give an historical account of the process by which the girl's domestic novel and the boy's adventure story transformed themselves into the pure children's novel, a process that involves an increasing acceptance of the reality and value of children's play.

5

The Nineteenth-Century Children's Novel

In the nineteenth century there appeared two diametrically opposed genres of children's novels, the boy's adventure story and the girl's domestic novel. The contrast could hardly be greater. Put most simply the adventure story encourages boys to leave home whereas the domestic novel encourages girls to stay home. Boy's adventure arises out of epic and romance and follows the archetypal pattern of the hero myth as described by Joseph Campbell in *The Hero with a Thousand Faces*. The hero leaves a safe and civilized place to cross "the threshold of adventure" into a dangerous "dream landscape of curiously fluid, ambiguous forms, where he must survive a succession of trials" (97). The protagonist of the boy's adventure story must confront monsters only slightly less mythic, cannibals and pirates. In the more realistic domestic novel the monsters are much tamer and the family is the safe haven that keeps them at bay and, if the protagonist is tempted to leave home for a wider world, that ambition is always sacrificed to the need for keeping the family intact. As a corollary to this difference, only girls need to grow up. The play of boys is not seen to be fundamentally different from the business of men whereas the adventurous perversity of young girls must always be tamed in order to produce proper wives and mothers.

In *Children's Literature Comes of Age*, Maria Nikolajeva describes this difference more abstractly by pointing out that "male time is linear" and "male space is open" whereas "female time is circular" and female "space is closed and confined" (125). The plot of the boy's adventure story is the suspense plot, linear and goal directed, shot like an arrow at the target (treasure). Various obstacles are placed in the way of this forward movement to construct a series of Freytag's pyramids, a series of climaxes of increasing intensity. To read a boy's adventure story is to climb a series of higher and higher mountains. In contrast, the plot of the adult domestic novel is typically a plot of revelation, the Austen plot, one in which some discovery makes us look back in time and reassess what has happened. Interestingly, the girl's domestic novel does not use this plot but rather one in which "time is cyclically closed and marked by recurrent time indications: ('It was spring again,' 'It was Christmas again')" (Nikolajeva, 125). Also, these seasonal cycles spiral over a number of years with the circles becoming increasingly constrictive. For example, in *Anne of Green Gables* the seasonal cycle begins in June and the first twelve chapters take place during an idyllic three weeks in June (89 pages). We then slowly cycle through year one in nine chapters marked by the various months (87 pages). Time speeds up in year two (7 chapters; 50 pages) and more so in year three (2 chapters; 20 pages) and year four (2 chapters; 14 pages. Year five sees some relief from these tightening circles (5 chapters; 34 pages) but it difficult not to see in this pattern a tightening noose designed to fix the protagonist in the immobility of maturity, or perhaps as a sign of the final circle that is her fate, the ring on her finger.[1]

The above analysis would seem to suggest that nineteenth-century girls got a raw deal in their genre and in the socialization that it implies and certainly it would be easy to make the case but it is also possible to argue that boys did not get a much better deal. As Martin Green has pointed out in *Dreams of Adventure, Deeds of Empire*, the boy's adventure story is clearly an imperialistic fantasy celebrating personal aggrandizement, exploitation of others and military triumph. In reality, when you left home looking for adventure what you actually found were people who already thought they were home and no matter how you might disguise the fact by pretending the island was deserted so the treasure was yours or demonizing the natives as cannibals deserving of annihilation, what you were really doing was stealing. Moreover, all the protagonists of the girl's domestic novel are intelligent and imaginative, assets that seem largely irrelevant to the protagonist of the boy's adventure story who needs little more than cour-

5. The Nineteenth-Century Children's Novel

age and luck. Indeed, when Jim Hawkins is bragging to the pirates about how he has thwarted them, one cannot help wondering whether courage is not just another name for stupidity. Also, when I discuss these questions with my students, there are very few of them, whether male or female, who are willing to argue that Anne Shirley made the wrong decision when she gave up her academic career in order to look after Marilla. Perhaps, what the world needs is not more Anne Hawkins but more Jim Shirleys.

But as interesting as these questions are I am not primarily concerned with thematic questions but with an analysis of narrative technique in the children's novel and how those techniques are related to the nature of children's play. The boy's adventure story begins with *Robinson Crusoe* and so a good place to begin would be with an analysis of what one must do to the adult novel in order to turn it into a children's novel and that will be the main thrust of my argument but first I would like to consider a specific aspect of its narrative technique, its use of a first-person narrator. To some degree, this choice is merely an accident following from its use by Defoe who uses it to confer an element of autobiographical realism to the new form of the novel and it is quite possible to write an adventure story in the third-person. On the other hand, the persistence of this narrative technique suggests that it might have a special function and to explore this possibility I shall jump ahead to *Treasure Island* (1883) and Stevenson's own critical comments upon what he was trying to achieve in this novel.

Of course, the first step in creating a boy's adventure story is to make your first-person narrator a child and to confer a certain amount of autonomy upon this child with the inevitable result that the protagonist must be older than the typical protagonist of the pure children's novel. This fact has led Wall to conclude that "writers of adventure stories were in fact less writers for children than writers for adolescents" (66) but this is a mistake and the adolescent novel is an entirely different genre which does not really appear until after the Second World War. Clearly young boys, and for that matter young girls, had no difficulty in identifying with these older protagonists as evidenced by the fact that they actually adopted their stories as the scripts for their own dangerous play. Moreover, a clever writer like Stevenson could avoid the problem by simply failing to tell us how old Jim

Hawkins is, a trick adopted by Ransome with John. The real function of the first-person narration is to avoid the rendering of consciousness and, in the process, creating complete identification with the protagonist. It is for this reason that we insist upon calling boy's adventure a "story" rather than a "novel," thus asserting its roots in earlier narrative traditions like epic and romance.

Wall makes much the same point when she observes that

> by choosing to use a first-person narrator, Ballantyne was enabled to eliminate the digressions and much of the moralizing which had plagued, and continued to plague, adventure stories, and to let his young readers enter the "regions of fun," identifying with the participants and not distracted from the excitement and from enjoyment of horrors by questions of reality [69–70].

I would agree but it should be pointed out that Defoe uses a first-person narrator without achieving this effect so further analysis is required. Also it is somewhat odd to characterize this technique as an elimination of a "plague" and then to go on and find fault with it because "there is scarcely a pretence of reality" (70). Rather it is an effect that is entirely in keeping with the logic of the children's novel and I shall allow Stevenson himself to argue the point.

An interesting debate took place between Robert Louis Stevenson and Henry James on the subject of the proper nature of fiction, a debate analysed by Felicity Hughes in her article "Children's Literature: Theory and Practice." James, in his desire to establish the novel as "high" art, sought to carry the conventions of realism further. Hughes cites the "The Art of Fiction" as the manifesto in which James argues that "the novel should not be presented by its author as 'just a story' or as 'make-believe,' but as something akin to history" (544). The result of this authorial commitment to a new, improved realism will be increased alienation on the part of the reader. As Hughes observes "James required that characters in novels be presented 'objectively' in a way that prevents the reader from entering into any extraordinary sympathy with them" (545–46). Stevenson responded by defending "the notion of the novel as 'make-believe'" (545) and argued in "A Gossip on Romance" that the "illusion" of the story is designed to absorb the reader, to take us "rapt clean out of ourselves" (Stevenson, 9: 134). As Hughes points

5. The Nineteenth-Century Children's Novel

out, he wished to write novels that "make intense demands of sympathy and identification" (545). Hughes concludes:

> While it is difficult to see the consistency of either writer's position, it is clear enough that they were opposed on the two points under discussion. James claimed that novels are serious in so far as they attempt to provide "the intense illusion of real life." Stevenson denied this claim. Secondly, James required characters to be "objective" and the reader to be detached, impartial and sceptical, whereas Stevenson saw reader involvement and the submersion of self to be the triumph of art [546].

Actually, these two opposed positions are entirely consistent with the difference between the children's novel and the adult novel. Stevenson's position is anti-realist and anti-ironic; thus, he would push this difference to the point of complete identification with vicarious fantasy, to turning the novel into a second-hand daydream. The way to accomplish this goal is to adopt a first-person narrator like Jim Hawkins as he implies in a letter he wrote to James:

> Could you not, in one novel, to oblige a sincere admirer ... cast your characters in a mould a little more abstract and academic ... and pitch the incidents, I do not say in any stronger, but in a slightly more emphatic key — as it were an episode from one of the old (so-called) novels of adventure? I fear you will not [24: 129].

Jim Hawkins is such a flat character though perhaps it would be preferable to adopt Stevenson's term and call him an "abstract" character since flat characters are generally limited, stereotypical characters. Indeed, Wall has characterized the protagonist of the boy's adventure story as "a stereotypic adolescent 'British Boy'" (66) and, although this is true, perhaps it would be more accurate to characterize his function as that of an "abstract" or empty "I," a subject position devoid of personality, a "blank" monitor of events who permits complete identification and thus vicarious participation in those events.

Of course, I remain skeptical that complete identification is possible in any reading experience and specifically, in *Treasure Island*, it ceases in Part Two, "The Sea Cook," when Stevenson replaces the suspense plot with a plot of revelation. Every child reader knows that Silver is the pirate that Jim Hawkins has been warned against and, especially at the beginning of chapter eight, is screaming at Jim to stop being so bloody stupid. And even during the suspense plot there are several moments when the intelligent reader stops and wonders why Jim is behaving the way he does since his behavior is consistently irrational, albeit lucky. The predominant effect, however, is to encourage complete identification with his dangerous play and the plot of the novel is largely an elaborate game of hide and seek in which "home free" is constantly changing and safe places become dangerous places so that the reader is constantly being asked to share with Jim the experience of leaving home, often for no good reason except for the thrill of leaving and returning triumphant.

Wall has resisted this analysis by emphasizing the fact that the narrator of the novel is "the older Jim Hawkins, looking back" with the result that "although the boy's consciousness appears to be dominant, it is the man's preoccupations which give the book its depth" (70). By selecting the right passages it is certainly possible to make this case as Wall does in the analysis that follows. As a result of this reading, the novel not only achieves more "depth" but in the process becomes darker and more ambivalent, so "it can simultaneously be a clean, straightforward, thrilling adventure story for a child, and a sombre comment on the pertinacity of evil and the futility of human greed for an adult" (71). It is because the novel supports such a reading that, out of all the hundreds of boy's adventure stories written in the nineteenth century, this is the one to be canonized but I suspect only literary critics would read it this way. My own reading is closer to that of Robert Kiely who, in *Robert Louis Stevenson and the Fiction of Adventure*, observes that "to try to speak seriously of good or evil in *Treasure Island* is almost as irrelevant as attempting to assign moral value in a baseball game" (78). Of course, there is no "right" answer in such a debate but I am inclined to Kiely's view of the matter. Indeed, the point could be made by simply comparing *Treasure Island* to the adult version of the same story, Conrad's *Heart of Darkness*.

At this point I would like to return to *Robinson Crusoe* and the process by which one converts it into a children's novel. This process, not surprisingly, is a process of cutting things out. My contemporary Dover edition of the children's story brings Crusoe to the point of shipwreck in seven pages compared to the forty-five of the adult version. There are many reasons for the various deletions and changes but I am only interested in one, the desire to de-emphasize the didactic elements

5. The Nineteenth-Century Children's Novel

of the plot in favor of the idyllic. Thus, what you cut out is fairly straightforward: any incident that is not conducive to getting Defoe to the island, any discussion of what properly belongs to "the Middle station" in life and, as much as possible while supplying a context, any moralizing about the impropriety of disobeying one's father and leaving home and any religious agonizing over God's inevitable punishment of such behavior. Any boy who has played the game knows what is important. You have to get to the island where there are no parents and you can build as many fires as you like; you have to climb the mountain so you know where you are and can draw a map and then you have to build your fort and wait for the cannibals and pirates to appear. Of course, the idyllic was always present as a sub-text of the adult novel or else one could not explain its powerful appeal to the fantasies of its readers but, in order to create the children's version, the idyllic elements must be brought to the surface and this is what Ballantyne did in *The Coral Island* (1858). There are many steps in getting from Defoe to Ballantyne but I am only going to consider one, Frederick Marryat's *Masterman Ready* (1841).

As he acknowledges in his Preface, Marryat follows *Swiss Family Robinson* (1812) and, in shipwrecking a family, manages to introduce children into his story. The didacticism also shifts from Defoe's concern with personal salvation to lectures on natural history as signs of God's Providence and in this way he also points to Ballantyne. In *Swiss Family Robinson* the father is the first-person narrator but Marryat replaces him with a third-person narrator. Since in his previous adult adventure stories such as *Peter Simple* he used a first-person narrator, this change in strategy clearly reflects the fact that he is now writing for children which, as his Preface indicates, he considers a very serious business and so he feels the need to replace the more intimate first-person father with an omniscient, third-person Father. As Wall observes "he invariably writes with a strong consciousness of the gap between himself and his implied child reader. The narrating voice is always grave and restrained, as if a lighter approach, a stance nearer to the narratee, might jeopardize the impact of the message" (48) As she astutely points out "it is ironical" (46) that when Marryat made the conscious decision to write for children he produced a book that is probably less attractive to them than were his earlier more humorous adult adventure stories.

The novel, then, would seem to be a step in the wrong direction but actually Marryat replaces the Peter Simple character with the title character, an elderly but equally "simple" seaman and in doing so actually paved the way for Ballantyne to introduce his equally "simple," first-person narrator Ralph Rover, who is also "a queer, old-fashioned fellow" (11), "old-fashioned" being used in its now obsolete sense of "having the ways of a grown-up person" (OED). Marryat thus points the way to the children's novel by constructing a nascent collective protagonist which is comprised of a didactic/idyllic fulcrum centered on the title character with the didactic arm represented by the sensible, twelve-year-old William who is always ready to listen to a lecture from Ready or his father and the idyllic arm represented by the perverse, six-year-old Thomas who is always getting into scrapes. Although the balance always weighs heavily on the didactic side of the fulcrum and no one would characterize this novel as humorous, there are times, especially in the beginning of the novel when Thomas provides us with moments of comic relief that point in the direction the children's novel will take.

For example, we are invited to laugh when Thomas throws stones at the caged lion and is frightened to death when it attacks him. Then a page later the serious William asks his father why some birds can swim, thus occasioning a lecture on natural history and "the wonderful provisions made by the Almighty hand," a lecture, however, that is placed in a humorous context when William asks his father to recollect that "when Tommy drove the hens into the large pond, they flounced about, and their feathers became wet and would support them no longer and then they were drowned" (13). Of course, such moments become rarer after they are shipwrecked and Tommy is treated considerably less sympathetically when work is essential for survival and play is merely disruptive. The ultimate triumph of the didactic occurs at the end of the novel when Tommy's playful perversity causes the death of Ready.

We can, however, see in the earlier novel the inspiration for Ballantyne's creation of his own collective character in *The Coral Island*. The center of the idyllic/didactic fulcrum is now the simple but "old-fashioned" Ralph Rover, a first-person narrator whom Wall characterizes as "a nonentity" (69). He occasionally appears as an adult looking back but, in this case, the adult "I" adds no depth to the story but "exists only to tell the story" (69). Actually, when the adult "I" appears, he can be quite prosy as at the beginning of chapter twelve:

> Rest is sweet as well for the body as for the mind. During my long experience, amid the vicissitudes of a chequered life, I have found that periods of profound rest at certain intervals, in addition to the ordinary hours of repose, are necessary to the well-being of man [106].

In the abridged Puffin edition of the novel, the seven sentences that follow this introduction are sensibly deleted as if in recognition of the fact that Ralph's primary function is to be the empty "I" with whom we identify. In this case, however, when we identify with Ralph we are rewarded with the company of two delightful friends, Jack Martin and Peterkin Gay. The use of the collective protagonist modifies the first-person narration so that the pronoun "we" appears just as often as "I" in the course of the action.[2]

The didactic component of this collective "we" is Jack, "a tall, strapping, broad-shouldered youth of eighteen" who "had a good education, was clever and hearty and lion-like in his actions, but mild and quiet in disposition" (15). The idyllic component is Peterkin who is "little, quick, funny, decidedly mischievous, and about fourteen years old" (15). Just how far we have come from Marryat is shown not only by the fact that the sensible Jack is allowed to play but that the perverse Peterkin is not merely tolerated but actually celebrated since his "mischief was almost always harmless, else he could not have been so much beloved as he was" (15). This relative affirmation of playful perversity is supported in two ways. First, Ralph, unlike Crusoe, is positively supported by his father and mother in his decision to leave home. Second, and most important, is the idyllic nature of the island upon which they have been shipwrecked. Crusoe on his island not only must work very hard but is in a state of constant anxiety. The boys, in contrast, are shipwrecked into "Paradise" (34), a vast playground in which it is always summer vacation.

That this is indeed the script for the play of generations of future boys is affirmed by a brief list of their activities. They build fires, construct bows and arrows, drink "lemonade" (34) that grows on trees and have feasts that are forced upon them in almost obscene abundance. They explore; they build a boat and fish and hunt. They even have their own swimming pool and so idyllic is this place that they do not even have to build their fort since one is provided for them in the form of a cave with an underwater entrance. Of course, none of this would be much fun if there were not some danger so there are sharks and skeletons and storms and even a strange sound that might be ghosts but turns out to be penguins. Because the island is so idyllic the first half of *The Coral Island* forgoes the suspense plot in favor a series of natural mysteries that must be solved such as the mystery of the penguins and a series of practical puzzles that must be overcome such as how to provide light. As it turns out, on this island even candles grow on trees.

The adventure really only begins once the cannibals and pirates arrive in the second half of the novel. This section is further divided into two separate plots, the first of which looks ahead to *Treasure Island*. The collective protagonist disappears when Ralph is kidnaped by pirates and becomes the sole protagonist. It is this part of the novel that Stevenson extracts as the inspiration for his novel and the relationship of Ralph with the "good" pirate, Bloody Bill, is clearly a precursor of Jim Hawkin's relationship with Long John Silver. This story ends with Ralph's triumphant return with the captured pirate ship which he celebrates with uncharacteristic mischievousness by firing the cannon to scare his friends. The collective restored, the boys then set sail to rescue Avatea but, at this point, Ballantyne's Christian didacticism hijacks the adventure story and the boys end up languishing in prison until suffering the ignominy of being rescued by a Christian missionary.

Of course, in order to get from *The Coral Island* to Ransome's *Swallows and Amazons*, one must deflect the course of boy's adventure into the realm of domestic reality and this deflection is what is accomplished in Twain's *The Adventures of Tom Sawyer* (1876). It is well known that Twain did not originally write this novel for children and the narratee is explicitly an adult when we are informed that "the reader probably remembers how to do it (whistling) if he has ever been a boy" (13). When, however, on the advice of his wife and his publisher Howells, he decided to issue the work as a juvenile, very little revision was necessary since from the beginning the focus of the novel was that of the children's novel. Admittedly, at times, the narrative voice is sarcastic to the point of being patronizing but that tendency is always balanced by an enthusiastic nostalgia for a boyhood that as Twain asserts

5. The Nineteenth-Century Children's Novel

in his Preface "really occurred." The result, as Wall would put it, is that "in this case the original address to adults has become dual address, a transformation made possible by Clemen's boyish enthusiasm for his story" (115), to which I would reply that no transformation was necessary since the point of view was always dual as it always is in the children's novel.

Wall has it that "nostalgia and satire together, in uneasy partnership, underlie the narrative" (113) but nostalgia and satire in partnership are always the emotional polarities that, respectively, construct the idyllic/didactic machine that is the children's novel. There is perhaps some merit, in this particular case, of seeing the partnership as "uneasy" if one is comparing it to the perfect poise of the Carroll narrator, but for the most part Twain's narrator, like Carroll's, is hovering between the point of view of the child and the adult. Humor is created by the simple trick of translating the leaving-home pattern of boy's adventure into the realm of domestic reality so that Tom is always running away from home and playing hooky from school. When he is not at home or in school, he is playing dangerously, following the scripts provided by boy's adventure. Tom plays the "General" (25) in their war games, "Robin Hood" (71), "the Black Avenger of the Spanish Main" (101), and "Indians" (127). If there is an uneasy relationship in the novel it might well be between this humorous description of his play and the actual adventure that ends the novel, a romantic fantasy that sees Tom defeat Injun Joe to achieve fame and fortune, a fantasy, moreover, that is considerably "darker"than anything in *Treasure Island*. Injun Joe is the one character from children's literature whom I clearly remember as giving me nightmares.

As a character, Tom is also a humorous translation from boy's adventure. I have already commented on Jim Hawkins bragging before the pirates, a scene that is directly descended from the epic harangue. In *Tom Sawyer* this quality is humorously exaggerated into Tom's "showing off," especially in his antic behavior as he courts Becky Sharp. Tom is quintessentially the object of everyone's gaze. At the same time, even though he is the humorous object of a third-person narrator, he remains a curiously "abstract" character like the empty "I" that is Jim Hawkins. In the "Introduction" to the novel, Lee Clark Mitchell observes that "given the intense focus of everyone's attention on Tom Sawyer, it may come as something of a shock to realize how little he is actually seen or shown, how minimally in fact the novel ever describes or specifically places him" (xx). This quality encourages vicarious identification or as Mitchell puts it "Tom's very emptiness as a physical signifier encourages readers to project their separate ideas and fantasies, to fill in the faceless shape that Mark Twain so vaguely delineates" (xxi). With *Tom Sawyer* we have taken a large step toward the pure children's novel as represented by Ransome's *Swallows and Amazons*.

If *Tom Sawyer* represents a humorous mixture of domestic reality, adventurous play and actual adventure, *Bevis, The Story of a Boy* (1882) has the honor of being the first boy's novel entirely dedicated to a realistic representation of the play of children and, being the first, it is not surprising that Jefferies does not entirely get it right. *Bevis* exists in a kind of limbo. As Wall points out "Jefferies neither encourages the kind of alliance in which adult writer and child reader together are amused by a character, nor exploits the gap between adult writer and child reader by marking his ironies for adult appreciation only" (122–23). In other words, the novel has the potential to move in either of two directions. If Jefferies had exploited "the gap" as Wall puts it, he would have created something very much like Grahame's *The Golden Age* but if he had encouraged the "alliance" of "adult writer and child reader" he would have created something very like Ransome's *Swallows and Amazons*. Thus the earlier novel points in both directions without realizing either with the result that the idyllic/didactic tension is entirely lacking as is the humor. The tone is entirely dead-pan as if we are being presented with a detailed case study in the nature of boyhood. Irony is present since the boys fail as often as they succeed in realizing their fantasies and they have very brief attention spans and easily drop one game to take up another but the irony is never noted, nor does it make a point; rather, we are simply presented with the reality of boys at play.

This representation is, in some ways, more realistic than in the typical children's novel but in others quite fantastic. The idyllic harmony of spirit that is found in the boys of *The Coral Island* is missing. Although Bevis and Mark are inseparable, they fight quite often and Bevis treats his friend imperiously and cruelly and Mark bitterly resents his subordinate position. Also more realistic is the fact that the scripts they work with are much less coherent than those found in Ransome's

5. The Nineteenth-Century Children's Novel

novels. They constantly change scripts and discard ones that are not working. We are not told what age they are. Wall thinks "Bevis is about twelve, a clever, wilful and passionate child" (120) but in the first few chapters he appears to be a petulant six-year-old and by the end of the novel he is an accomplished young man, despite the fact that all the events take place in the course of one summer. What seems most unrealistic is the almost complete lack of restraint that is put on their exceedingly dangerous play. They whack one another with wooden swords, make a gun, kill animals for the sheer pleasure of it and almost end up shooting Loo so involved are they in their tiger hunt. Perhaps, in the interest of maintaining the Empire, Victorian boys played harder than boys today but if they had actually played like this it would be a wonder if any survived. Admittedly, Bevis has some minimal sense of restraint. When asked why they cannot use arrows and spears in the battle he explains that "eyes will get poked out, ... and there would be a row. If anybody got stuck and killed, there would be an awful row" (126). One is never entirely sure if Jefferies is joking at moments like this and at times one sees in the text yet a third possibility, the possibility that leads to *Lord of the Flies*.

Their play, even more so than in the later novels by Grahame and Ransome, is predicated upon class and it is made quite clear that the elaborate play of the boys is supported by ample leisure and money. It is summertime so school is never mentioned though Bevis is clearly well educated, has access to a large library, and has read extensively in the literature of adventure, including Homeric epic. The importance of class is foregrounded very early in the novel when Bevis enlists the services of the stableboy to pull his raft to the stream. When the boy hesitates, Bevis, with typical unpleasantness, stamps his foot and insists "I'm your master." When the boy points out that it is actually Bevis' father who is his master, his response is: "You do it this minute," said Bevis, hot in the face, "or I'll *kill* you; but if you'll do it I'll give you — sixpence" (10). Once the raft is launched, the stableboy is clearly intrigued and wants to join in the play but Bevis ignores him until the Bailiff appears, grabs him by the neck and drags him back to work. We are then informed that "Bevis and Mark were too full of the raft even to notice that their assistant had been haled off" (11). This oblivion to others is fairly typical of the boys when they are engrossed in their play although there are moments when Bevis's egotism is balanced by a sense of compassion.

Rigid class distinctions are not unusual in the British children's novel but seldom are they asserted so explicitly and ruthlessly. Much more unusual, however, is what happens when class and gender mix. The result is a sexual explicitness that is seldom found in the children's novel. In a number of scenes the boys are the objects of the gaze of slightly older, lower-class females. On the first occasion the boys are exploring their newly discovered land and arrive at the cottage of the witch. The following scene ensues:

> "Granny, don't you know who they be?" said a girl, coming round the corner of the cottage. She was about seventeen, and very pretty, with the bloom which comes on sweet faces at that age. Though they were but boys they were tall, and both handsome; so she had put a rose in her bosom. "They be Measter Bevis and Measter Mark. You know, as lives at Longcot" [66].

The boys are oblivious to her but she is clearly fascinated by them and accompanies them to show them the way home. When they part company, Bevis offers her the standard sixpence whereupon we are told:

> She took it, but her eyes were on him, and not on the money; she would have liked to have kissed him. She watched them till she saw they had got into the straight road, and then went back [69].

We meet her again when the boys are pretending to be savages and accidently intrude upon "a group of haymakers resting for lunch" (100). She is being courted by one of the laborers and is described in vivid detail:

> Her large eyes, like black cherries—for black eyes and black cherries have a faint tint of red behind them—were immediately bent full on Bevis as she rose and curtseyed to him. Her dress at the throat had come unhooked, and showed the line to which the sun had browned her, and where the sweet clear whiteness of the untouched skin began. The soft roundness of the swelling plum as it ripens filled her common print, torn by briars, with graceful contours. In the shadow of the oak her large black eyes shone larger, loving and untaught.
> Bevis did not speak. He and Mark were a little taken aback, having jumped through the gap so suddenly from savagery into haymaking. They hastened through a gateway into another field [100–101].

In this case the boys are not quite so oblivious though it is made clear

5. The Nineteenth-Century Children's Novel

that they are not yet ready for the "haymaking" game. Also, although they are the objects of her gaze, she in turn is more fully the object of the gaze of the male narrator.

Later, there is a similar, though much more intense scene, with the fourteen-year-old Loo who is helping them to make their gun. We enter her consciousness as she has masochist fantasies about the boys:

> She would have put her arm on the anvil to receive a blow from the hammer; she would have gone down the well in the bucket if they had asked her. Her mind was full of this wonderful work — what could they be making? But her heart and soul was filled with these great big boys with their beautiful sparkling eyes and white arms, white as milk, and their wilful, imperious ways. How many times she had watched them from afar! To have them so near was almost too great a joy; she was like a slave under their feet; they regarded her less than the bellows in her hands [232].

The last sentence suggests that the point of all this is an ironic observation on the indifference of boys to girls but, in proportion, the emphasis is on the sexual fascination of the girl. Later in the novel, she will actually become their slave on the imaginary desert island.

As the gun-making scene continues, Loo has fantasies about the boys kicking her and pulling her hair. She imagines that "she would put her naked foot so they could step on it; then if she cried out perhaps they would stroke her" (233). This fantasy is actually enacted at the end of the chapter but not quite how Loo would wish:

> At night they went for the barrel. Loo brought it, and Bevis, as he thought, accidentally stepped on her naked foot, crushing it between his heel and the stones at the door. Loo cried out.
>
> "Oh dear!" said he, "I am sorry. Here — here's sixpence, and I'll send you some pears."
>
> She put the sixpence in her mouth and bit it, and said nothing. She indented the silver with her teeth, disappointed because he had not stroked her, while she stood and watched them away [233–34].

Again the boy's oblivion to the desire he has evoked is in marked contrast to the conscious, though unsuccessful, contrivance the girl has used to satisfy it. Given that Bevis is purportedly a biographical construct, one might wonder whether these fantasies have more to do with Jefferies or the Victorian age. In any case, they entirely disappear in Grahame and Ransome, who replace these girls with safe sisters of the same class and the same competence in adventurous play.

Then again perhaps they do not so much disappear as they are simply effaced. Jacqueline Rose has invited us to think of *Peter Pan* in terms of homoerotic fantasy and the boy's adventure story certainly supports a similar analysis. Bevis and Mark bathe together every morning and the description of this activity invites comparison with Marlowe's description of Leander swimming the Hellespont. They "glided buoyantly, lifted by the water as swallows glide on the plane of the air" and Bevis is described as "lost in the ecstacy of motion" (286). Similarly, in *The Coral Island*, the boys bathe together and we are told that

> there was, indeed, no note of discord whatever in the symphony we played together on that sweet Coral Island; and I am now persuaded that this was owing to our having been tuned to the same key, namely, that of *love*! Yes, we loved one another with much fervency while we lived on that island; and, for the matter of that, we love each other still [126].

Boys who play together stay together.[3]

But perhaps this kind of analysis is too limited and what is most intriguing about the representation of sexual fantasy in *Bevis* is not its explicitness but its ambiguity. One could interpret it as an homoerotic fantasy projected upon lower-class females, a sado-masochistic fantasy or, simply, a fantasy of Victorian, middle-class males about lower-class women. Similarly, in the Alice books, as Empson has pointed out, in some scenes, like the one with the Gnat, Alice is the object of Carroll's desire, whereas in others, like the one with the Duchess and the flamingo, Carroll is Alice, unwillingly made the object of female desire. In discussing Rose's theory, Kimberley Reynolds observes that "it seems to be precisely *because* childhood is presumed to be innocent that so many writers have felt it safe to let their private fantasies find expression in writing for children" (24). Certainly the myth of childhood innocence effaces the reality of childhood sexuality but rather than concluding that this effacement is in the service of the private fantasies of individuals, or of males, or of the Victorian age, we get closer to the truth about the children's novel if we conclude that it is in the service of the very principle of fantasy itself. The polymorphous perverse is not called "polymorphous" for nothing. The sexuality that is effaced by the myth of innocence is not any particular sexuality but, rather, all possible sexualities at once. What *Bevis* makes rather uncomfort-

5. The Nineteenth-Century Children's Novel

ably explicit is that the idyllic of boy's adventure is the pure pleasure principle of unrepressed fantasy.

In marked contrast, the reality principle is firmly in control in the girl's domestic novel but one of the more comforting aspects of Freudian theory is that it asserts that we all start out in the same place; in the beginning we are all perverts. Children, whether male or female, do not need a script in order to play dangerously; all can equally, to the horror of their parents, climb to the top of the monkey bars and crow their triumph. And, although the function of the girl's domestic novel is to repress such behavior, ultimately, it must be repressed in all of us. This is the reality that underlies the realistic domestic novel, in both its adult and children's versions, and a logical place to begin an analysis of the domestic novel is with a comparison of the different visions of this reality manifested in the different narrative techniques of *Pride and Prejudice* and *Little Women*.

A comparison between *Pride and Prejudice* and *Little Women* is certainly justified by the similarities of the novels. Both are novels about the education of a group of female siblings placed in a domestic context and involved in a number of courtships leading to marriage. Both share similar views about class and what it means to be a "lady" and represent this social ideal in specific social contexts such as "balls" and "visits." Both make the main protagonist the second eldest sister, the clever-but-not-so-pretty one whose temper must be tamed. The differences, however, are much more striking. In *The Rhetoric of Character*, Nikolajeva begins her analysis of Alcott's use of the collective protagonist, with the observation that "we can clearly see the difference between the four March sisters and the five Bennett sisters in *Pride and Prejudice*, in which Elizabeth is by almost every criterion the sole protagonist, while her sisters have supporting roles" (74). Furthermore, in *Pride and Prejudice*, three of the siblings are the objects of scathing irony whereas in *Little Women* all the siblings are the objects of affectionate amusement. Nikolajeva goes on to point out that "by contrast, the protagonist in *Little Women* consists of four entities, each representing specific traits" (74).

While I certainly agree that there is a collective protagonist, Nikolajeva, here and in her subsequent argument, tends to overemphasize the centrality of this protagonist and to see this difference as an absolute one, whereas it is, as usual, a matter of degree. There is considerable evidence in the novel that Jo is the main protagonist and even in the first chapter this fact is signaled by the simple fact that she speaks first and that, when the narrator sketches their characters, Jo's sketch is twice as long as that of her siblings. Moreover, the Bennett sisters will occasionally appear as a collective, as when "every lady" saw Wickham for the first time and "all were struck with the stranger's air"(54). Indeed, the sisters appear collectively a number of times at the beginning of the novel, usually for ironic effect. For instance, the narrative summary that begins chapter three ends with the statement that "nothing could be more delightful! To be fond of dancing was a certain step towards falling in love; and very lively hopes of Mr. Bingley's heart were entertained" (5). This statement could be construed as narrated monologue ironically expressing the triteness of the collective female consciousness though, as is often the case in Austen, the irony is redoubled as the statement is literally true since in this restrictive society dancing *is* the only way to fall in love.

But I do not wish to quibble and there clearly is a difference between the two novels in Alcott's use of the collective protagonist. Nine of the twenty-three chapters of the first volume of *Little Women* belong to the collective protagonist (1, 2, 4, 10, 11, 12, 15, 16, 22) whereas Jo only gets five (3, 5, 8, 14, 21). But that is more than her siblings: Meg gets two (9, 23); Beth gets three (6, 17, 18) as does Amy (7, 19, 20). Laurie, who, as a boy, is in an interestingly ambivalent relationship to the collective, only gets one (13).[4] There is also some evidence of self-consciousness in Alcott's use of this technique in the way she weaves the individual stories into the story of the collective. The importance of the collective protagonist is further attested to by the fact that it almost disappears in volume two, in which only the first and last chapters belong to the collective. In volume two, we would more properly refer to multiple protagonists, which is a predictable development as the children get older, and, for this and other reasons, I am going to restrict my analysis to volume one. Alcott also gives her collective protagonist a collective consciousness, as in the opening of the novel when all the siblings join in "thinking of father far away, where the fighting was" (5) but she only does this for a total of 58 lines in the first volume and perhaps is not consciously aware she is doing it.[5] Sub-

5. The Nineteenth-Century Children's Novel

sequent writers, following her lead, will become more self-conscious about the ways the collective protagonist can be used and it will become more prominent in writers like Nesbit and Ransome. Also, subsequent writers will lower the age of their protagonists and the lower the age of the protagonists the more prominent the collective character will become as a representation of the children's play group.

As important as the collective protagonist is in differentiating between the narrative techniques of our two novels, it is secondary to, though connected to, the difference in voice and focus. The generalizations I am about to make will not seem startlingly original and merely confirm what most readers already intuitively know but it is useful to put what is already intuitively known in the context of a theory and to support it with empirical evidence. The famous first sentence of *Pride and Prejudice* immediately locates our narrator on the magisterial heights of irony from which we are invited to join her in looking down upon the imbecility of the poor mortals struggling in the social maze below. In marked contrast, the narrator of *Little Women*, in the amused but affectionate voice that Wall characterizes as "the equivalent of a fifth sister" (90), provides us with an intimate view of the conversation of four sisters but what soon becomes clear is that what this narrator loses in height she makes up for in breadth and the narrator of the children's novel is considerably more intrusive. After two formal and sarcastic sentences that establish her authority, the narrator of the adult novel descends into a ridiculous dialogue which needs little in the way of narrative asides. The narrator of the children's novel need not descend but the dialogue that begins the novel is hedged about with asides that establish not only who is speaking but how. This difference in voice and focus can be felt subjectively but is easily established objectively by simply counting lines where everything in quotation marks is dialogue and everything else is narration. If we compare in this way the first two chapters of *Pride and Prejudice* with the first chapter of *Little Women*, we discover that the adult novel has 35 lines of narration to 124 lines of dialogue whereas the children's novel has 180 lines of narration to 203 lines of dialogue. There is considerably more telling than showing in the children's novel and if this is what we intuitively expected we can just as easily turn to common sense to explain the difference by asserting that the inexperienced child reader needs more help than the adult. There is, however, an alternative and more positive explanation of this difference.

The comparison given above is simplified by the fact that there is no representation of consciousness in the first two chapters of *Pride and Prejudice* and only 15 lines of such in the first chapter of *Little Women*. If we are to compare the entire novels, we must divide the narration into narrative summary and the representation of consciousness and this is a somewhat less objective task than differentiating narration from dialogue and I doubt that any two readers would come up with exactly the same count. The task is made simpler if we remember that psycho-narration, quoted monologue and narrated monologue are purely grammatical categories and do not necessarily imply focalization, especially in the case of psycho-narration. For example, in chapter three of *Pride and Prejudice* we are told what Mrs. Bennet is thinking on two occasions for a total of eight lines of psycho-narration but there is no suggestion that we are to share her point of view or that what she is thinking is anything other than stupid. On the other hand, when we are told what Elizabeth is thinking we are usually expected to focalize and share her point of view even when she is wrong. I think that it is clear that there is considerably more focalization in the adult novel than in the children's novel but it would be difficult to demonstrate that objectively so I am going to give a purely grammatical count. The result is quite striking in itself. In *Pride and Prejudice* there are 2950 lines of narrative summary, 5111 lines of dialogue and 2869 lines of the representation of consciousness through psycho-narration, quoted monologue or narrated monologue for a proportion of 27%, 47% and 26% respectively. In the first volume of *Little Women*, the respective numbers are 3172, 3715 and 882 for a proportion of 41%, 48% and 11%. The amount of dialogue is about the same in the children's novel and the adult novel but there is a disproportionate amount of narrative summary in the children's novel and the reason for this is that the children's novel is not interested in the representation of consciousness. As a result, the narrator of the children's novel will always be more intrusive.[6]

The importance of point of view to the play of the novel is attested to by the fact that my assignation of protagonists to the various chapters is largely based upon this factor. In the chapters I have assigned to

5. The Nineteenth-Century Children's Novel

the collective character there is no focalization on any particular character. For example, in chapter one there are fifteen lines of psycho-narration of which the collective gets 3, Amy 1, Meg 3, Beth 3 and Jo 5. The fact that Jo gets the most is another subtle clue that she is the main protagonist and no one will be surprised to discover that we enter her mind more often than that of any other character but, even in proportion, it is no where near as often as we enter the mind of Elizabeth Bennett. Of the 2869 lines of the representation of consciousness in *Pride and Prejudice*, 2268 belong to Elizabeth, 79% of the total. Of the 882 lines in *Little Women*, 298 belong to Jo, 34% of the total and of those only about two-thirds involve focalization.[7] At the beginning of chapter two, there is a brief moment of focalization as Jo gets 7 lines of psycho-narration describing her waking to Christmas day but the rest of the chapter belongs to the collective which gets 3 lines, Beth 2, Meg 2, Mrs. March 1 and Jo 2 more. Chapter three, however, clearly belongs to Jo as we focalize on her for a total of 37 lines, including a long paragraph of psycho-narration as she surveys the ball (28) and another paragraph in which she surveys Laurie which ends as follows:

> Curly black hair, brown skin, big black eyes, long nose, nice teeth, little hands and feet, tall as I am; very polite for a boy, and altogether jolly. Wonder how old he is? [30].[8]

The purest example of the use of the collective protagonist occurs in chapter ten, which is purely humorous and which has no representation of consciousness. Instead, we enter the minds of the protagonists by reading texts they have written (I count this as dialogue) and this will become a much imitated source of humor in the children's novel.

The principle I am describing is fairly clear and there is no point in tediously analysing it for all the chapters in which it operates but there are a few anomalies that are worth considering. Chapter seven clearly belongs to Amy and hers is the only consciousness we enter but only for 20 lines and there is no focalization. Rather, Amy is objectified and the tone of this chapter comes very close to that we expect from the pure children's novel. The moral center of the chapter comes in two paragraphs of what I have called reluctant psycho-narration:

> That was dreadful; it would have been bad enough to go to her seat and see the pitying faces of her friends, or the satisfied ones of her few enemies;

> but to face the whole school, with that shame fresh upon her, seemed impossible, and for a second she felt as if she could only drop down where she stood, and break her heart with crying. A bitter sense of wrong, and the thought of Jenny Snow, helped her bear it; and, taking the ignominious place, she fixed her eyes on the stove-funnel above what now seemed a sea of faces, and stood there so motionless and white, that the girls found it very hard to study, with the pathetic little figure before them.
>
> During the fifteen minutes that followed, the proud and sensitive little girl suffered a shame and pain which she never forgot. To others it might seem a ludicrous or trivial affair, but to her it was a hard experience [68].

Before the narrator intrudes to distance us from the mind of the protagonist and to point the moral, "the pathetic little figure" has become an object of our gaze and even in the psycho-narration that precedes that description there is an element of objectification that is simultaneously comic and pathetic. We could term this technique "mock-heroic psycho-narration" since it is achieved by the use of an over-dramatized and inflated language to describe Amy's thoughts and feelings: "with that shame fresh upon her," "drop down where she stood" and "a bitter sense of wrong." To describe the situation as "ignominious" is a particular joke at the expense of the vocabulary-challenged Amy.

This technique is commonly used in the children's novel to enter the consciousness of young children and is fairly characteristic of how Amy is treated throughout the first volume of the novel. For example, we are told that "Amy suffered deeply at having to wear a red instead of a blue bonnet" (41) and that she "went on with her work, in the proud consciousness of virtue" (43). When Jo fails to forgive her for burning her book, we are told

> Amy was much offended that her overtures of peace had been repulsed, and began to wish she had not humbled herself, to feel more injured than ever, and to plume herself on her superior virtue, in a way that was particularly exasperating [75].

Again it is no surprise that we enter the minds of the youngest siblings, Amy and Beth, the least but even Jo, who comes the closest to being a reliable, central consciousness, is also subject to a certain amount of objectification.[9] Just over the page from the above example, we find the following example of reluctant psycho-narration:

5. The Nineteenth-Century Children's Novel

> Jo heard Amy panting after her run, stamping her feet, and blowing her fingers, as she tried to put her skates on; but Jo never turned, and went slowly zigzagging down the river, taking a bitter, unhappy sort of satisfaction in her sister's troubles. She had cherished her anger till it grew strong, and took possession of her, as evil thought and feelings always do, unless cast out at once [76].

In the last sentence we feel the narrator draw us back from Jo's consciousness in order to condemn it. Alcott is developing the techniques that subsequent writers for children will use.

Some might give chapter thirteen, "Castles in the Air," to the collective since it is about their collective dreams but I give it to Laurie because we focalize on him at the beginning and end of the chapter in 42 lines of psycho-narration and quoted monologue. As we watch Laurie spying on the girls at the beginning of the chapter, we can see Alcott again experimenting with objectification, in this case to signal Laurie's ambiguous relationship to the collective. Similarly, in the previous chapter, she objectified the girls in the consciousness of Miss Kate, in this case to signal their relative freedom as American girls. She will experiment with the device again in the next chapter, "Secrets," as we watch Jo submit her manuscript through Laurie's eyes though here the reader's pleasure lies in knowing he has got things wrong. Although this is clearly Jo's chapter, she only gets 20 lines of consciousness and the reader's desire to focalize on her is constantly being resisted by the narrator's attempt to objectify her, a technique that is again simultaneously comic and pathetic as we are both laughing at her success (there can be no sequel because "the hero and heroine were dead") and sympathetically admiring it like Beth who "got excited, and skipped and sung with joy" (152). The subplot of the chapter is also served by this objectification as Jo is laughed at for her refusal to accept the fact of Meg's romance, a joke that will continue through the rest of the volume.

The only other exceptions to the rule (that the use of the collective protagonist involves no focalization and that a single protagonist is focalized) relate to Beth. Chapter six presents no problem as we do enter Beth's consciousness in 30 lines of psycho-narration. In chapters seventeen and eighteen, however, we do not focalize on her; rather, she, in her illness, becomes the object of the concern of others and in chapter eighteen we actually focalize on Jo (25 lines) especially in the scene when she thinks her sister is dead (182). Of course, this fact is no surprise since Beth is literally unconscious toward the end but more than that her unconsciousness is a rhetorical device meant to represent the essentially unthinking nature of her spiritual goodness. This is a rhetorical trick designed to idealize Beth and, as Alderson has pointed out "the real Beth may have been their 'angel in the house,' but she was never the shy, retiring little mouse that Alcott made her" (xxiv). Just as Amy is typically objectified by mock-heroic psycho-narration, Beth is typically objectified by negative psycho-narration. Even in chapter six, which belongs to her in the conventional sense, she is so characterized:

> She never knew that Mr Laurence often opened his study door to hear the old-fashioned airs he liked; she never saw Laurie mount guard in the hall, to warn the servants away; she never suspected that the exercise-books and new songs which she found in the rack were put there for her especial benefit [60].

Beth's function in the novel is to forget herself as in the scene when she cheers up Frank by talking about buffaloes and she "forgot herself, and was quite unconscious of her sister's surprise and delight at the unusual spectacle of Beth talking away to one of the dreadful boys" (133–34). Her unconscious goodness must be rendered in the consciousness of others. These devices of objectification are what Alcott bequeathed to later writers of the children's novel and are part of the general tendency of the children's novel to avoid the rendering of consciousness even as it is being done.

 I have suggested that the narrator of the children's novel will always be more intrusive than the narrator of the canonical adult novel though, clearly, I have used that term in an unusual way, but even by more usual measures of intrusiveness, Alcott's narrator is quite intrusive, though not as much so as the Nesbit narrator. She refers to herself as "I" fifteen times in the first volume. Probably the reason that early novelists for children instinctively adopted this technique is that it helps to establish the gap between the child and adult, not a gap between narrator and narratee but between the narrator/narratee and the child protagonist. It is a confiding voice and is successful only to the extent that it is not condescending. In that regard one cannot help but think

5. The Nineteenth-Century Children's Novel

of the narrator at the beginning of *The Lion, the Witch and the Wardrobe* and how one cringes every time he mentions that damn wardrobe door. Of course, it is not necessary for the narrator of the children's novel to be so obviously intrusive but she will always be intrusive to the extent that there is a disproportionate use of narrative summary, and, increasingly as we approach the pure children's novel, the function of that narrative summary will be the humorous description of children at play. Play is essentially a thoughtless activity, even though it is the ground of all thought.

Of course, although play is described in *Little Women*, one could not say that it was central to the novel and this is not surprising since the novel arises out of a didactic tradition that is fundamentally hostile to play. The whole point of the girl's domestic novel is to convince young girls to give up their play so as to become proper ladies and good wives and mothers. Many of my students find the novel intolerably preachy but, compared to its immediate predecessors, it is a breath of fresh air. Susan Warner's *The Wide, Wide World* (1850) is a grim and humorless novel whose ten-year-old protagonist is only allowed to be happy when she is praying or reading Bunyan. At least Alcott allowed her girls to play the Bunyan game. As Foster and Simons point out, however, "it is one of the earliest and best examples of what was to become probably the most popular nineteenth-century fictional genre in America — the sentimental/domestic novel, written by women for women, and implementing an archetypal plot in which an unprotected heroine overcomes suffering and tribulations to achieve spiritual perfection and moral maturity" (37). This plot, thus, becomes the template for the plots of subsequent domestic novels for children, including Alcott's. This "archetypal plot" includes what seems to be a persistent, novelistic, female fantasy of marrying one's adopted, older brother who has been responsible for molding you into this figure of spiritual and moral perfection. We think of Evelina and Orville and Emma and Mr. Knightley, but when the protagonist is a ten-year-old as she is in Warner's novel, the fantasy seems somewhat disturbing to the modern sensibility, though, if we consider the matter, we realize that, when Emma was ten, Knightley was in his twenties, the same age discrepancy that exists between Ellen and John. Then again we do not imagine Knightley hugging and kissing Emma in the way that John does

Ellen. In any case, this fantasy, in some variation, persists in subsequent sentimental, domestic novels for children. It is the relationship of Jo to Bhaer and of Rebecca to Alan. We finally feel that we have entered the twentieth century when Montgomery finally rejects it.

Aside from this sexual fantasy, this archetypal plot also includes the placing of the sensitive and imaginative child in the care of a grim, unloving spinster aunt. Again, although no subsequent aunt is nearly as grim and unbending as Aunt Fortune, this plot is repeated over and over again in subsequent children's novels, though in a softened and more humorous form. In Warner there is no suggestion that Ellen can win over Aunt Fortune as her descendant Anne wins over Marilla with her charming perversity. There is absolutely no concession to childhood perversity in this novel and, again as Foster and Simons point out, "whereas in *Little Women* and *What Katy Did*, maturity is represented as a state of restraint and limitation in contrast to the utopian freedom of childhood, *The Wide, Wide World* does not romanticize its heroine's early years" (38). For this reason, despite the fact that the novel contributes elements of theme and plot to subsequent children's novels, most people would not consider it to belong to that category.

Moreover, the narrative technique of the novel is unlike that of subsequent novels. The voice makes no concession to a child reader and the focus, though not exactly the ironic, centered consciousness of an Austen novel, is closer to it since we do spend a considerable amount of time in Ellen's consciousness. The novel begins with two long paragraphs in which we enter into Ellen's consciousness as she stares out the window at a gloomy city street. Later we are told that she had watched "the children that played in the yards" (16) but receive the distinct impression that she has never joined them. The tone of the novel lightens somewhat when we arrive in the country despite the implacable grimness of Aunt Fortune. The countryside tempts her to play and she explores the trough that leads to the spout and "she played awhile with the water, which had great charms for her" (107). At this moment it would appear that Warner is going to allow her to play like a child but the moment is short-lived as she "plunged into the mire" of a ditch. As a consequence, her aunt dyes all her white socks grey.

This pattern is repeated throughout the novel. When she meets the mischievous Nancy she is led into play that results in her falling

5. The Nineteenth-Century Children's Novel

into the brook. During the Christmas holiday at the Marshmans she makes a more suitable friend in Ellen Chauncey but they do not play together but work on their New Year's presents. The other children play but Ellen remains aloof. Of course she is allowed to play on Christmas day when "there was a great call for games, and young and old joined in them" (305) but this dispensation is short-lived. In the next chapter, it is confirmed that in Evangelical families children were not allowed to play on Sunday. The "wicked" children are resentful of this fact and George invents a guessing game that involves characters from the Bible. Ellen sits silently through the ensuing game despite the fact that she knows the answers and when questioned about her behavior she affirms that she believes that "Sunday was meant to be spent in growing better and learning good things" (310) and not in playing. The other children reject her as a prig but we are clearly supposed to be on her side in the matter. One can only hope that Ellen is not an accurate representation of the real nature of Evangelical childhood.

Indeed, that hope is confirmed to some extent in Charlotte Yonge's somewhat less puritanical *The Daisy Chain* (1856), a work that is equally influential on Alcott and subsequent children's novelists. In the short preface, Yonge perceptively calls *The Daisy Chain* "an overgrown book of a nondescript class, neither the 'tale' for the young, not the novel for their elders, but a mixture of both" (vii), a statement that suggests that she cannot conceive of a children's novel at the same time that she has created something that exists outside of the present categories of adult novel and moral tale for children. Never does she achieve a narrative voice that could be said to address children yet, at times, she exactly captures the element of childhood that will later become the subject of the children's novel. Time after time we see the younger children playing and, occasionally, the adults are even allowed to join them, especially if they are male. Mary is allowed to be one of the "boys" when she is ten and Harry will always remain one. Dr. Spenser appears as the first pervert, the forerunner of the playful "uncles" that will appear in later novels, and Ethelred, the clever-not-the-pretty daughter, becomes the archetype for future female protagonists, and like Jo in *Little Women* is clearly the author herself. Alcott is obviously indebted to Yonge and though we must be pleased that she cut down the number of siblings from eleven to four, this might have more to do with biographical fact than novelistic good sense. Obviously with eleven siblings you are going to have multiple protagonists rather than a collective but Yonge anticipates the collective protagonist in her description of the riotous play of the younger siblings, Harry, Mary and Tom who "the family collectively termed 'the boys'" (4). Alcott also found a more even balance between tears and laughter. In Yonge every laugh is paid for with a dozen tears, as in the very funny episode in chapter twenty-five when Harry dresses up as a girl in order to find out what the Andersons are saying about the Mays. In this episode, we come very close to the spirit of the children's novel but, when his impersonation frightens Margaret, he is severely rebuked and a bit of fun generates pages of moralizing. In the end he is punished by being denied Confirmation but his contrition is so great that in the end he is allowed to be confirmed, thus preventing his eternal damnation.

Wall does not consider these earlier novels in her study and I think that omission contributes to her difficulty in placing *Little Women*, which she deals with as a unique phenomenon in a section of her book called "Adolescent Chatter" (89–91). When compared to its predecessors, it certainly deserves to be called a children's novel, especially if one is dealing only with volume one, but when compared to what is to come, it might more fittingly be called an adolescent novel. But since it appeared at a time when those categories were not yet clearly formed it might be more useful to consider the techniques Alcott developed that influenced later writers of the girl's domestic novel. Also, although I have no evidence that it is the case, I like to think that Alcott could not have written this novel, could not have so clearly moved it away from the tradition of the sentimental, domestic novel toward that of the pure children's novel, if she had not read *Alice in Wonderland* before writing it.[10]

As didactic as the work might seem to modern taste, it caused some shock at the time and, according to Valerie Alderson in her "Introduction" to the novel, "Sunday-school teachers and librarians objected to the 'play-acting,' which apparently offended their moral sensibilities" (xi). Certainly chapter two is one of the funniest in the novel, one in which the tone comes very close to that of the pure children's novel though it must be remembered that the amusing half is preceded by an equally long didactic, pathetic scene in which the girls sacrifice their

5. The Nineteenth-Century Children's Novel

Christmas dinner to relieve the Hummells. Indeed, this is the basic formula of the novel which constantly oscillates between humor and pathos, a formula that is actually articulated by Alcott in her description of Jo as someone whose "life was a series of ups and downs, which were both comic and pathetic" (39). Jo and Amy, as the perverse sisters, generate most of the humor but all of them are allowed to oscillate through the spectrum. Alcott is actually quite good at being humorous and pathetic at the same time as in chapter seven, "Amy's Valley of Humiliation," whose inflated title borrowed from Bunyan signals her coming mock-epic mortification. This scene of school punishment will become a set-piece in the girl's domestic novel and Katy Carr, Rebecca Randall and Anne Shirley will all be subjected to a similar mortification.

The perfect balance between humor and pathos that is so characteristic of the novel is foreshadowed in the opening chapter. *Little Women* begins with three pages of dialogue framed by brief comments by the narrator. The children are all given pretty much equal billing though Jo gets the first line and longer speeches. The opening dialogue is followed by three paragraphs of summary description by a slightly intrusive narrator who begins by addressing her "young readers" and referring to herself as "we" (7). The four sisters are "sketched" by the narrator by order of age, with Jo again getting the longest treatment. These physical descriptions end with the narrator archly suggesting that "what the characters of the four sisters were, we will leave to be found out" (8) though the sketches merely confirm what the reader already knows from the opening pages of dialogue. The characters are already fixed and though they will mature they will not change. They exist as four "humors," sympathetic but at a slight comic distance. Their characters have been delineated not only by what they say and what the narrator says about them but by a kind of psycho-narration based upon body language. Meg is still; Jo cannot be still. Beth sighs and Amy primps. This technique is quite common in the children's novel in which the psyche is revealed not by what characters think or feel but by external signs such as blushing or frowning. In the opening scenes humor is predominant as they complain and bicker. In the dialogue that follows the narrator's intrusion, pathos is predominant as they all agree selflessly to spend their Christmas money on presents for their mother but actually what strikes one in both scenes is the perfect poise that Alcott has found that balances these two emotional tendencies.

We have seen Alcott experimenting with various techniques of objectification and she clearly knew how to use the device to generate both humor and pathos, a trick she probably learned from Dickens whom she much admired. Tears are evoked by making an impossibly innocent child the object of the gaze of an irascible adult who undergoes a spiritual conversion as a consequence. So when the shy Beth wraps her arms around the neck of Mr. Laurence and kisses him we are told:

> If the roof of the house had suddenly flown off, the old gentleman wouldn't have been more astonished; but he liked it — oh dear, yes! He liked it amazingly; and was so touched and pleased by that confiding little kiss, that all his crustiness vanished; and he just set her on his knee, and laid his wrinkled cheek against her rosy one, feeling as if he had got his own little granddaughter back again [62–63].

My students tend to be a hardhearted bunch and will never admit to crying at such moments but it is clearly a powerful rhetorical trick and can become the central device of a children's novel, as it is in *Little Lord Fauntleroy* and *Heidi*. Also, in subsequent domestic novels there are a number of grim aunts waiting to have their hearts melted.

The Beth character, however, will disappear from what I have called the pure children's novel and evoking laughter will become the central concern. In this case you make the perverse child at play the object of the gaze of an adult who can be either bewildered or amused depending upon whether he or she is a pervert or not. Amy, of course, is the perfect candidate for this kind of treatment:

> So busy was she on this day, that she did not hear Laurie's ring, nor see his face peeping in at her, as she gravely promenaded to and fro, flirting her fan and tossing her head, on which she wore a great pink turban, contrasting oddly with her blue brocade dress and yellow quilted petticoat. She was obliged to walk carefully, for she had on high-heeled shoes, and, as Laurie told Jo afterward, it was a comical sight to see her mince along in her gay suit [188].

This is the road that will lead to Nesbit.

Alcott developed many of the narrative techniques that will be

5. The Nineteenth-Century Children's Novel

imitated by subsequent writers, and just four years after the appearance of *Little Women*, Susan Coolidge's *What Katy Did* (1872) took us one step nearer to the pure children's novel as written by Nesbit; indeed, if you were to consider only the first half of the novel, you would think you were already there. This is the aspect of the novel that I am most interested in but it is worth noting that my female students find what happens to Katy much more shocking that what happens to Jo even though they are thematically the same thing and Foster and Simons in their analysis tend to emphasize the similarities between the novels whereas I would tend to emphasize the differences. One reason my students give for seeing Jo's experience as more "natural" than Katy's is the fact that most of the sermonizing belongs to Marmee who they tend to see as an attractive character who has positively undergone the same transformation that is expected of Jo. I would tend to see the removal of the Marmee character as a definite improvement because it helps to create the illusion of childhood autonomy that is so crucial to the pure children's novel. Also, Jo and her descendants, Rebecca Randall and Anne Shirley, are treated ambiguously so that the illusion is generated that, although they have been transformed into potential wives and mothers, they have not really changed at all. For example, when Jo promises Beth to renounce her writing she reneges but what she writes is the "good" book we have been reading rather than the "bad" ones that Bhaer has warned her against. Katy's experience is much more painfully "broken-backed" though it should be noted that humor does not entirely disappear in the second half of the novel. Like Jo, her transformation into "angel of the house" is marked by culinary disaster and her wish that "somebody would invent a new animal" (179) is in keeping with the spirit of the pure children's novel.

In any case, my analysis will concentrate on the first half of the novel and the qualities that point the way to Nesbit, the most important of which is that she, much more so than Alcott, is very much aware that her subject as a children's novelist is play. We do not have to believe she read the Alice books since she tells us she has when she alludes to *Through the Looking-Glass* by telling us that Katy's drawer "reminded one of the White Knight's recipe for a pudding (114). As further evidence of the strangely split nature of this narrative, this allusion occurs just before she falls off the swing. Once she has been crippled, she is given *The Wide, Wide World* for Christmas (156). I like to think that the intrusive and strangely oblique introduction to the novel, in which the narrator tells us she was inspired to tell the story by listening to two katydids, is an allusion to Alice's conversation with the caterpillar, as if Coolidge is trying for a Carrollian whimsicality that is unavailable to the author of a realistic novel. But most telling is the poem that precedes the novel which in subject and sentimentality imitates Carroll's, and, like his, is in marked contrast to the novel itself.[11] Coolidge, like Carroll, gives us an idealized account of the origin of her novel, in this case the play of a group of siblings in a Cleveland suburb:

> SIX of us once, my darlings, played together
> Beneath green boughs, which faded long ago,
> Made merry in the golden summer weather,
> Pelted each other with new-fallen snow.

The fact that Coolidge is remembering her own childhood play accounts for the refreshing realism of her description of it in the opening seven chapters and despite several hints from the intrusive narrator that Katy is going to suffer for her perversity, the description of her play is remarkably uncritical; indeed, it is this relative lack of initial criticism that makes what happens to her so shocking. There are many ways in which Katy is like Jo (she is clumsy; she does not care about clothes; she plays like a boy; she writes; she is "fond of building castles in the air" (10) and like Jo dreams of being famous) and Coolidge's indebtedness to Alcott is not surprising since they shared the same editor but there are also many ways in which she moves away from her predecessor toward Nesbit. She makes her children younger and thus makes play more central to the novel. Katy, the eldest sibling, is twelve but is "as heedless and innocent as a child of six" (9–10). Indeed, in one of the funniest scenes in the novel, we get a retrospective of Katy at five, when she and her sister Clover "adopt" Marianne O'Riley. Theoretically, the younger age of the siblings should make the collective protagonist more prominent and Coolidge does experiment with it at the beginning but Katy always steals the show and Katy is much more central to the novel than Jo is to hers. Indeed, the collective pretty much disappears after her accident. The practical result of this difference is that it makes for a novel of a more typical length for a children's novel than *Little Women* is.

5. The Nineteenth-Century Children's Novel

We also see Coolidge moving further toward the objectification of her protagonists than Alcott, though using some of the same devices Alcott devised. The first chapter is almost all objectification as the narrator first establishes her authority at an amused but affectionate distance from the events she is about to relate and then removes all of Alcott's dialogue so that all that remains are the narrator's character sketches. The first sketch serves to remove the Marmee character and to replace her with the more amusing Aunt Izzie, a strategy that seems to place Coolidge firmly on the side of the anti-didactic:

> Aunt Izzie had been a gentle, tidy little thing, who loved to sit, as Curly Locks did, sewing long seams in the parlour, and be told she was a good girl; whereas *Katy* tore her dress every day, hated sewing, and didn't care a button about being called "good," while Clover and Elsie shied off like restless ponies when anyone tried to pat their heads. It was very perplexing to Aunt Izzie, and she found it quite hard to forgive the children for being so "unaccountable," and so little like the good boys and girls in Sunday-school memoirs, who were the young people she liked best, and understood most about [4].

Coolidge's anti-didacticism is then confirmed by the addition of Dr. Carr, the largely absent but authoritative father who "wished to have the children hardy and bold, and encouraged climbing and rough plays" (4–5). The rest of the chapter consists of sketches of the various members of the collective protagonist who are represented collectively "perched on the top of the ice-house, like chickens on a roost" (6).

Katy is revealed as the main protagonist much more blatantly than Jo is, not only by the title, but also by the fact that she is not initially a member of the collective, which is represented as unable to act until she finishes her chores and joins them. Thus her sketch is the climactic one and is three times as long as that of her siblings. Admittedly, the sketch of "Poor little Elsie" (8) is almost as long as Katy's. Initially, one might simply read this fact as a way of setting her up as Katy's whining and unadventurous foil but, in retrospect, this is also a sign of her eventual prominence in reconciling us to Katy's accident because one of its consequences is to make her nicer to Elsie. Katy's sketch is an extended example of reluctant psycho-narration. We are told what she "felt" and dreamed and "was fond of" but are never allowed to focalize on her as the narrator draws us back, as when we are told that "she had fits of responsibility about the other children, and longed to set them a good example, but when the chance came, she generally forgot to do so" (10). She is viewed from a middle distance of sympathetic mockery.

Chapter two, "Paradise," is a representation of the children at play and belongs to the collective protagonist though it is made clear that Katy is the leader and her will is the collective will and this with only the slightest hint that this self-assertiveness is a fault that must be corrected. The chapter proceeds largely through narrative summary and dialogue, the latter including the final joke of the chapter, the text of Dorry's "jurnal" (21), a text that is considerably younger than any found in Alcott. The chapter self-consciously alludes to chapter thirteen of *Little Women*, though again the dreams are markedly younger. There is no focalization and what consciousness is represented belongs to the collective, 20 lines of psycho-narration and four of narrated monologue. The latter is an interesting development though it probably is not a conscious decision and, as is often the case in the children's novel, it is not at all clear what is narrated monologue and what is narrative summary. I have given the children the bare minimum as represented by the following lines: "Who knew what the fairies might not have done since any of them had been there to see?" (13) and "oh, delightful surprise!" (17). The chapter ends with the end of the day and the end of their play as the children's collective regret and anticipation of future Saturdays is rendered in eight lines of psycho-narration which gently modulate into the narrator's nostalgic explanation of the chapter's title, the equation of children's play with a return to the garden of Eden, a romantic vision that is typically at odds with the didactic clouds that are gathering though, even here, the fall is anticipated in the allusion to "an angel with flaming sword" (23).

It is not until chapter three that we focalize on Katy in order to see her confront her first moral lesson and even here the focalization is resisted by devices of objectification and is oddly oblique to the actual lesson to be learned. We gradually move toward the moment of focalization with brief lines of psycho-narration as we are told that "this vexed Katy very much," "this made Katy crosser than ever" (27) until

> her conscience gave such a twinge that she was forced to get up with the rest, and see a black mark put against her name on the list. The tears came

5. The Nineteenth-Century Children's Novel

into her eyes from vexation; and, for fear the other girls would notice them, she made a bolt for the yard as soon as the bell rang, and mounted up all alone to the wood-house roof, where she sat with her back to the school, fighting with her eyes, and trying to get her face in order before the rest should come [27–28].

Even this is not quite focalization since her inner turmoil is largely represented by external body language. At this point the narrator intrudes to describe the wind "seizing her sun-bonnet," a description that ends with descriptive psycho-narration as "Katy, flying after, saw it lying a crumbled lilac heap in the middle of the enemy's yard" (28). It is at this point that Coolidge does something strikingly original:

> This was horrible! Not merely losing the bonnet, for Katy was comfortably indifferent as to what became of her clothes, but to lose it *so*. In another minute the Miller girls would be out. Already she seemed to see them dancing war-dances round the unfortunate bonnet, pinning it on a pole, using it as a football, waving it over the fence, and otherwise treating it as Indians treat a captive taken in war. Was it to be endured? Never! Better die first! And with very much the feeling of a person who faces destruction rather than forfeit honour, Katy set her teeth, and, sliding rapidly down the roof, seized the fence, and with one bold leap vaulted into Miss Miller's yard [28–29].

One might be tempted to call this mock-heroic narrated monologue but clearly the effect is somewhat different from what Alcott is doing with Amy. There is little objectification here but rather almost complete focalization and thus complete identification with Katy at her moment of heroic decision. Of course, the narrator cannot resist some intrusion and "Katy was comfortably indifferent as to what became of her clothes" and the last sentence belong to the narrator but the rest is psycho-narration and narrated monologue representing Katy's thoughts. In the purely objective description of the actions that follow there are mock-heroic elements as "out poured the Millerites" full of "wrath and indignation at this daring invasion" and "with a howl of fury they precipitated themselves upon Katy" (29). Also there is a certain contextual mock-heroic element in the fact that the object of this daring coup is a bonnet not a scalp but, for the most part, we are pretty much invited to identify uncritically with Katy's decision, and what she has decided is to behave like a boy in a boy's adventure story.

Foster and Simon point out that Katy, unlike Jo, never expresses the desire to be a boy but, in this moment, in a way that Jo never is, Katy simply *is* a boy. All the elements are present: the reference to an appropriate script ("Indians"), the glorification of bravery (Katy's "bold leap" (29) in defense of her "honour") and of physical strength (Katy's awkward tallness is now an asset), the indulgence in violence (Clover rapping knuckles with a hammer) and in personal aggrandizement (Katy being "praised and petted by the big girls" (30)). To allow almost complete identification with such a decision is a very subversive act, especially since it is largely cut loose from the didactic argument of the chapter. She is not punished but rewarded for this action and the only connection to her subsequent, punishable actions (the Game of Rivers) is that the first made her "perfectly reckless" (30). Focalization, in this instance, serves to resist the whole didactic thrust of the novel and, for a moment, sixty years before time, Coolidge invents Ransome's Titty.

In the rest of the chapter Katy is objectified, both humorously and pathetically, as "old Father Ocean" who "capered like a lunatic" (32) and "poor Ocean" who "sobbed" "all the way home" (35) until Dr. Carr appears, in the place of Marmee, to deliver the final sermon. Chapter four, "Kickeri," largely belongs to the collective but, in the end, Katy is focalized on as the guilty instigator of the dangerous play:

> Katy did not even pretend to be asleep when Aunt Izzie went to her room. Her tardy conscience had waked up, and she was lying in bed, very miserable at having drawn the others into a scrape as well as herself, and at the failure of her last set of resolutions about "setting an example to the younger ones." So unhappy was she that Aunt Izzie's severe words were almost a relief; and though she cried herself to sleep, it was rather from the burden of her own thoughts than because she had been scolded [51].

This is the second example of focalization in the novel, though even here there is some reluctance; however, unlike the first, this is in support of the didactic argument and the very fact that Katy is thinking about her moral condition is a sign of the gathering didactic clouds, though, again, the final and definitive lecture is given by her father. Almost as if she wishes to hold off the gathering clouds, in chapter 5 Coolidge reverts back to the collective protagonist as in chapter 2 and gives a purely humorous account of the children's play based upon a reading of their texts.

Chapter six belongs to Katy and there is some focalization on her

5. The Nineteenth-Century Children's Novel

as she becomes dimly aware that there is something wrong with the romantic Imogen but the main emphasis is upon what she does not know. The moral center of the chapter is a moment of objectification as we enter Dr Carr's consciousness as he overhears Imogen in the parlour telling her tale of the Brigand, a moment introduced quite appropriately by a bit of negative psycho-narration:

> Katy forgot to listen for Aunt Izzie. The parlour door swung open, but she did not notice it. She did not even hear the front door shut when Papa came home to dinner [86].

Katy's unthinking involvement in the story places the narratee at a comic distance from her, a distance that is shared with Dr. Carr as we listen with him to the silly story. Later, after her transformation, when Imogen reappears, Katy herself shares this position as she comes to the realization of "how queer" (195) Imogen is but at this point the moral must be enunciated by Dr. Carr in yet another final lecture.

In chapter six, "Cousin Helen's Visit," there is a marked increase in the representation of consciousness as if to signal that the episodic plot dealing with the representation of play is about to come to an end and that we are now going to concentrate on Katy's moral transformation. There is considerable focalization on Katy who gets 56 lines of psycho-narration, 12 lines of quoted monologue and 5 lines of narrated monologue but she is not the only character whose consciousness we enter. The collective protagonist is still present with 11 lines of psycho-narration and 4 of narrated monologue. Katy and Clover together get 2 lines of psycho-narration, Clover 2, Elsie 1, Helen 2 and Aunt Izzie 4. Fairly consistently we enter into the characters' consciousness in order to discover their reactions to Cousin Helen, who now enters the novel as Katy's moral ideal and replaces Dr. Carr as the novel's didactic voice. For example, on page 96 we focalize on Katy for 18 lines of psycho-narration as she comes to the realization that Cousin Helen is not the pious prig she had anticipated. Later, her coming ordeal is foreshadowed by 3 lines of quoted monologue:

> "It must be *awful* to be sick," soliloquized Katy, after Papa was gone. "Why if I had to stay in bed a whole week—I should *die*, I know I should" [105].

The chapter ends with 9 lines of quoted monologue as Katy resolves to be as good as her Cousin Helen.

Coolidge also uses the representation of consciousness to subtly suggest some of the novel's central themes. For example, Elsie's role as the character most benefitted by Katy's transformation and Helen's role as the agent of that transformation are represented by a quick modulation through their three minds in the following paragraph:

> Little Elsie clung with a passionate love to this new friend. Cousin Helen had sharp eyes. She saw the wistful look in Elsie's face at once, and took special pains to be sweet and tender to her. This preference made Katy jealous. She couldn't bear to share her cousin with anybody [107].

Earlier, Helen's role as a positive spiritual force is represented in an amusing episode rendered through the consciousness of Aunt Izzie, the collective protagonist and Clover:

> Aunt Izzie, dropping in about eleven o'clock, found them having such a good time that, almost before she knew it, *she* was drawn into the game too. Nobody had ever heard of such a thing before! There sat Aunt Izzie on the floor, with three long paper quills stuck in her hair, playing "I'm a genteel Lady, always genteel," in the jolliest manner possible. The children were so enchanted at the spectacle that they could hardly attend to the game, and were always forgetting how many "horns" they had.
> Clover privately thought that Cousin Helen must be a witch [102].

Thus, Helen is represented as an agent of play at the very moment that her appearance signals its end.

As one might expect, in the next chapter that sees Katy's accident, the level of focalization increases slightly (80 lines of psycho-narration, 22 of quoted monologue and 6 of narrated monologue); however, a certain degree of objectification continues in the unceasingly intrusive narrative asides and this will set the pattern for the remainder of the novel. We will continue to focalize on her to some degree but the psycho-narration will often be reluctant or negative, her inner life will often be rendered by external body language and the story will be carried predominantly by narrative summary and dialogue. The general principle is fairly clear. In the first part of the novel we do not focalize on Katy because she is playfully unthinking. Once she has her accident and can no longer play, she can begin to think and so we begin to focalize on her more often, though never to the extent we focalize

5. The Nineteenth-Century Children's Novel

on an Elizabeth Bennett. The tendency begun in *Little Women* continues and is carried a bit further in *What Katy Did*.

The above analysis suggests the ways in which Coolidge follows Alcott but at the same time moves us closer to Nesbit. The same tendency can be found in her narrator who, though somewhat more didactic than Nesbit's, basically shares her voice and focus. The Coolidge narrator is much more intrusive than the Alcott narrator. She refers to herself as "I" 28 times in chapter one alone and, although this falls off in subsequent chapters, she consistently maintains an I/you relationship between narrator and narratee throughout the novel. Her observations can be straightforwardly didactic ("But I am sorry to say that my poor, thoughtless Katy *did* forget" (38)) or mildly sarcastic ("all of which, as may be imagined, was exceedingly improving" (25)) but they are consistently introduced by such phrases as "I think," "I don't think," "I fear," "I can't begin to tell you" (34) or "I can't pretend to tell" (44), all of which have the effect of foregoing omniscience, of suggesting that the adult narrator cannot possibly begin to understand the children. One of the best examples of this technique, and one that clearly foreshadows the Nesbit narrator, is the long intrusion that follows the description of the loft where the children play on rainy days:

> This was the place, which for some reason I have never been able to find out, the Carr children preferred to any other on rainy Saturdays when they could not play outdoors. Aunt Izzie was as much puzzled at this fancy as I am. When she was young (a vague, far-off time, which none of her nieces and nephews believed in much), she had never had any of these queer notions about getting off into holes and corners and poke-away places. Aunt Izzie would gladly have forbidden them to go to the loft, but Dr Carr had given his permission, so all she could do was to invent stories about children who had broken their bones in various dreadful ways by climbing posts and ladders [57].

Given what is about to happen in that wood-shed, this intrusion is rather more ominous than what one finds in Nesbit but, if we ignore that fact, we can hear the voice of Nesbit's narrator. She is an adult and therefore cannot understand the children's "queer" and passionate devotion to their reckless play. At the same time, she can understand it better than Aunt Izzie who is the victim of the narrator's anti-didactic irony. The narrator is placed in the middle between the idyllic and didactic and, of course, her narratee is there with her.

The principle that Coolidge has invented can be articulated more precisely. Wall suggests that Alcott's narrator speaks with the voice of an older sister. In contrast, Coolidge's narrator speaks to her readers in a voice that one might attribute to a playful, unmarried younger sister of one's mother (there being in English no adjective for the female version of "avuncular"). Indeed, Nesbit actually articulates the principle at the beginning of *Five Children and It* when her narrator clearly distinguishes herself from that other kind of aunt who is older than one's mother:

> Now that I have begun to tell you about the place, I feel that I could go on and make this into a most interesting story about all the ordinary things that the children did — just the kind of things you do yourself, you know — and you would believe every word of it; and when I told you about the children's being tiresome, as you are sometimes, your aunts would perhaps write in the margin of the story with a pencil, "How true!" or "How like life!" and you would see it and very likely be annoyed [22].

This is the voice of an adult narrator who is complicit with the children in taking their side against adults who do not know how to play and who prefer realistic, didactic stories to fantasy but it is also a narrator who knows that children can be "tiresome" and is prepared to teach "you" lessons on the subject. On the other hand, this narrator is never going to make "you" the victim of the kind of teasing that she inflicts on the protagonists such as her mockery of the irascible Robert or of the pompous Cyril when he explains about "germans" (104). This is the narrator that Coolidge invented.

But as accurate as Coolidge is in describing the play of children and as sympathetic as she is to that play she cannot allow herself to move all the way toward the pure children's novel because she cannot escape the Evangelical tradition that her genre belongs to. Her description of the children's Sunday is not as dour as Warner's but they still must give up their play. Again there is as certain ambivalence since as much as she insists that "Sunday was a sweet and pleasant day, and the children thought so," she also recognizes that as a result of its quietness the children "woke up on Monday full of life and mischief, and ready to fizz over at any minute, like champagne bottles with the wires just cut" (42). This is an insight worthy of Nesbit and, it is important to remember that even in Nesbit's novels the didactic does not simply disappear; rather, it is the boundary that circumscribes the action, just as play is the ground upon which the action unfolds but play is never the problem that generates the action. In Nesbit, the problem that generates the plot is often something fairly inconsequential, like a lack of money in the *Treasure Seekers* or simply boredom. In Coolidge play remains the problem that generates the plot and so play itself must destroy Katy's ability to play in order that she can be transformed into the angel of the house and this unmitigated assertion of the danger of play, this absolute triumph of the didactic, is ultimately what is so shocking about the novel.

The next novels I consider, *Rebecca of Sunnybrook Farm* (1903) and *Anne of Green Gables* (1908), are contemporary with the novels of Nesbit but are clearly different from hers in that they still belong to the genre of the domestic novel and, although humor predominates over pathos, especially in Montgomery, the plot still hinges on the moral transformation of the protagonist. The first seven chapters of *What Katy Did* are more like Nesbit than anything in these later novels but they are of interest because they represent mature examples of their genre and thus a polished and self-conscious use of the techniques of objectification first developed by Alcott. Also both novels deviate from the line that leads to Nesbit by forgoing the intrusive, younger-sister-of-your-mother narrator invented by Coolidge in favor of an older, more sarcastic narrator that seems to be based upon the narrator of *Tom Sawyer*. The influence of Twain is also felt in the way that they have both made their small towns central to the action in a way that Alcott and Coolidge did not. I consider them simultaneously since they are so much alike and Montgomery is clearly indebted to Wiggin although apparently that indebtedness was no where acknowledged.[12]

Both novels begin with identical extended scenes of objectification as we are introduced to our chattering protagonists through the consciousness of two bemused and tongue-tied males who are driving them to their new homes. Of course, there are some significant differences between Mr. Cobb and Matthew but in terms of narrative technique their function is identical, to establish the child as the perverse Other that provokes both laughter and sympathy. The protagonists are both confronted with the archetypal Aunt though Wiggin has taken Coolidge's inconsistent and disjointed Aunt Izzie and split her into two, the implacable Miranda, who hearkens back to Aunt Fortune, and the more sympathetic Jane. Montgomery then brilliantly merged them again to produce the more satisfyingly complex Marilla, who is a Miranda with a Jane struggling to get out. In both novels we first enter the consciousness of the protagonists in two almost identical scenes of reluctant psycho-narration when, alone for the first time, they contemplate their new rooms with the result that Rebecca "stripping down the dimity spread, precipitated herself into the middle of the bed and pulled the counterpane over her head" (26) and Anne "sprang into bed where she burrowed face downward into the pillow and pulled the clothes over her head" (27). This comic/pathetic scene gives way to pure humor as at this precise moment we switch to the consciousness of Miranda/Marilla, who, in Miranda's case, opens the door to see "a white and tempestuous ocean of counterpane, an ocean breaking into strange movements of wave and crest and billow" (26–27) and in Marilla's "various skimpy articles of raiment scattered most untidily over the floor and a certain tempestuous appearance of the bed were the only indications of any presence save her own" (27). In keeping with their different characters, Miranda goes on to react with humorous horror as she rebukes Rebecca whereas Marilla, treated with more subtlety, reacts with stoic silence and even some sympathy but, then again, Anne has had the good sense to take her clothes off first.

There is no point in laboriously listing the similarities of the two novels or all the ways they are indebted to Alcott, Coolidge and Twain. In terms of narrative technique, both novels demonstrate a mature and self-aware use of objectifying devices such as reluctant psycho-narration, mock-heroic psycho-narration and narrative asides. A few further examples aside from the one above will make the point. When Rebecca is punished at school we are told that her "head was bowed with shame and wrath. Life looked too black a thing to be endured. The punishment was bad enough, but to be coupled in correction with Seesaw Simpson was beyond human endurance" (38–39). The last two sentences could be taken as narrated monologue but it is so overwritten that its effect is to distance her, to put us in the position of laughing at her, and this is often the case when we ostensibly enter her consciousness. Later we are told that "Miss Dearborn stole a look at Rebecca's bent head and was frightened. The child's face was pale save

5. The Nineteenth-Century Children's Novel

for two red spots glowing on her cheeks. Tears hung on her lashes, her breath came and went quickly, and the hand that held her pocket handkerchief trembled like a leaf" (39). When we see her through the eyes of an adult, we feel the closest to her and her pain, as the overdone "shame and wrath" of her supposed internal consciousness is translated into a child's body language.

Anne, even more than Rebecca, is also given to extravagant self-dramatization. In one characteristic scene, her ostensible punishment in being made to apologize to Mrs. Lynde is turned to moral triumph in her idyllic lack of self-awareness as she turns the moment into play. After giving a long and passionate speech begging for forgiveness, she bows her head and waits for judgment. The reader is then invited to see the scene through the eyes of Marilla:

> There was no mistaking her sincerity — it breathed in every tone of her voice. Both Marilla and Mrs. Lynde recognized its unmistakable ring. But the former understood in dismay that Anne was actually enjoying her valley of humiliation — was reveling in the thoroughness of her abasement. Where was the wholesome punishment upon which she, Marilla, had plumed herself? Anne had turned it into a species of positive pleasure [74].

The reader laughs and understands that Marilla's perception is a sign that she can be redeemed and, indeed, the point is made again when we discover that "Marilla was dismayed at finding herself inclined to laugh over the recollection. She had also an uneasy feeling that she ought to scold Anne for apologizing so well; but then, that was ridiculous!" (75). The use of the phrase "valley of humiliation" is an allusion not only to Bunyan but to Alcott and to Amy's own mock-heroic "abasement." Similarly, Wiggin subtly gives credit to Twain by using his own phrase, "Let us draw the curtain of charity over the rest of the scene" (*Sawyer*, 41), after Rebecca throws her pink parasol into the well:

> We will draw a veil over the scene that occurred after Rebecca's return from school. You who read may be well advanced in years, you may be gifted in rhetoric, ingenious in argument; but even you might quail at the thought of explaining the tortuous mental processes that led you into throwing your beloved pink parasol into Miranda Sawyer's well [90].

Of course, as funny as the novels are, they are domestic novels and the protagonists must be cycled through the years until they are transformed into proper women and as they get older we will spend more

Playing with Books

and more time in their consciousness. The trick in the domestic novel, however, is to effect this transformation while, at the same time, suggesting that nothing has really changed. Never can the protagonists achieve the "consciousness" of an Elizabeth Bennett because to do so would be to destroy that playfulness which we most admire in them. One rather crude way of achieving this effect is simply to assert it as when Adam Ladd looks into Rebecca's eyes and discovers "they were still those of a child" (224). This is not very convincing when one considers that she is seventeen and has already displayed some jealousy over his relationship with Huldah Meserve. A more satisfactory way of achieving this effect is through a particular use of narrative technique, a use that can be demonstrated by an analysis of the end of *Anne of Green Gables*.

One narrative technique that Montgomery is fond of, and one that could be seen as related to the embedded texts used by Alcott, Coolidge and Wiggin, is the use of retrospective narrative. For example, when Anne goes to Sunday school for the first time we are allowed very little access to her thoughts and feelings until she returns home and recounts them to the appalled Marilla. As she gets older, we are allowed more access to her consciousness and a marked change takes place after the incident of the sinking punt, an event that might well be symbolic of her reaching puberty. It is also the last moment we see her playing. When the punt begins to sink, we are in Anne's mind for a full paragraph, though even here focalization is resisted by the sarcastic and anti-romantic narrator who tells us that "it was necessary for Elaine to scramble to her feet" (223). But at this moment of greatest excitement, suddenly the principle of the children's novel asserts itself and we listen to her recount the experience to Mrs. Allan the next day. This amusing account is followed by an equally amusing return to the action as we enter the collective consciousness of the horrified Ruby, Jane and Diana. We then return to Anne's consciousness in a paragraph of narrated monologue just before the actual rescue but then she is objectified again in the eyes of Gilbert and in the sarcastic narrative aside "It was certainly extremely difficult to be dignified under the circumstances" (225), though again, if one wants to be generous, one could construe this as narrated monologue and give the insight to Anne. Montgomery's technique in this crucial scene is to oscillate between focalization and objectification and this will be her practice through the rest of the novel.

The scene ends with Gilbert asking if they could be friends and we suddenly meet an Anne that we have not met before:

> For a moment Anne hesitated. She had an odd, newly awakened consciousness under all her outraged dignity that the half-shy, half-eager expression in Gilbert's hazel eyes was something that was very good to see. Her heart gave a quick, queer little beat. But the bitterness of her old grievance promptly stiffened up her wavering determination [225].

This is certainly a "newly awakened consciousness" but Montgomery cannot afford to lose her child to adolescence so the overture is rejected as the old Anne reasserts herself; however, from this moment on, Anne begins to fade and the book becomes decidedly less amusing. Montgomery handles the transition with poise and manages to half convince us that Anne has not really changed and although we begin to spend much more time now in the mind of a mature Anne the techniques of the children's novel are not entirely forgone. For example, in the next chapter when Anne attends the Exhibition in Charlottetown, mock-heroically described as an "epoch" in her life, we do not view the events through her consciousness but, rather, Anne relates them to Marilla after the fact. Also, she never quite loses a certain flamboyance in her speech and that quality has been the main joke in the novel. Anne, like Alice, is unable to prevent herself from thinking out loud and at great length. Indeed, Montgomery alludes to this technique when she makes it one of the signs of Anne's maturity that, as Marilla puts it, she does not "chatter half so much" and Anne replies that "it's nicer to think dear, pretty thoughts and keep them in one's heart, like treasures" (254). Admittedly, fifteen is rather late to develop this ability but it is perfectly in keeping with the logic of the children's novel that Anne continues to chatter to the end, albeit somewhat more sedately.

I end my analysis of the girl's domestic novel with Nesbit's *The Railway Children* (1906) because it is the only domestic novel she wrote and thus is useful in defining more clearly the parameters of the genre and its difference from the pure children's novel. Also, although I have largely restricted my analysis to narrative technique, ultimately it cannot be divorced from thematic considerations and so with this novel I will reconnect the genre with its gender. Foster and Simons point out that "in its focus on a heroine who at the age of twelve is poised between childhood and the awakening sexuality of full adolescence, and its use of a traditional sentimental structure, unusual for Nesbit's work, *The Railway Children* forms an extensive examination of the concept of 'unmanliness,' in both its social and literary dimensions" (131). In other words, unlike in her previous novels in which gender difference plays almost no role, when Nesbit chooses to write a sentimental, domestic novel, gender difference becomes a central concern. It would be interesting to speculate whether or not Nesbit chose to write in a different genre, and one that had been the subject of satire in her previous novels, in order to address gender issues, or whether those issues merely got dragged along because she switched genres. In any case, the change in narrative technique is quite marked. In the fantasy series, Anthea is the main protagonist and the most sensitive of the siblings but this distinction is only subtly hinted at whereas Roberta/Bobbie is clearly the central protagonist and the most developed and individualized of the three siblings. Indeed, it would seem that the three siblings that make up the collective protagonist have been quite consciously chosen not so much to represent different character traits but rather to represent the three genres I have been considering, with the ten-year-old Peter representing the spirit of boyish adventure, the youngest, Phyllis, representing the child pervert, and Roberta representing the moral ideal of the domestic novel. Thus, the novel becomes a self-reflexive study of the various possibilities of the children's novel.

 The fact that she wrote this novel in the same year that she wrote *The Story of the Amulet* suggests that it might reflect a similar desire to rise to a higher seriousness than in her previous novels and while I deplored that aspiration in relation to her subsequent fantasies, in this particular case I cannot regret the decision since this is arguably her finest novel. Earlier I suggested that this novel exists on the generic boundary between the pure children's novel and the domestic novel and it would be useful to explain exactly what this assertion means by discussing the ways in which it is both like and unlike her previous novels. The most important difference is the introduction of a pathos that has little or no place in her previous novels and not only at the end but throughout the novel, especially in the description of the rescue of the Russian and Perks's birthday party. Nesbit is self-consciously aware

5. The Nineteenth-Century Children's Novel

that pathos is at the moral center of the domestic novel and, although this novel is still very humorous, it insists on characterizing Bobbie as the "good girl" of the domestic novel because she is capable of pity.

The other concessions to the tradition of the domestic novel are more superficial. Of these, the most important is the reintroduction of the Marmee character though a somewhat less preachy version. Also, although the Mother is now a central character in the novel, that fact does not prevent the children from enjoying much the same degree of autonomy they enjoyed in the previous novels. Nesbit also throws in Aunt Emma "who was much older than Mother" (9) and therefore disagreeable and a couple of references to religion, the fact that Uncle Edward is in Heaven (126) and that they are all "in a book that God's writing" (171). Of course, the novel is realistic as is the domestic novel but somewhat less so in its use of coincidence and emphasis upon adventure rather than the minutiae of day-to-day life. Her most significant divergence from the domestic novel is her refusal of the seasonal, cyclical plot. The action all takes place during the spring and summer and thus she solves the central problem of the domestic novel. Bobbie does not have to become a "good girl." She already is one from the beginning and she exists throughout the novel as simultaneously Roberta/Bobbie with no suggestion that Bobbie must die so Roberta can be born.

The way Nesbit uses the collective protagonist in this novel suggests that she is very much aware of the various possibilities of the traditions she has inherited. As Foster and Simons point out Peter consistently "constructs his identity according to the model of the hero in a tale of daring and mystery" and in the coal stealing episode "when discovered *in flagrante delicto,* however, his fictive status is exposed, and from being the glamorous bandit of his fantasy he is reduced ignominiously to, 'something small and dark ... scrambling and rattling furtively among the coal' (40)" (136). In contrast to this satire of Peter and boy's adventure, Nesbit recognizes that the domestic novel, in both its adult and children's version, asserts the value of what Dorothy Van Ghent, in reference to Elizabeth Bennet, has called "emotional intelligence" (103), a quality that is seen as essentially female. Of course, one would like to think that such a quality is not gender specific and so, although Nesbit tended to celebrate boy's adventure and dangerous play in her previous novels, in writing a domestic novel she can, through her representation of Peter, satirize it as a device for socializing boys into emotional stupidity, that stoic, stiff-upper-lip quality so valuable in future managers of Empire. At the same time, she can avoid the equation of sensitivity with passivity by having both of the sisters always actively involved in all the adventures, though Phyllis is always humorously reluctant.

Indeed, Foster and Simons tend to see Phyllis as a character "bound by the captivity of the feminine," in contrast to her sister who "experiments during the course of the narrative with different female identities" (137). If this is her role, and in some ways she reminds us of Amy, it is certainly secondary to her main role as child pervert and there is nothing particularly "feminine" about the joke consistently associated with her, the fact that her shoe laces are always coming undone. If anything the problem she has with her clothing in general would connect her with her predecessors Jo and Katy, who suffer similar problems. Rather, Phyllis, like Alice, is characterized as unthinking, as someone who is unable to prevent herself from thinking out loud. This humorous quality could be seen as morally positive, a sign of childlike truthfulness, as in "The Emperor's New Clothes," but in this domestic novel it is characterized as insensitivity. As a consequence, the more "conscious" Bobbie must resort to kicking her sister under the table, to which she characteristically responds by asking "What are you kicking me like that for, Bob?" (38). Phyllis is the preconscious child who is the protagonist of the pure children's novel and as such is a source of humor but this quality is somewhat devalued in contrast to the emotional intelligence of her sister Bobbie. As one might expect, in the course of the narrative, we never enter the consciousness of Phyllis because she, characteristically, has no mind to enter.

In marked contrast, we spend a great deal of time in the consciousness of Bobbie and we focalize on her more than on any other of the previous protagonists we have considered. For this reason, this novel could be seen as looking forward to the postwar "problem novel" and its adoption of the narrative technique of centered consciousness. I choose to consider it as looking back on the tradition of the domestic novel because, although Bobbie has a problem, the absence of her father, it is a problem entirely external to her own personality which is characterized as positively empathetic, that is capable of pity. To create the problem novel one must shift the emotional polarity toward fear and it is the unpleasant Mary of *The Secret Garden* (1911) that looks ahead to the postwar novel which I will be analysing in the next chapter. Also, although Bobbie is less objectified than previous protagonists she is still not an Elizabeth Bennet but a twelve-year-old girl and the voice of the intrusive narrator always keeps us at a slight distance from her. For example, after the scene described above, when the mother agrees to let the children walk on the railway tracks, the narrator intrudes to tell her reader "I dare say you think that she ought not to have said it. But she remembered about when she was a little girl herself, and she did say it-and neither her own children nor you nor any other children in the world could ever understand exactly what it cost her to do it. Only some few of you, like Bobbie, may understand a very little bit" (54). The narratee is invited to feel superior to Bobbie who, after all, only understands "a very little bit" though that is considerably more than Phyllis understands.

The presence of the intrusive narrator always keeps us at a slight distance from Bobbie even as we focalize on her. When the narrator intrudes to tell us what we already know, that Roberta is the main protagonist, she says:

> I hope you don't mind my telling you a good deal about Roberta. The fact is I am growing very fond of her. The more I observe her the more I love her. And I notice all sorts of things about her that I like [84].

This is followed by eight paragraphs of psycho-narration and quoted monologue that show us what we are to like about Roberta but before she shows us the narrator feels compelled to tell us:

> For instance, she was quite oddly anxious to make other people happy. And she could keep a secret, a tolerably rare accomplishment. Also she had the power of silent sympathy. That sounds rather dull, I know, but it's not so dull as it sounds. It just means that a person is able to know that you are unhappy, and to love you extra on that account, without bothering you by telling you all the time how sorry she is for you. That was what Bobbie was like [84].

Bobbie remains an attractive character precisely because she is not *too* conscious of her moral superiority.

Thematically, there is much to admire in this novel and Foster and

Simons have many positive things to say about Bobbie's characterization and its contrast with Peter's but, ultimately they have a problem with the novel's "overriding conservatism" (147) and the problem is that Nesbit makes explicit what is largely only implicit in the domestic novel, that its celebration of pathos is ultimately a celebration of motherhood, a condition that is seen as biologically predetermined. The statement that seems to unequivocally make this point belongs to the Doctor as he explains sexual differences to Peter after he has been behaving in a typically insensitive manner:

> "Well," said the Doctor, "you know men have to do the work of the world and not be afraid of anything — so they have to be hardy and brave. But women have to take care of their babies and cuddle them and nurse them and be very patient and gentle."
> "Yes," said Peter, wondering what was coming next.
> "Well, then, you see. Boys and girls are only little men and women. And *we* are much harder and hardier than they are" ... "and much stronger, and things that hurt *them* don't hurt *us*. You know you mustn't hit a girl —"
> "I should think not, indeed," muttered Peter, indignantly.
> "Not even if she's your own sister. That's because girls are so much softer and weaker than we are; they have to be, you know," he added, "because if they weren't, it wouldn't be nice for the babies" [168].

Foster and Simons claim that "it is difficult to read this as innocent or devoid of irony" (135) and, indeed, Peter's attempt to translate "these scientific facts" (169) for his sisters is ridiculously mangled but there is no indication that Nesbit does not share the Doctor's opinion, albeit the theory is presented in a rather puerile manner as befitting its audience. Nor is it necessarily alarming to suggest that there is a biological propensity for mothering since this only makes good evolutionary sense for mammals, especially for human infants, the most helpless of mammals. It becomes somewhat more problematic when it is suggested that this biological difference translates into a difference in psychological dispositions but this is precisely the assumption that lies at the heart of the distinction between the two genres we have been considering. Of course, it would be desirable to reconcile the difference and one is always pleased to discover courageous girls and emotionally intelligent boys but to erase the difference would be to erase the genres and one is reluctant to go that far. Indeed, Foster and Simons in their study of the domestic novel tend, quite rightly, to accentuate the positive and it is easy enough to make a case for the moral superiority of the girl's domestic novel over the imperialistic fantasies of boy's adventure. On the other hand, who would forgo the hopeful thrill of the child teetering on top of the monkey bars that is the spirit of boy's adventure?

6

The Twentieth-Century Children's Novel

After the Second World War the children's novel took a turn toward the didactic and a new, darker tone became common, with the result that we ended up inventing a whole new category, the adolescent novel. To put it simply, writers suddenly became less interested in the fact that children play and became more interested in the fact that they have problems. Of course, children had problems before the Second World War but writers were more interested in the play of preschoolers as the model and subject for their writing and the "problem" appears only as a limiting horizon that acknowledges that play can be dangerous and that it must come to an end. The result was a children's novel clearly demarcated from the adult novel, with its own rhetorical strategies and its characteristic tonality of humor rather than irony. The function of the adult novel is to construct "individuals," moral agents who successfully or unsuccessfully confront their problems. The children's novel is not interested in "individuals." The children's novel, as I understand it, is amoral and growing up is not a matter of solving problems. It is merely an inevitability that unfortunately cannot be avoided and one must be prepared to accept it with a certain amount of grace, which is to say that although you must stop playing you can try to do so without forgetting how. The humor that results from this vision is certainly less unmitigated in the postwar novel but I do not think that it has disappeared. Some of the most popular writers for children remain humorists and one thinks of Beverly Cleary, Louise Fitzhugh, Judy Blume, and Roald Dahl and even writ-

6. The Twentieth-Century Children's Novel

ers that might be thought of as more serious such as Lucy Boston, Nina Bawden, Philippa Pearce, William Mayne and Katherine Paterson retain a core of humor in their work. The idyllic/didactic machine still remains the fulcrum upon which the children's novel is constructed, with perhaps a somewhat different tuning. Before I analyse this change more fully, I would want to consider the historical problem raised by it. Why is it that after the war children suddenly seemed to get older?

One could perhaps assert that the world had become a darker place. After the Holocaust and the vision of Anne Frank's childhood it might seem callous to frolic with Pooh Bear. With nuclear destruction impending it is perhaps more difficult to evoke "secret gardens" of play.[1] But to make that kind of statement is to evoke an adult nostalgia that is alien to the nature of the children's novel and, in any case, a darker world might be all the more reason to turn to the children's novel in the sense that after reading something like *The Chocolate War* I feel a strong urge to refresh the mind by rereading *The Phoenix and the Carpet*. Perhaps the answer lies in the fact that children's play has changed. One of the things that I agree with Neil Postman about is his condemnation of the evil of organized sports for children and all the other adult organized activities that we seem intent on forcing upon them. But again this development is not entirely new. The nineteenth-century schoolboy suffered the same coercion and, in *Stalky & Co*, Kipling exactly captured the true spirit of childhood perversity in the boys' unwillingness to play games. Perhaps the world has simply become a more dangerous place. One expert in childhood play informed me that the playgrounds now stand empty for fear of predators. I do not know if that is true but if it is then the fear of modern parents would constitute just the same kind of abuse as the piety of Evangelical parents. I roamed free as a child and so did my children and I am skeptical that things have changed. Children will play, with or without the co-operation of their parents. If none of these explanations satisfy it is perhaps because they all depend on the mistaken theory that texts are representations that reflect the real nature of childhood and it might be more interesting to start at the other end of the problem.

If we think of the children's novel, not as a representation, but as a toy to be played with then, as has been noted, one aspect of that play is of particular interest in its difference from the play of the adult novel.

From Carroll to Boston the children's novel carefully avoided the preferred narrative point of view of the canonical, adult domestic novel, omniscient third-person centered consciousness. Theoretically, it was always possible to adopt this technique. All one would have to do is to flatten the ironic voice and focus through the mind of one's child protagonist but no one did this, except for Burnett and Wilder, until Boston did in *The Children of Green Knowe* (1954) and there is some question whether Boston actually intended to write a children's novel. Hunt agrees in seeing Boston as the seminal figure who influenced Pearce, Garner and Mayne (136–137) but he does not mention the point of view as the crucial element. It might simply be that this is another lucky accident or writers had simply become bored with the old strategies and wanted to try something new. The old strategies involved narrative techniques that objectify the protagonist, and spread the interest around to several protagonists, often siblings. The effect is to prevent the construction of the "individuals" that the adult novel is interested in. Suddenly, after the war, centered consciousness became the rage in a kind of reversal of what was happening to the adult novel. As the adult novel repudiated the classic realistic novel, the children's novel discovered it. It is almost as if the post-modern novel discovers the old children's novel at the very moment that the new children's novel discovers the old adult novel. To some degree, by adopting centered consciousness one is almost forced to create an "individual," a round, three-dimensional subjectivity, and once one has created an "individual" it is almost inevitable that you will give her problems. So it is not the problem that created the new children's novel but the new narrative technique that dragged the problems of childhood along with it.

But as fond as I am of the above theory, it is perhaps too literary for my taste and in the end I will return to a simple materialist explanation for what happened after the war. I have argued that the social must always accommodate itself to the somatic and, indeed, it is impossible to understand the social without understanding this process of accommodation. Of course, there is considerable social flexibility to childhood and Mitterauer warns against taking the view that "the phenomenon of youth" is "a one-sided interaction of the somatic and the social in which the former is the constant and the latter is the variable"

6. The Twentieth-Century Children's Novel

(6). The particular phenomenon he is referring to is the age of reaching puberty and the fact that "in some parts of Europe female maturity has been brought forward by more than four years since the first half of the nineteenth century" (3). Moreover, records show that in the eighteenth century children of the urban middle class reached puberty a year earlier than children of the rural laboring class. The two factors that Mitterauer identifies as causing this situation are nutrition and workload. Meat and sugar eating among the urban middle class contribute to early maturity as does the fact that they send their children to school since physical labor retards puberty. The increasing discrepancy between the somatic and the social in bourgeois childhood, between the age of reaching puberty and the age of leaving school, is probably one of the main reasons for that historically unprecedented postwar accommodation that we call the sexual revolution.

In terms of the problem we are considering one sees an inkling of its solution in these facts. I have argued that the pure children's novel developed out of the new material reality that developed as children left their play behind to attend school. There is some lag time here since the children's novel does not really appear until 1865 with the appearance of *Alice in Wonderland* but what that novel does is take the parodic perversity of the play of preschoolers and translates it into the book that literate children play with and thus creates the formula for the children's novel. Meanwhile, over 150 years, there is a gradual lowering of the age of puberty and again we have a time lag but this process begins to accelerate as more children become schooled meat-eaters until by the middle of the twentieth century the average age of puberty has been lowered from sixteen to twelve. I think that it is safe to say that the pre-literate child who is not abused nor abandoned is fairly problem free. The child in school is not so fortunate and is, indeed, constantly being given problems to solve but these are nothing compared to the problems of the child who reaches puberty. At puberty the personality constructed during the oedipal stage must be torn down and rebuilt and the *Sturm und Drang* of adolescence is a cultural universal. In a sense, the classic domestic novel *is* the adolescent novel of the old adolescence. Evelina is sixteen when her story begins. Today she would be twelve. What has happened is that children now get older faster and this is probably the only sense in which Postman is right about the disappearance of childhood. So the answer to my original question is that children do not merely seem to be older; they simply are older.

The fact that the subject of puberty never arises in the children's novel of the Golden Age is not merely a result of Victorian prudery. When you have the luxury of locating your protagonist anywhere on the spectrum from seven to sixteen, the specter of puberty never arises to darken the humor. When the choice has shrunk to seven to twelve it is hard to avoid seeing it on the horizon and the humorist must develop new tricks. In *Are You There God? It's Me, Margaret*, Judy Blume embraces puberty with the enthusiasm of the cheerleader she is, but even in her case the novels with younger protagonists are noticeably funnier. In *Harriet the Spy*, Louise Fitzhugh solves the problem by making her eleven-year-old sexually and socially naive for her age and gains in humor what she loses in realism. In *Matilda*, Roald Dahl, who could not care less about realism, breaks the rules with a four-and-a-half-year-old protagonist who is also a prodigy that can read better than most adults. In *Antar and the Eagles*, more subtly and more successfully, William Mayne manages a six-year-old without even a hint of cuteness. And even if you accept the inevitable and cross the divide, it does not necessarily mean the end of humor, simply that it will be balanced with more pathos and anxiety. In *Jacob Have I Loved*, once Sarah Louise has gotten her period and falls in love with the Captain, she suffers very stormy weather but that does not prevent the scenes in which her grandmother torments her from being hilariously funny. Even in the postwar novel, the spirit of humor, so marked in the Golden Age, still persists.

But these large historical generalizations need to be supported by particular analysis of children's writers of the twentieth century. This analysis cannot be exhaustive and I apologize for neglecting many good writers or for merely mentioning them in passing. I wish to make the historical case but my primary interest is in rhetorical analysis and so must limit myself to a handful of writers for close analysis. I have chosen writers who I consider to be both good writers and also seminal figures in the development of the children's novel. Thus I will consider Dahl as a writer who continues the tradition of the children's novel as invented by Carroll and I will also consider Wilder as the exception to

6. The Twentieth-Century Children's Novel

my rule, a writer who uses centered consciousness and thus anticipates the general adoption of this narrative technique in the postwar novel. Considering the explosion of new writers that appeared on the scene after the war my choices might seem even more arbitrary, but I largely limit myself to Boston, Pearce, and Mayne, and even the amount of time I spend on them might seem woefully inadequate given the contributions they have made to the development of the postwar children's novel.

The possibility of the postwar problem novel always existed from the moment the formula of the children's novel was devised since it simply exists on the didactic side of the idyllic/didactic polarity. To make this point, it would be useful to compare the two very different novels of Frances Hodgson Burnett, *Little Lord Fauntleroy* (1886) and *The Secret Garden* (1911). The first is a domestic novel though an unusual one in that it makes a sensitive boy the protagonist. Perhaps for this reason it also forgoes the cyclical, seasonal plot and Fauntleroy only ages one year so he remains throughout the perverse Other who generates pathos and humor. This is accomplished through the same devices of objectification that I have been describing as he is made the object of everyone's adoring gaze. Wall seems to think this is a flaw and that the book is really addressed to adults because "though Fauntleroy is almost always the center of attention, he presented from the outside. The narrator looks at him, not into his mind, and is therefore always at a little distance from him" (169). This is another example of how Wall's thesis leads her astray as she contradicts herself and finds a flaw in Burnett what was a virtue in Carroll. This is simply the technique of the children's novel and the result is no different from the way we look at Alice or any protagonist in the children's novel. The only real variation in the technique lies in whether you choose to make your child good, bad or perverse.

The perverse child who generates humor is poised right in the center of the idyllic/didactic polarity. The "good" child shifts the polarity toward the idyllic to generate pity whereas the "bad" child shifts toward the didactic to generate fear, though, in both cases, never to the point of reaching the tragic. Of course, this shift is not an absolute but just a predisposition and didactic anxiety can be found in the domestic novel as in the book-burning episode in which Jo almost kills her sister or in Katy's mistreatment of Elsie. In Burnett's two novels, however, these predispositions are almost pure. In *Little Lord Fauntleroy* Burnett makes her protagonist an exemplary child with the result that the tone oscillates between humor and pathos. In *The Secret Garden* she explores the other end of the spectrum by creating an unpleasant protagonist who is often alone and, as a result, we quite often view the world through her eyes, though she is an unreliable consciousness in the beginning. The novel might well have been inspired by *What Maisie Knew*, since Burnett admired James and was a friend of his. Thus, in this novel, she anticipates the postwar, problem novel and the tone oscillates between humor and anxiety. Foster and Simon quite sensibly include *The Secret Garden* in their study of the domestic novel but actually it is the domestic novel in reverse. In the domestic novel the perverse child must stop playing in order to be "good"; in *The Secret Garden* the "bad" or unhappy children must learn to play in order to solve their problems.

Of course, *The Secret Garden* is still a long way from *What Maisie Knew* and it cannot be viewed as an example of centered consciousness if only because there are two protagonists. I do not count Dickon since he is not so much a character as a personification of Magic itself and as such has no consciousness to enter. We do, however, enter into the consciousness of two unpleasant, ten-year-old children with problems and so it is impossible not to view this novel as an exception to the generalization I have made about the history of the children's novel. However, it is also true that the narrator can be said to enter reluctantly into the consciousness of Mary and Colin and Wall has noted that the situation creates the need for the narrator "to keep her distance" and treat the children "objectively" (175). For instance, at the moment when Mary's transformation begins, she hears the robin redbreast:

> She stopped and listened to him and somehow his cheerful, friendly little whistle gave her a pleased feeling — even a disagreeable little girl may be lonely, and the big closed house and big bare moor and big bare gardens had made this one feel as if there was no one left in the world but herself. If she had been an affectionate child, who had been used to being loved, she would have broken her heart, but even though she was "Mistress Mary Quite Contrary" she was desolate, and the bright-breasted little bird brought a look into her sour little face which was almost a smile. She listened to him until he flew away [35–36].

6. The Twentieth-Century Children's Novel

There is a certain amount of reluctance in the psycho-narration. She is not thinking of herself as "a disagreeable little girl." We are seeing and hearing what she sees and hears but her feelings are not fully understood by her but by a narrator looking at her from a middle distance as "this one" rather than "her."

Similarly, after his last tantrum, Colin's feelings are described as follows:

> That night Colin slept without once awakening and when he opened his eyes in the morning he lay still and smiled without knowing it — smiled because he felt so curiously comfortable. It was actually nice to be awake, and he turned over and stretched his limbs luxuriously. He felt as if tight strings which had held him had loosened themselves and let him go. He did not know that Dr. Craven would have said that his nerves had relaxed and rested themselves [169].

Again the narrator keeps her distance by twice telling us what Colin does not know. Also, not only is this entering into the children's consciousness reluctant, it does not happen all that often and the narration generally proceeds through dialogue and description. Finally, although the novel is not primarily humorous, it does create humor by techniques quite often used in the children's novel. The antics of the children are viewed through the consciousness of various uncomprehending adults such as Mrs. Medlock, Dr. Craven and the nurse, while the adult pervert, Ben Weatherstaff, is allowed to join in their play since, though unpleasant himself, he also knows how to talk to the robin.

According to Wall "*The Secret Garden* had shown how a writer might write unsentimentally, unselfconsciously and effectively *to* children, without using either first-person narration as Ewing had done or an obtrusive narrative personality like Nesbit's.... Burnett's is a straightforward, comfortable, modern voice, content, for the most part, to address a child audience without regret, and without the need to assert adult superiority by defining an adult presence" (176). I would agree that Burnett is the first to achieve a "modern voice" and the contrast between this voice and the Victorian voice of *Little Lord Fauntleroy* is quite marked to the point that one is amazed that these two novels were written by the same author. But the main novelty of this voice is that it actually enters into the consciousness of two unpleasant children who must solve their problems by learning to play together. Far from inaugurating the beginning of a new kind of children's novel, in fact, it is an anomaly and nothing quite like it will appear until Philippa Pearce decides to rewrite the same story 47 years later. *Tom's Midnight Garden* adopts much the same technique, though in an even more modern way since Pearce reverses the gender of the two protagonists, gets rid of the Dickon character, that idealized child of nature, and substitutes a kind of telepathic time-traveling for Burnett's religious Magic. Burnett is the first to write the "problem" novel and her accomplishment is the exception that proves the rule: the children's novel is not interested the consciousness of "individuals."

The other exception we must consider is the series of novels written by Laura Ingalls Wilder.[2] If we look, however, at the first novel in the series, *Little House in the Big Woods* (1932), we can see that, although she uses third-person centered consciousness, she adapts it to the nature of the children's novel. Wall devotes an entire chapter to "The Child-Centred Novel," by which she means a novel that uses third-person centered consciousness. In a way, her analysis supports my thesis since she points out that novels with children as protagonists are not necessarily children's novels and cites works by Henry James, L. P. Hartley and Jane Gardam to prove her point. In each case, the use of centered consciousness creates a work addressed to adults rather than children. But she ends with the work of Laura Ingalls Wilder to demonstrate that it is possible to center on a child's consciousness and still write a children's novel and so Wilder could be said to anticipate the common adoption of this technique in the postwar novel.

Most of the time, as Wall observes, Wilder "maintains the tone of the confiding adult talking to children throughout, while presenting events as Laura would see them" (243). This assertion needs more careful analysis. The first chapter contains 265 lines of narration, 23 lines of dialogue, of which only two do not belong to Pa, and 28 lines of psycho-narration rendering Laura's consciousness, most of which is merely descriptive. These proportions would seem to take the principle that the children's novel tells rather than shows to an extreme but, actually, Wall's subjective insight that we see "events as Laura would see them" is correct and can be objectively explained. Also though it is true that "Laura is still a very little girl" I do not think it is entirely true that "the narrator addresses a narratee of similar age" (243). Practically speaking the narratee would have to be older than Laura since she turns six in the novel and cannot read. While it is true that Wilder asks us to identify with her central character more than is typical of the pure children's novel, quite often we observe her with the same bemusement that we observe an Alice or Anne Shirley.

The reason that we get the impression that we are seeing things through Laura's eyes is that the author has simplified her narrative voice to an unprecedented degree with the result that we read most of the narrator's statements as narrated monologue. On a number of occasions I have remarked that in the children's novel it is often difficult to distinguish between narrative summary and narrated monologue and this would be a good place to explain why. There is no such problem in the adult novel as a passage from *Pride and Prejudice* will demonstrate:

> Mr. Darcy corroborated it with a bow, and was beginning to determine not to fix his eyes on Elizabeth, when they were suddenly arrested by the sight of the stranger, and Elizabeth happening to see the countenance of both as they looked at each other, was all astonishment at the effect of the meeting. Both changed colour, one looked white, the other red. Mr. Wickham, after a few moments touched his hat — a salutation which Mr. Darcy just deigned to return. What could be the meaning of it?— It was impossible to imagine; it was impossible not to long to know [55].

Of course, the forgoing of omniscience at the end is a clear indication that we are not listening to the narrator but also the distinction between the formal style of the narrator and the simpler style of the internal monologue is also a strong indicator. If the narrative voice is already simple, the distinction becomes more ambiguous.

Of course, context also helps as we can see in the following passage from *Little House in the Big Woods*:

> At night, when Laura lay awake in the trundle bed, she listened and could not hear anything at all but the sound of the trees whispering together. Sometimes, far away in the night, a wolf howled. Then he came nearer and howled again.
> It was a scary sound. Laura knew that wolves would eat little girls. But she was safe inside log walls. Her father's gun hung over the door and good old Jack, the brindle bulldog, lay on guard before it [2].

As in the Austen example, the use of psycho-narration to introduce narrated monologue is a good indicator and most readers would assign all of the above to Laura's consciousness. But as one reads on, one realizes that there is very little to distinguish the voice of the narrator from the representation of Laura's thoughts. As a result, we end up reading a great deal of what could be narrative summary as narrated monologue and, thus, the novel becomes an example of centered consciousness.

In the second chapter, I gave a theoretical account of what it means to make a voice simple without providing much in the way of textual analysis to support the theory. I failed to do so both because it would be tedious and the techniques used are so varied, subtle and multiple as to make generalization beyond the particular case almost impossible. In this particular case, we could note a few factors. The "Once upon a time" opening leads to an expectation of folktale simplicity. A simple diction as in the use of "scary" above and an extensive use of simple sentences and one sentence paragraphs are grammatical factors. One simple trick Wilder uses is to have the narrator refer to the father and mother as "Pa" and "Ma" and one of the few occasions in which the narrator clearly distinguishes herself and her narratee from her protagonist is when she explains this trick:

> The little girl was named Laura and she called her father, Pa, and her mother, Ma. In those days and in that place, children did not say Father and Mother, nor Mamma and Papa, as they do now [2].

The consequence of adopting this narrative technique is to diminish the humor and though it is not entirely lacking it is certainly not central to the novel and usually has more to do with the antics of Pa than of the children. Also, this novel is unusually didactic for a Golden Age novel. The postwar novelists I am going to consider next do not imitate Wilder though Philippa Pearce makes a rather good stab at it in *Here Comes Tod!* (1992) when she takes on a pre-school protagonist rather than her usual gloomy ten-year-olds. What Ingalls has done, essentially, is to come up with a third-person narrative technique equivalent to Blume's first-person technique. The advantage of the third-person narration is that we are not hopelessly stuck in the mind of the protagonist but can achieve some distance. On the other hand, of all the children's novels that I teach, this is the only one that a significant number of students find boring.

Perhaps, they would find it less boring if I taught one of the later novels since, predictably, as Laura gets older she becomes more of an "individual." As a result, we spend increasing amounts of time in her consciousness, which in turn becomes more sophisticated but then so does the narrative voice, with the result that the distinction between narrative summary and narrated monologue remains ambiguous. There are, however, some subtle changes. In *The Long Winter* (1940), when Laura is fourteen, throughout the novel we center on Laura's consciousness of the sound of the blizzards, thus generating a sense of anxiety that differentiates this novel from the first one. The plots also become less episodic and more centered on some specific problem. In *Little House in the Big Woods*, there is really no plot but merely episodes strung together by a description of the various kinds of work that go with the various seasons of a single year, most of which consists of descriptions of gathering, preparing, preserving and eating food. The children are portrayed as playing but this is not the central interest of the novel; rather, the novel consists of loving and detailed descriptions of the work required for survival. But there is nothing grim about this presentation and the enduring delight that this novel evokes has a great deal to do with how it turns the grueling work of pioneer life into a kind of play and, thus, into an object of nostalgia.

Everyone seems to agree that Lucy Boston did something startlingly original in *The Children of Green Knowe* (1954) and Wall's excellent analysis of her accomplishment need not be repeated except to support her subjective impressions with objective evidence. In terms of the analysis I have been presenting, what she managed to do was to center on the consciousness of her seven-year-old protagonist without simplifying her narrative voice as Wilder did and without objectifying him as Burnett did with her protagonists in *The Secret Garden*. The result is a novel in which "it is the presentation of events through Tolly's eyes, in language not far removed from what the child himself could understand, though not use, rather than the presence of specifically child or adult narratee, which determines the style" (Wall, 220) Wall also correctly points out that Boston adopts a more typical narrative stance in her subsequent children's novels which are more clearly addressed to a child narratee.

One important difference is that Tolly is not a perverse child, and the novel is not particularly humorous, but neither is he particularly good nor bad. As Wall would put it "Tolly's is in a sense a blank mind" and the result "is a book about wonder" (221). On the other hand, he is an unhappy child. He is first described as "alone as usual" (1) and is essentially without a family and the novel is pervaded by a sense of mild anxiety. It is, after all, a ghost story but the ghosts turn out to be benign and provide him with the siblings he is missing and so his problem is solved by finding someone to play with and, in this way, the novel belongs to the same genre as *The Secret Garden*. The major difference is the "blankness" of his mind and this is an effect achieved by a particular narrative technique.

The novel is unusual in not being divided into chapters but if we take the embedded stories as signaling moments of narrative closure then the first "chapter" (35 pages) consists of 303 lines of narrative, 461 lines of dialogue and 332 lines of the representation of consciousness (205 psycho-narration, 17 quoted monologue and 110 narrated monologue). These are the same proportions as the Austen novel as we might expect in a novel that employs the technique of centered consciousness. I have arrived at these numbers, however, by adding in the narrated monologue even though it is just as ambiguous as in Wilder's novel and different readers would arrive at higher or lower counts. The simplified voice of the narrator is not achieved, however, by a simplification of her language but by a single trick that is also used, to a lesser degree, by the Wilder narrator. The narrator never comments but only describes and this must be the most unintrusive narrator to be found in the children's novel. Even the dialogue is relatively free of narrative comment. Since the psycho-narration is also predominantly descriptive, the effect is created of merging the mind of the protagonist with the voice of the narrator since they are always seeing the same thing.

As Wall observes, the danger of this technique is that it might lead to a certain blandness but Boston "avoided a too bland texture, and monotony, ... by presenting Mrs Oldknow as narrator of stories about the house and its inhabitants to the young Tolly. This brings into the story a more usual adult-child, narrator-narratee relationship" (224). Even more importantly, the Mrs. Oldknow character is necessary since the plot of this novel, like the Austen plot, is one of revelation and in

6. The Twentieth-Century Children's Novel

order to solve the mystery Mrs. Oldknow must provide the clues that the narrator cannot, clues that are, of course, correctly interpreted by the reader before they are by Tolly. Also, now and then, the narrator very subtly differentiates herself and her narratee from the protagonist by the use of the pronoun "you" rather than "he" as in the following statement: "it was so cleverly carved that you could see every hair, and it felt like fur to stroke" (11). In subsequent novels she will use this technique more often. Also, though the psycho-narration is predominantly descriptive, we are also briefly allowed access to what Tolly is feeling, most often his feelings of wonder at his new home but also his feelings of fear and frustration. Still, this novel brings the children's novel much closer to the adult novel, although, its emphasis on Tolly's "wonder" fills it with a kind of nostalgia, a nostalgia for a comfortable though oddly archaic home that was the original impetus that led the author to write this story. If you want to get even closer to the adult novel you must turn to the even darker novels of Philippa Pearce.

I am going to consider three of Pearce's novels in chronological order in order to show how the logic of her narrative technique carries her farther and farther away from the realm of the children's novel. In *Tom's Midnight Garden* (1958) she borrows her plot from Burnett and her narrative technique from Boston with the result, as Wall puts it, she has created what "is generally regarded as one of the finest children's novels of the postwar period" (194). It is certainly an example of centered consciousness but Pearce's narrative voice is much more easy to distinguish from Tom's consciousness than is Boston's and Tom himself is a very unpleasant protagonist like Burnett's Mary. As a result, Tom is objectified to some extent and the narratee certainly understands him better than he understands himself. His problem is that he has been denied an opportunity for play by his brother's illness and the solution to his problem is to find an opportunity to play in a garden that is far superior to the one he has been denied. The problem and the narrative technique used to address it are clearly delineated in the opening two paragraphs of the novel:

> If, standing alone on the back doorstep, Tom allowed himself to weep tears, they were tears of anger. He looked his goodbye at the garden, and raged that he had to leave it — leave it and Peter. They had planned to spend their time here so joyously these holidays.

> Town gardens are small, as a rule, and the Longs' garden was no exception to the rule; there was a vegetable plot and a grass plot and one flower bed and a rough patch by the back fence. In this last the apple tree grew: it was large, but bore very little fruit, and accordingly the two boys had always been allowed to climb freely over it. These holidays they would have built a tree house among its branches [7–8].

The tone of Tom's internal petulance is in marked contrast to the voice of the narrator that explains it. Wall suggests that Pearce's narrator "has a bland explanatory manner not far removed from the tone of oral telling" (194) and certainly one would not describe her voice as ironic though it can be sardonic and there is a certain dramatic irony in the contrast between this garden and the delights of the one Tom will discover. Moreover, this narrator, unlike Boston's, can provide clues and always keeps herself and her narratee at slight distance from her struggling protagonist as when we are informed that "in following the course of Tom's historical researches and his reasoning, we have gone a little ahead upon the order of events — as Tom perceived them in the garden" (113). This narrator can also provide hints that Tom and Hatty's idyllic sojourn in their garden is to be short lived: "So, at once, their play began again in the garden, and went on as though the garden and their games need never end" (116). If this is short of irony, it comes very close.

The novel is not without humor in its middle portion but the ending is bittersweet and the beginning is dreary. Not only is Tom not a particularly likeable character at the beginning of the story but nothing much happens. Although the discovery of the garden and the mystery of time it evokes awakens some interest there is really no story until Hatty appears. Slowly one becomes aware that this is not Tom's story at all: it is Hatty's story and Tom is the agent through which we see her story. In an ingenious twist the narrative focus is created long before the protagonist appears and the effect is uncanny and mysterious though the voice remains flat and matter-of-fact. Hatty suddenly appears within the focus and the story comes to life. The result is a plot of revelation which is challenging to both the child and adult narratee. Admittedly, I guessed that Hatty was Mrs. Bartholomew from the moment that Hatty appeared but I am a fairly practiced reader and my knowledge in no way detracted from my delight in how the mystery

6. The Twentieth-Century Children's Novel

unfolds. The child narratee is in much the same position and presumably will discover the answer before Tom does. It does not really matter when the discovery is made since the pleasure lies in the discovery. The main clue is the double reference to Mrs. Batholomew dreaming, first on page 18 and then again on page 35 when we are told "she was dreaming of the scenes of her childhood" but there are many such clues and the mystery is complex and many-layered.

Of course, from the moment that Hatty falls from the tree and we hear James talking about her and realize how old she has become, the story switches direction and Tom becomes the protagonist. At this point I imagine most readers will know that Hatty is going to grow up and get married but I suspect that children interpret the remainder of the story differently than adults, in which case we have a form of double address even though the voice and focus remain the same. If we agree that children are not nostalgic, then they will interpret what Tom is doing as an attempt to keep a friend that he has enjoyed playing with. In which case, the story has a happy ending in the sense that, thinking he has lost her, he finds her again. From the adult point of view, what Tom is doing is a futile attempt to retain his childhood. The adult reading contains a more poignant irony but the ending remains a happy one in the sense that Mrs. Bartholomew *is* still Hatty, that the child has remained alive in her. This adult insight is expressed in the uncomprehending words of Aunt Gwen at the end of the novel: "Of course, Mrs Bartholomew's such a shrunken little old woman, she's hardly bigger than Tom, anyway: but, you know, he put his arms right round her and he hugged her good-bye as if she were a little girl" (229).

Pearce has pushed the children's novel about as far as it can go in the direction of the ironic adult novel. Evidence that she still remains within the parameters of the children's novel lies in the fact that she still understands the importance of play to children. Also Pearce is basically playing with the same problem that is evoked in *Through the Looking-Glass*, the question of whether Alice is dreaming of the Red King or the Red King is dreaming of Alice, a problem that reveals Carroll's awareness that the formula he devised is based upon a tension between the desires of the adult and the child. Tom's intense desire for a garden to play in evokes the nostalgic dreams of Mrs Bartholomew which he is allowed to enter as a dream child. But the garden is as much his dream in the sense that whenever he falls asleep in that dream he awakens back in reality. In the end, as in the Alice books, we awaken to reality and so *Tom's Midnight Garden* can be seen as a darker, more poignant enactment of the fact that at the end of the children's novel play must always come to an end.

If anything, her next novel, *A Dog So Small* (1962), is even bleaker than *Tom's Midnight Garden*. As in that novel, we center on the consciousness of a child as he uses his imagination to create a play space but play is now seen as predominantly dangerous rather than innocent. Part of the difference arises from the fact that Ben is playing with an imaginary dog rather than another child and that play is taking place in the city rather than the garden. The result is far from idyllic since play results in neurotic behavior, a serious accident, and nightmares. Moreover, Ben is treated ironically in the second half of the story. He does not realize that his mother and grandmother had concocted a plan to enable him to have a dog and when he gets it he does not want it. He wants his imaginary dog Chiquitito. As his grandmother puts it "'people get their heart's desire,' she said, 'and then they have to begin to learn how to live with it'" (153). He finally does learn but not before some bitterly cruel irony. In the end, "he saw clearly that you couldn't have impossible things, however much you wanted them. He saw that if you didn't have the possible things, then you had nothing" (155). Just as the real dog is slipping away, he calls him back. The didactic message is asserted very much at the expense of the idyllic, and didactic anxiety is more characteristic of Pearce than is humor. She speaks to the child but always to a child hemmed about by a bleak and inevitable adult reality and she apparently feels it is necessary to teach a child the vanity of human wishes. The publishers have assigned this novel as one intended for younger readers and that choice is a sign of the confusion that surrounds the question of assigning an age to readers. They presumably arrived at this conclusion because Ben is not an adolescent; indeed, if measured by the quality of his petulance, he appears even younger than Tom. They also perhaps thought that tiny dogs must be cute but there is nothing cute about Chiquitito. If we consider the novel in terms of the vision of childhood it presents then this novel is considerably older than *Tom's Midnight Garden*.

It might well be for this reason that Wall feels the need to qualify her praise of Pearce. She begins her analysis by asserting that "there can be no question of the implied author's acceptance that her implied reader is a child, nor of the narrator's perfect poise and self-possession in addressing a child narratee without regard to a possible adult reader" (194). She ends by concluding: "I believe Pearce's achievement to be admirable; yet her very success raises questions, for perhaps the comforting consoling voice and the presence of an overt narratee are a valuable, even perhaps necessary, part of writing for the majority of children" (197). Hunt quotes this same passage to express his own doubts (137) and there can be no question that Pearce pushes the children's novel to its very boundary with the adult novel, which is why she is so admired by literary critics. It might be useful to compare her accomplishment with that of Dahl, who though not popular with literary critics, is most definitely popular with child readers. If Pearce is always on the verge of losing her child narratee, Dahl is always on the verge of losing the adult. In contrast to Pearce's cool, slightly ironic narrative voice, Dahl adopts the voice of an exuberantly playful adult child, a kind of perpetual Cat in the Hat. In contrast to Pearce's didactic anxiety, Dahl is pretty much nothing but "funny bits." Dahl aligns himself entirely with the child with the result that his adults, if not good, are selfish and stupid grotesques. Pearce who understands the power and the danger of the child's imagination always portrays her adults as loving and helpful, though perhaps a bit helpless in the face of the child's reticence. This quality perhaps compensates for the lack of comfort in her narrative voice. Between them they define the large range of affect that is possible within the limits of the children's novel.

Her next novel, *The Way to Sattin Shore* (1983) is a very fine novel but it is one that clearly passes beyond those limits. The blurb at the beginning says that it is "a mystery lightened by humour" but that seems wishful thinking since there is precious little that is humorous about this story. It does have a happy ending but it is arrived at darkly. The beginning makes use of an ingenious third-person present tense:

> Here is Kate Trantor coming home from school in the January dusk—the first to come, because she is the youngest of her family. Past the churchyard. Past the shops. Along the fronts of the tall, narrow terrace houses she goes. Not this one, nor this one, nor this...
> Stop at the house with no lit window.

> This is home.
> Up three steps to the front door, and feel for the key on the string in her pocket. Unlock, and then in. Stand just inside the door with the door now closed, at her back [7].

This goes on for two more paragraphs and then reverts to third-person, centered consciousness for the rest of the novel. At first we are looking at Kate from a distance with the camera far above her; then the voice becomes imperative and we are in her head listening to her order herself into the unwelcoming house, as we hear the ominous irony of "This is home." The effect is alienating and involving at the same time and perfectly captures our uneasy relationship with the protagonist who exists in a state of almost neurotic anxiety caused by the mysterious "beam of darkness"(8) emanating from her grandmother's bedroom. As in *Tom's Midnight Garden*, we have a plot of revelation but one considerably darker and more opaque. Also, gone are the loving and helpful adults; all the characters are flawed. The protagonist is nine or ten, though we do not discover that until the end of the novel. She desperately needs to play but her fear prevents her. She does make a friend but mainly through Anna's persistence and the friendship is perfunctory and must end anyway as Anna is moving away. Her preferred playmate is the cat Syrup but, being a cat and not a dog, he is aloof and prefers his own adventures. In a sense Syrup is the only child left in this novel since he goes on long excursions through the neighborhood and is loved by everyone but even he is subject to irony as his adventurous spirit leads him to the attic where he is locked in and almost starves to death. There is one moment of relief from the oppressive atmosphere of the novel when Kate goes tobogganing and overcomes her fears in a moment of exhilarating play, but the moment is passing and her fears return. Of course, the story has a happy ending but that is not enough to characterize it as a children's novel.

Nor can we solve the problem by simply classifying it as a novel for young adults. It would be useful to compare it with the widely acclaimed novel for young adults by Katherine Paterson, *Jacob Have I Loved* (1980). It also has a bitterly unhappy protagonist and an evil grandmother but is very different in how it handles these materials. First of all, Sarah Louise is fourteen, not nine, and in the first half of the novel though she has her problems she is basically happy in her friendship with Cal. It is only upon reaching puberty that her troubles begin and the second half of the novel is much darker but, even then, the scenes in which the grandmother torments her for her love of the Captain are hilariously funny. It would be fair to say that this novel is "lightened by humor." Moreover, Paterson retains a black and white characterization in that the mother and father are good and the grandmother is the absolute incarnation of evil, though I suppose one could argue that she is merely senile. In Pearce's novel all the characters are flawed and, although the grandmother is the source of evil, she is not its incarnation; she is merely another flawed character. Even she has a moment of redemption when, as a parting gift to Kate, she gives her the tray she tobogganed with and, after warning her not to use it for tobogganing, she "cackled with laughter" (186). This novel is characterized by the moral ambivalence and irony of the adult novel and we can see how Pearce has seemingly been unable to resist the logic of her narrative technique which pushes her with each novel closer to the realm of the adult novel until, with *The Way to Sattin Shore*, she has reached a point that is perhaps closer to *What Maisie Knew* than it is to *Tom's Midnight Garden*. By this statement I do not mean that children could not read this novel and take pleasure in it but that it is characterized by rhetorical techniques that do not arise from the vision of childhood typically found in the children's novel, a vision that acknowledges the value and dangers of play. Then again, when we compare Pearce's didacticism to that of the early nineteenth century, we must acknowledge that it is brilliantly subtle in comparison.

After considering Pearce, it is perhaps appropriate to go to the opposite extreme and consider the novels of Roald Dahl, who more than any other postwar novelist, has affirmed, perhaps even to the point of exaggeration, the anti-realist and anti-ironic qualities of the classic children's novel. In his case, it does not even make much difference if he chooses to tell a story in the first person or the third person since the "I" in *Danny the Champion of the World* (1975) who intrudes to tell us "I must pause here to tell you something about Mr. Victor Hazell" (42) is indistinguishable from the "I" in *Matilda* (1988) who intrudes to tell us "I think I might enjoy writing end-of-term reports for the stinkers in my class. But enough of that. We have to get on" (9). The first "I" is a wise child and the second is a big kid. Perhaps it is because his focus is so one-sided that he has to rely so heavily on the scatological and the violent for his humor, as some of his critics have complained. Dahl has a knack of bringing out the prig in his adult readers. His main joke is still the "wise child" joke of the Alice books but whereas Carroll could tease Alice and Nesbit could tease Oswald, in Dahl the child is always wise and the adult is always stupid, unless, of course, he is still a child like Danny's father. Thus *Danny the Champion of the World* is an exception to my rule that in the pure children's novel a first-person narrator is always unreliable.

In terms of developing a theory of the children's novel, *Danny* is very useful because it is an example of the rare occasion when an adult short story, "Champion of the World," has been rewritten as a children's novel. Shavit makes this transformation a "test case" and analyses the resulting changes in some detail (43–59). The changes are quite predictable and in keeping with what I have described as the rhetoric of the children's novel. The events in both are much the same and both use first-person narrators but the narrator in the adult story is an adult who views the poaching obsession of his friend Claud ironically from a position of intellectual superiority whereas the child narrator of the children's novel looks up to his father and enters into poaching with complete enthusiasm. As a result, as Shavit observes, in the adult version poaching is always treated ambiguously "either as a game or as stealing" (52). What is either a game or a crime in the adult version, through a flattening of the irony, becomes in the children's version pure play. Also, as a consequence, the novel becomes considerably less realistic than the short story and it turns out that everyone in the village is a poacher, or, we might say, a pervert, including the policeman and the vicar's wife. Also, as you would expect in a children's novel, they actually get to eat some of the pheasants at the end. Shavit seems to think that these changes somehow contribute to "the reinforcement of the poor self-image of the children's system" (59) but I fail to see the logic of that assertion and Dahl himself seems to have no problem in simply switching from one way of telling a story to another; indeed, if he were to describe what he has done he might well point out that he has simply added more "funny bits."

As I pointed out earlier, in *Matilda* he actually has his protagonist articulate my theory of the children's novel. The first novel Matilda reads is, unsurprisingly, *Great Expectations*, as Dahl gives credit to the ultimate source of the tradition he is writing in as he did earlier in *The BFG* (1982) when the Big Friendly Giant, who clearly is meant to represent Dahl himself, tells us that he learned how to write by reading *Nicholas Nickleby*. *Matilda* is one of his more realistic novels and except for the telekinesis, which rather arbitrarily appears and disappears, the other occurrences are typically exaggerated versions of reality. Of course, grabbing a little girl by her pigtails and throwing her over the fence is rather over the top and Matilda is far more precocious than any child could actually be. As Miss Honey observes, she is "a grown-up child" (195), a term that one could well apply to Dahl himself. We are occasionally allowed access to her consciousness but not very often and more often she is the object of adult observation, which, in the case of the villains, her father and Miss Trunchbull, is a state of narrow incomprehension and in the case of the sympathetic adults, Mrs Phelps and Miss Honey, is a state of bemused wonder. Dahl has a very clear sense, if a somewhat limited one, of what it means to be a children's novelist.

After the war there was not only an increase in the number of children's novels being produced but these novels reflected a larger spectrum of affect as I have suggested in my comparison of Dahl and Pearce. I have not been entirely fair to Pearce in my analysis since she is capable of encompassing a large range of tonalities, from the simplicity of the picture book to her darker, more ironic novels. Margaret Mahy is another writer who is comfortable with a wide range of tonalities. On one hand, she can manage the nuttiness of Dahl in *The Blood-and-Thunder Adventure on Hurricane Peak* (1989) and, on the other, she can manage the sinister eeriness of Garner in *The Tricksters* (1986). She is also quite comfortable in the middle in the Ransome-like, playful realism of *The Pirate Uncle* (1977). Also, within this wider spectrum of affect, there is considerably more experimentation with different narrative techniques as one might expect as the tradition of the children's novel becomes longer and writers look for new ways to tell their stories. Perhaps most notable in this regard is what Mary Norton did in *The Borrowers* (1952) which, unlike Boston's *The Children of Green Knowe*, remains predominantly humorous but plays with narrative technique in a way that makes her equally influential on subsequent children's novelists. Wall analyses her accomplishment at some length and suggests that she "is one of the most sophisticated of modern writers for children. Her achievement in making the art of narration itself part of the subject of her fictions for children ... is a fine one" (266). I would like to end my chapter, with an analysis of some works of William Mayne who, like Norton, consistently makes "the art of narration itself part of the subject," indeed, so much so, that he very seldom repeats himself from novel to novel.³

In his earlier novels, such as *The Member for the Marsh* (1956), he is pretty much following Ransome's lead though somewhat more realistically with songs and feasts and fires and rafts rather than pirate adventures but as his career progressed he experimented with a number of sub-genres and narrative techniques until in the 1980's he produced three works that demonstrate his extraordinary range, *Drift* (1985), *Gideon Ahoy* (1987) and *Antar and the Eagles* (1989). Wall points out that in Mayne "while an ironic narrative stance can sometimes be detected there is never an ironic narrator" (215) and though, to some degree, that is true of all good writers for children, what Wall is trying to suggest are the subtle nuances of Mayne's style and the way he achieves a complexity of narration without ever leaving the parameters of the children's novel. Just as Norton could be seen as trying to adapt the boxes-within-boxes narrative technique of an adult novel such as *The Heart of Darkness* to the formula of the children's novel, so we see Mayne constantly making similar experiments.

For example, in *Drift* he tells the same story from two different points of view, with an effect, according to Ann Donovan, "not unlike that of Lawrence Durrell's *Alexandria Quartet* or John Fowles' *The Collector* or *The French Lieutenant's Woman*" (296). In "Narrative Strategy in *Drift* by William Mayne," Donovan analyses this strategy in great detail but the main trick, as she points out, is that "although the story is told in the third person, the voice of the author is effaced until it seems almost as if it is a first-person narrative" (296). Thus the narrator provides us with no information beyond what Rafe can surmise of his situation as he is suddenly thrust into the reality of Native American life. Although it is clear that Rafe's surmises are unreliable (in fact, he is seldom right about anything), there is no way for the reader to know just how unreliable he is until the entire story is retold from

6. The Twentieth-Century Children's Novel

Tawena's point of view. This method of narration is more than just a clever trick since it is thematically functional as a way of expressing the vast cultural gap that exists between the whites and the Native Americans.

As is often the case with Mayne, it is difficult to assign this work to a particular genre since, although it could be characterized as a realistic historical novel, it takes place in no specific time or place but some sort of generalized New World. Also, although the novel is characterized by humor and a gritty realism, the description of the perceptual acuity of the native people is perhaps exaggerated to the point of fantasy. Perhaps for these reasons, Hunt has characterized this novel, along with *Antar and the Eagles*, as "quasi-myth" (146). The first 13 chapters belong to Rafe who exists in a state of humorous bewilderment at the same time as he faces very real dangers. Gradually he learns to survive under the tutelage of the two native women, a mother and daughter, who return him to his home but he never realizes that it is Tawena who is intervening to save his life. In the last eight chapters the entire story is retold from the point of view of Tawena who turns out to be the real hero of the novel. Rafe, however, does change and through his experiences manages to escape the narrow prejudices of the white colonists but the ending is ambivalent and ultimately Rafe and Tawena go their separate ways, unable to bridge the cultural gap between them.

In *Antar and the Eagles* he leaves the fantastic realism of his historical novel in order to try his hand at animal fantasy. Mayne is doing *The Jungle Book* but with no philosophical axe to grind and with unexpectedly intriguing and humorous incongruities created by what happens when eagles attempt to raise a six-year-old and to teach him to fly. The very fact that the protagonist is only six creates difficulties that Mayne solves with his usual aplomb, though not in the same manner as Wilder and Boston solve the problem of their young protagonists. There is some simplification of the narrative voice but one can always distinguish the narrator from the thoughts of the protagonist who is objectified to some degree in his lack of knowledge and his implacable stubbornness. The following scene early in the novel is fairly typical:

> He went on climbing. He stopped when he hit his head on something and almost let go.

> It is the sky, he thought. I have reached it.
> It was not, of course. He had come up under the ball at the top of the steeple, which was there in the style of his country. His head had bumped on the new lead [13].

The narratee always knows more than Antar but we certainly center on his consciousness and share his anxiety in the early part of the novel when he thinks the eagles intend to eat him, though there are numerous clues that they have no such intention. Once their real intention becomes clear the novel becomes more humorous, though Mayne, as is typical of him, is in no hurry and we must wait until Antar learns their language to discover that intention.

In fact, Mayne makes the age of his protagonist a part of the joke since the eagles need a young but resourceful child who does not weigh much and so they put him on a strict diet. The clash between human and eagle culture is the source of much of the humor, and Mayne's interest in attempting to bridge this mutual incomprehension reflects a similar interest in *Drift*. In the end, Mayne resists the temptation of having his hero fly home in triumph because, after his adventures and after reluctantly serving as egg-mother to the fledgling future leader of the eagles whose egg he has rescued and inadvertently hatched, he has grown too heavy to fly and must ignominiously walk home. Also the plot is not as episodic as *The Jungle Book* and has a coherent and very exciting adventure plot that places it in the category of high fantasy but without any swords or sorcery and a wry humor and gritty realism that reminds one of *Watership Down* but written in a voice addressed to the child.

The fact that Mayne can so successfully combine humor, fantasy and adventure is a sign that he possesses that poise that is so characteristic of good writers for children. The result is that Mayne has written a work of fantasy that is completely devoid of that "religious" feeling that raises the tone and, according to Bob Dixon, ethically taints the fantasy of Tolkien, Garner, Le Guin, L'Engle, Adams and Lewis (145), most of whom do not write for children in any case. To put it in Matilda's terms, Mayne does a Tolkien with all the "funny bits" left in. The effect he creates is evoked by a comment that Garak, Antor's friend and mentor, makes to him near the end of the novel: "With you, sometimes you have said things that made my feet walk up and down on

6. The Twentieth-Century Children's Novel

their own, and forced my eyes to close. Eagles do not know much of laughter or friendship, but perhaps they were what I experienced" (151). Mayne has said things that give the reader the same experience.

Gideon Ahoy! takes us into Pearce territory though without the need for fantasy since Mayne has found a narrative technique that evokes the gap between the desires of the adult and the child without a recourse to magic. There has always been a close connection between the children's novel and fantasy and it is not entirely an accident that the first such novel should be a work of fantasy. If play is merely daydreaming out loud, the pure pleasure principle of unrepressed fantasy, then it is logical to represent the idyllic with a magic that makes dreams come true. Nesbit began her career by writing realistic stories about the play of children and this was a logical choice since she was parodying the realistic domestic novel of the nineteenth century but, as pointed out earlier, this choice created difficulties that she solved by switching to fantasy. Ransome wrote realistic stories about the play of children but he was working in the tradition of the boy's adventure story with its roots in romance and an exaggerated sense of the possibility of heroic triumph. At the other extreme, although they are dealing with the real problems of childhood, both *The Children of Greene Knowe* and *Tom's Midnight Garden* are fantasies, though it is easy enough to forget that fact. Also it is not surprising that, as Pearce's novels get darker and more ironic, she forsakes fantasy for realism though, in *A Dog So Small*, Ben's ability to evoke his imaginary dog is perhaps fantastically exaggerated. The problem then is how to write a children's novel which balances the idyllic and didactic without having recourse to fantasy. Mayne provides an ingenious solution to that problem in *Gideon Ahoy!*

Mayne devises a double narrative technique that combines third-person centered consciousness, things seen through the eyes of twelve-year-old Eva, alternating with a present tense narration of participial phrases used to delineate the world as lived by the brain-damaged and deaf Gideon and by the younger twins Mercury and Tansy. The following example is typical:

> Gideon happy with the boat, listening to him, copying his actions of sleeping, getting up, and coming after that. Tansy and Mercury stood beside and imitated. Gideon, not liking to be mocked, shouting "Rauh" at

them and sending them scurrying back to Mum. Mercury limping horribly, Tansy looking in the palm of her hand at an imaginary safety pin.

Eva thought, She isn't very religious: nothing will happen like nails going through; but saints would be like Tansy and Mercury — a naughty kind of saint [84].

The notion that preschoolers are like naughty saints is typical of Mayne's wry humor and is an excellent way of expressing what I mean when I call them perverts. The third person narrator appears briefly and simply in the second sentence and then reappears at the end in the centered consciousness of Eva. This example is somewhat misleading because in fact, in the whole novel, the past tense narration is considerably more common than the present tense narration and his narrative technique is not as complicated as it might seem. It makes perfect sense if you understand the context and, at the beginning of the novel, the principle is clearly explained:

Eva sat up, looked at her clock, saw it was seven, and got up. For Gideon all times of the day were the same, particularly when he was hungry. It was all Now to him. He had no system for time. Tansy and Mercury had very undeveloped systems, and the result was the same. Eva had a system that said Now was about to begin, but not just yet, please, so there was no need to worry about it. Time was all Then for her.

Next door Tansy and Mercury began to kill each other, which always sounded as if it would happen Now, but never had, and probably wouldn't Then. They became quiet, both dead or finding something else to do [8–9].

Eva, the Then child, is sandwiched between her fifteen-year-old brother who is stuck in a perpetual Now and the preschoolers, who can be Then if they want but prefer to be Now because it is more fun. The result is certainly playful and humorous and perfectly accessible to the child reader though the philosophical play on the fact that "Then" means both "in the future as a consequence" and "back then in the past tense of story" is perhaps somewhat sophisticated for a child but then it probably is for most adults too.[4] In practice, the Now language of the playing children is constantly being translated into Then language by the narrator, by the thoughts of Eva, and by the oral statements of the mother. What Mayne has done, in effect, is to adapt the stream of consciousness of the adult novel to the children's novel by constantly stopping the stream and explaining it, though that is not exactly what he is doing since strictly speaking the siblings have no consciousness since they exist in a state of pure play. But that is not exactly true either since Gideon has feelings of love, anger and jealousy but they never appear as consciousness but as states of the body and as Wall has observed Mayne's ability to translate feelings into "bodily sensations" is one of his strengths as a writer for children (213). The twins are particularly perverse but in a way that is subtly different from the prewar novel, in that their play is presented as a surreal nuttiness that is utterly alien, though comprehensible, to the mature Eva. Indeed, throughout the novel she is reading a science-fiction novel, which is pretty much the only kind of play that she is permitted, and when the three siblings go missing she "had a picture of all three being put aboard the saucer to Novendore, since they were obviously aliens" (108).

Mayne's style is as playfully innovative as his narrative technique and he has a good ear for the oral which is always an advantage to the children's writer. His linguistic playfulness is more subtle and richer than Dahl's and unlike Dahl he can also handle the pathetic as easily as the comic. This is a problem novel in that it deals with a loving but dysfunctional family burdened with a child that will never grow up and an absent father. The result is that Eva has had to grow up too soon and certainly the play of her siblings is represented as both a treasure and a burden to her. Near the end, the tone comes very near the tragic but everything is made right by a stratagem that allows the father to stay home and ensures Gideon's future with the consequence that Eva will presumably be left free to live her own life and to enjoy her family. Actually, in a way typical of the children's novel, there is some question if Eva is the protagonist of the novel since she is always a mature observer and does not change in the course of the novel. The title would suggest that Gideon is the protagonist and he is the one who has adventures, or, rather, misadventures, and in the end returns from near death with his hearing miraculously recovered. Also Tansy and Mercury have a claim to the role since they are ones who effect Gideon's rescue. Actually, we could see in the four siblings a kind of parodic collective that parallels that of *The Railway Children*, with Gideon as Peter, the twins as Phyllis and Eva as Roberta.

Mayne has managed to write very sophisticated narratives while happily remaining within the typically humorous tonality of the children's novel. He is clearly writing *for* children but has demonstrated that one can do so without sacrificing creative innovation and he is clearly a serious writer who fortunately understands that to be so characterized has nothing to do with being serious. His accomplishment should make it clear that the children's novel is not some inferior subcategory but a unique genre with its own characteristic formula and techniques. Moreover, all the many successful practitioners of this art, from Carroll to Mayne, are clearly those writers who have never forgotten how to play like a child.

Conclusion

Although the theory of the children's novel I have presented is one that begins with the assumption that children's novels are written *for* children, this assumption in no way implies that those children are of any particular age. Practically speaking, since the humor of the children's novel depends on the fact that the narratee is older than the protagonist, the effect is dependent upon arriving at a certain level of reading competency and that could vary considerably from person to person but otherwise the age of the reader is irrelevant in regard to the enjoyment of children's novels. Of course, literature can be produced for children who are just learning to read but such would not constitute the children's novel. Also some children's novels might well be easier to read than others but good writers of children's novels do not set out to accommodate their work to the reading ability of their audience, which is why most of them claim that they are not writing for children at all. A good novel for children is one that conveys a vision of childhood that is honest to that experience, which is not to say that it tells the truth about childhood since writers naturally select particular aspects of childhood that interest them. Of course, as I have argued, the fact that children must learn to read is a factor in the historical construction of the category of the children's book and a factor reflected in the nature of the children's novel but that is not the same thing as to say that one can identify the particular age group that a novel is addressed to. Reading ability, of course, should properly be the concern of the teacher who selects books for children but it is irrelevant to the concerns of the literary critic.

If the above statements seem to contradict my assertion that children's books are written *for* children then perhaps the distinction I am asserting would be made clearer by relating my own experiences as a reader. Again, I am well aware that my experience was not typical any more than my experience of play was typical. Just as my play was that of a middle-class boy living in a newly built suburb so my reading was that of a person who is going to grow up to be an English professor but just because my experience was atypical, and whose is not, I should not be prevented from generalizing from that experience. One should properly be skeptical about one's memory of childhood and I will admit that I cannot remember the precise age at which I read particular books, but I can be fairly confident about what I read between two general age groups, the period from nine to twelve and from twelve to sixteen. By the time I was nine I was reading four novels a week and the reason I know that is that it was the maximum permitted by the local bookmobile and I think I could probably have managed more despite spending a considerable amount of time watching television. I was a binge reader and when I discovered a writer I liked I would read everything by them that was available. I was a great fan of Blyton and Trease but before them I had read *Alice in Wonderland, Ivanhoe, Black Beauty*, and *Little Lord Fauntleroy*, all of which were part of a set of classics my mother had given me for a birthday present.

Naturally, under these circumstances, by the time I was eleven I had pretty much exhausted the children's side of the bookmobile and, at that time, there was no such category as fiction for young adults. The rule was that when you reached grade eight you were permitted to take out books from the adult side, a rule that for me meant I had to wait until I was twelve. The rule seems to indicate that the librarians were not concerned about the content of the adult books but were making an assumption about reading ability. They assumed that by the time you were in grade eight you had learned to read well enough to read adult books, an assumption which for me was a terrible imposition. In desperation, I began to secretly read the books my mother had borrowed from the bookmobile. In this way I came to read Norman Mailer's *The American Dream*. My mother would have been appalled to discover this fact but, like all children, I was not interested in protecting my innocence and was good at keeping secrets. The book made quite an impression on me and perhaps I would have read more Mailer if there had been any way of acquiring him. On the other hand, I suspect I would have preferred more Blyton and Trease, if I had not exhausted the supply. In any case, the point is that I was reading Mailer at the same time I was reading Blyton and, although they were clearly different experiences, they were equally accessible. The main difference, is that at the age of eleven I found Blyton to be more fun, to have more play in her.

I entered the second period of my reading when I turned twelve, entered grade eight and began taking out books from the adult side of the bookmobile. Early on I discovered Jane Austen. I loved her novels though I do not think I admired her for her intricate irony because, when I was appalled to discover that she had only written six novels, I happily replaced her with the seemingly endless supply of regency romances by Georgette Heyer. At thirteen, I entered High School whose well-stocked library now provided me with a whole new supply of children's novels. It was there that I discovered *The Lion, the Witch and the Wardrobe* and promptly devoured the whole Narnia series. Again, just as I felt no incongruity in reading Mailer with Blyton, I found none in reading Austen with Lewis. Given my experience, I must be skeptical that writing *for* children is in any way involves taking into account their reading ability; rather it simply means writing a book they would wish to play with. Also librarians have apparently become wiser and I have been informed that our local library system has no rules such as I suffered under. Children can take out any book they like.

On the other hand, the library clearly encourages children to read within their age bracket and clearly differentiates between the junior novel and the novel for young adults. I asked the librarian responsible for ordering the junior novels how this differentiation is made and apparently it is done on the basis of reviews and the main criterion seems to be the age of the protagonist. Thus the junior novel, which is intended for children from eight to twelve, would have protagonists in that same range and the novel for young adults would have protagonists between twelve and eighteen. She also pointed out, however, that this scheme is complicated by the fact that younger children tend to want to read up and by a certain ambiguity in the point of transition so that the period between eleven and fourteen constitutes a grey area. The content of the novel then must be taken into consideration and I strongly suspect that the determination is made on the basis of whether or not the novel is humorous or deals with problems. In support of this expectation we could look at an author like Philip Pullman who makes it into both categories and a comparison of his junior novels with his adolescent novels would give you a fairly clear sense of how the demarcation is made.

The distinction that separates the Pullman who writes for young adults and the Pullman who writes for children is quite marked and is in keeping with the theory of the children's novel I have presented and is clearly revealed by the critical comments on the jackets of his junior novels. *The Fire-Maker's Daughter* is "at once funny, suspenseful, and impossible to put down." *Count Karlstein* "blends humor and horror." *I Was a Rat* is a mixture of "fairy tale, satire, slapstick humor, and suspenseful melodrama." The writer of children's novels is still a humorist but more than that, Pullman, unlike the writers of the Golden Age, is also self-consciously a parodist who enjoys transgressing generic boundaries. Indeed, as the tradition of the children's novel lengthens, it is reasonable to expect that novel to become more self-reflexive and intertextual. Thus Dahl reveals his indebtedness to Dickens in *BFG* and borrows Norton's joke about "human beans." *The Fire-Maker's Daughter* is a rewrite of Kipling and *Count Karlstein* alludes to *Heidi* at the same time as it parodies nineteenth-century gothic romances. *I Was a Rat* is the *Rosencrantz and Guildenstern Are Dead* of children's literature as it explores the question of what happened to the rat who was turned into a page boy in *Cinderella*. Nor is this tendency limited to the children's novel. My own children's knowledge of literary tradition is largely based upon the parodies of that tradition found on *The Simpsons*.

Thus it is that the tradition of the children's novel that began with *Alice in Wonderland* in 1865 is still alive and well as we begin the twenty-first century. Moreover, it is quite clear that writers know exactly what they are doing when they write children's novels and that in good writers this has nothing to do with adapting their writing to the reading ability of children. The children's novel demonstrates its own, unique narrative techniques, techniques designed to present a vision of childhood based upon the nature of children's play. The writer of the chil-

Conclusion

dren's novel is a humorist who intentionally flattens irony and avoids the depiction of individual consciousness by the avoidance of interior monologue in favor of description and dialogue. As a result, the child is constructed as Other in the perversity of its play and both the adult and child reader are invited to recapture the pleasure of a phantasmagoric play that has been lost. The result is a novel that is different from but in no way inferior to the adult novel. Indeed, I have intentionally sub-titled this book *A Study of the Reader as Child*, rather than the other way round, in order to evoke the sense of how the children's novel can rekindle in us the pure pleasure of the play of the text, a pleasure that can all too easily be lost in a rage for interpretation. The children's novel exists to remind us all, child and adult alike, how to play with our books.

Chapter Notes

Chapter 1

1. Newbery is usually mentioned though credit should be given to Thomas Boreman, *The Gigantick history of the two famous giants, and other curiosities in Guildhall, London* (1740) and to Mary Cooper, *Tommy Thumb's Pretty Song Book* (1744).

2. This same view is expressed more recently by Maria Nikolajeva in *Children's Literature Comes of Age: Toward a New Aesthetic* (New York and London: Garland, 1996, 3) and Karín Lesnik-Oberstein has defended the Ariès methodology in *Children's Literature: Criticism and the Fictional Child* (Oxford: Clarendon Press, 1994).

3. Fortunately, this lack of historical imagination has been addressed by a number of scholars who have tried to recreate the pleasure that children once took in this literature. See Samuel F. Pickering, Jr., *Moral Instruction and Fiction for Children, 1749–1820* (Athens and London: U of Georgia P, 1993), Patricia Demers, *Heaven upon Earth: The Form of Moral and Religious Children's Literature, to 1850* (Knoxville: U of Tennessee P, 1993), Gillian Avery, *Behold the Child: American Children and Their Books 1621–1922* (Baltimore: John Hopkins U P, 1994) and Ruth B. Bottigheimer, *The Bible for Children from the Age of Gutenberg to the Present* (New Haven and London: Yale U P, 1996).

4. For a summary of Spufford's arguments see 65–66 of "The Rise of Children's Literature Reconsidered," *Children's Literature Association Quarterly* 26.2 (2001): 64–73.

5. According to Hanawalt (Growing Up, 113) even in fourteenth-century London, among the artisan and merchant classes, fourteen was the normal age to begin an apprenticeship and increasingly the ability to write was becoming a prerequisite.

6. It is impossible to be more precise than this. As the experience of William Morris suggests, it is possible that four year old children were sent to school for babysitting as much as for schooling. I also suspect that one year of schooling was more common than four. See Spufford's chapter on "Elementary education and reading skills" 19–43.

7. For a study of the epistemological and social changes in the seventeenth century that allowed the novel to distinguish itself from romance see Michael McKeon, *The Origins of the English Novel, 1600–1740* (Baltimore: John Hopkins U P, 1987). For the role of literacy and printing in this development see 43–45 and 50–52.

8. The "coach-and-six" reward for literacy is not restricted to Newbery and for a fuller account of middle-class concerns about literacy in eighteenth-century children's literature see Andrew O'Malley, "The Coach and Six: Chapbook Residue in Late Eighteenth-Century Children's

Notes — Chapter 2

Literature," *The Lion and The Unicorn* 24 (2000): 18–44.

9. Shavit makes the doubleness of the audience a central element of her analysis in *Poetics of Children's Literature* but seems to be less interested in analysing rhetorical duplicity for its own sake as an object of interest in children's literature as she is in showing how it can be reduced to a simplicity that children supposedly prefer. The double audience is also the topic of an entire edition of *Children's Literature*, 25 (1997) which discusses "cross-written" works, a term I suspect could be applied to all the works of children's literature that are considered "classics."

10. Crane documents the history of *Guy of Warwick* from its beginnings as a medieval manuscript to its last appearance in the late eighteenth century as a chapbook for children. Similarly, Spufford points out that the chapbook hero Bevis of Southampton thrilled adolescent males of the late twelfth century in the same way as he sinfully thrilled Bunyan at the end of the seventeenth (7).

11. Neil Postman would disagree with me on this point but then he sees "print" as the cause of everything. See *The Disappearance of Childhood* (New York: Vintage Books, 1994, 48).

12. Nodelman first developed this theory in *The Pleasures of Children's Literature* (155–159).

13. Eible-Eibesfeldt agrees that in the traditional societies he has studied "three-year old children are able to join in a play group, and it is in such play groups that children are truly raised" (600) and that "there is a children's culture, which is transmitted from the older children to the younger ones without adult intervention" (601). Unlike Harris, however, he feels this traditional children's culture has been threatened by "the development of anonymous mass society" (602). It is clear that there is a difference between the play of children in bourgeois culture and in traditional cultures but there is also considerable continuity and, although the parents in a urban neighborhood might not know each other, the children most certainly do. Indeed, Corsaro sees "the recent socioeconomic changes in Western and developing societies" as increasing "the development of extensive and complex peer cultures, which play a major role in the everyday lives of young children and preadolescents" (89).

14. Harris unfortunately does not give her sources but this generalization appears to be derived from Whiting and Edwards (199–200).

15. Eible-Eibesfeldt finds both courtship and sexual modesty to be cultural universals (238-261) and while this might well be pushing biological determinism too far, he does provide evidence that most "civilized" behavior finds at least a rudimentary correlative in traditional societies.

16. In *Of Grammatology*, Derrida coins the term "logocentrism" to describe the privileging of speech and the view that writing is "the dangerous supplement" that comes to "prey upon natural innocence" (168). I have coined the term "grammacentrism" to describe the privileging of writing as the site of rationality. There is no need to coin a term such as "logophobia" since, as my subsequent argument reveals, no such condition can exist.

17. This now seems to be the prevailing view but my own view is not new but merely a return to the old, pre–Ariès view of the matter. See Thompson, *The Making of the English Working Class* (New York: Vintage Books, 1966), 331–349. He ends his balanced account of child labor in this period with the assertion that "the exploitation of little children, on this scale and with this intensity, was one of the most shameful events of our history" (349).

Chapter 2

1. The way in which, in this episode, Lewis moralizes the ambivalence associ-

ated with the animal talker/talking animal distinction makes it clear that he understands that this "difference" is the psychological basis for racism and, although it is a road I have not taken, *Out of the Silent Planet* certainly invites analysis in those terms.

2. Cited by Bruno Bettelheim in *The Uses of Enchantment* (New York: Vintage Books, 1977, 144), and incorrectly attributed to Chesterton's *Orthodoxy* (London: John Lane, 1909). It is actually a "remark" attributed to Chesterton by J.R.R. Tolkien in "On Fairy-Stories" (*Tree and Leaf*, Boston: Houghton, 1965, 44).

3. The Opies's insight is supported by the findings of Maureen and Hugh Crago who explore the history of their daughter's experience with books in *Prelude to Literacy: A Preschool Child's Encounter with Picture and Story* (Carbondale and Edwardsville: Southern Illinois UP, 1983). They found between the ages of two and four "a need for *consistency*" and that "Anna also began to correct us if our reading deviated by even a single word from the text which she knew and expected to hear." They also remark on "her desire that pictures be whole, not fragmented; texts invariable; fictions governed by a single, not multiple, rules" (256).

4. A quick survey of *Twentieth-Century Children's Writers* (3rd ed., Chicago: St. James, 1989) would reveal many writers who deny the "difference." Indeed, so marked is this tendency that in her preface to that work Naomi Lewis observes that "the greatest children's writers rarely care much for children — give or take the selected child or two. Their works, they claim, were not aimed at the young at all. (It is only frankly commercial writers who firmly state the reverse)" (xi).

Chapter 3

1. As Deleuze puts it "*sense is both the expressible or the expressed of the proposition, and the attribute of the state of affairs.*

It turns one side towards things and one side towards propositions. But it does not merge with the proposition which expresses it any more than with the state of affairs or the quality which the proposition denotes. It is exactly the boundary between propositions and things.... It is in this sense that it is an "event": *on the condition that the event is not confused with its spatio-temporal realization in a state of affairs.* We will not ask therefore what is the sense of the event: the event is sense itself. The event belongs essentially to language; it has an essential relationship to language. But language is what is said of things" (22).

2. I first made this connection before I had read *A Thousand Plateaus* and, at the time, I thought it was purely fortuitous but that is not the case since, as Massumi points out "the word 'plateau' comes from an essay by Gregory Bateson's on Balinese culture, in which he found a libidinal economy quite different from the West's orgasmic orientation" (7). See *A Thousand Plateaus*, 158 which in turn directs you to *Steps to an Ecology of Mind*, 113.

3. It might well have been true of late nineteenth-century, Viennese, middle-class males and throughout history one can identify times in which an effort is made to repress all manifestations of play, even among children. Thus in English history one can identify such periods as that of late seventeenth-century Puritanism and early nineteenth-century Evangelicalism.

4. There has, for example, been an effort to develop a theology of play. See David Miller, *Gods and Games: Toward a Theology of Play.*

5. In *The Would-be-Goods* Nesbit reveals her understanding of the idyllic and didactic, of the pleasures and dangers of play, in the following assertion by her child narrator: "In some ways the good times you have with grown-ups are better than the ones you have by yourselves. At any rate they are safer. It is almost impos-

sible, then, to do anything fatal without being pulled up short by a grown-up ere yet the deed is done. And, if you are careful, anything that goes wrong can be looked on as the grown-up's fault. But these secure pleasures are not so interesting to tell about as the things you do when there is no one to stop you on the edge of the rash act" (201). As Nesbit well knew, the children's novel is "interesting" because it places you "on the edge of the rash act."

6. I am not particularly interested in the stages of play development since I am primarily interested in the pretend play of children from three to six. David Cohen, for example, would not recognize this as an example of play because it is "an activity that the infant is 'unconscious' of. During this period, it seems likely that the child, when playing, has an attentive 'alert face' rather than a 'play' face." The next crucial stage would be when infants "first recognize the signal that it's time to play," and he cites the work of Bruner (1975) on the peekaboo game. "The next crucial landmark is, it seems, when the child can initiate play and is able to 'emit' a play signal" (188), which he claims his son Reuben was able to do at 18 months. Finally, "between two and three, Reuben moved from just recognizing a play signal to being able to initiate play and, even, to comment on his intention of doing so. He had become a conscious player" (189). It is at this point that the child has a complete grasp of the difference between fantasy and reality and is aware of the existence of other 'minds.'

7. Harris does not give her sources but the anecdote about the girl is taken from an article by Vivian Paley, "Is the Doll Corner a Sexist Institution?" (1973). Paley, in the spirit of the rising feminism of the time, decided to abolish the doll's corner in her daycare and to convert it into a library. What happened is that the girls took blocks from the boy's play area and reconstructed their doll's corner, leading Paley to conclude what would still be anathema to most literary critics today, that "there are differences between little boys and girls" (576).

8. That children enjoy playing "baby" is confirmed by Cohen's observations of his son Nicholas who "between 6:0 and 6:3 ... adopts this babyish game, laughing as he does it. He says he doesn't 'wanna brush teeth. He grabs his pyjamas out of my hand, twirls them and adds: 'I don't wanna 'jammas.' And laughs" (136).

9. In relation to this particular example, it might be useful to quote David Cohen who points out that "psychoanalysts have tended to see the different toys that different sexes like as a reflection of their fundamental biology. Erik Erickson observed (1977) that boys and girls played very differently with blocks. Boys tended to create tall, long shapes — the Lego phallus — while girls tended to make dumpier structures with enclosed spaces. John plays at making rockets; Jill at building a house. Erikson suggested these were biological differences and, also reflected the basic male/female divide. The boy thrusts aggressively into the world while the girl envelops it with love" (59–60). Stated so bluntly such assertions are rightly treated with incredulity but, given the historical and cultural persistence of such distinctions, the opposite assertion that such differences are purely cultural, should be received with equal incredulity. Given the present state of research into this question, any extreme affiliation with either side of the nature/nurture debate should be received with profound skepticism. Also, although Erikson might well have said something like Cohen suggests, he does not do so in *Toys and Reason* as Cohen asserts.

10. For empirical evidence of this assertion see Joseph Shepher, who describes what happened when a decision was made not to repress childhood sexuality in the Israeli kibbutzim (60–61).

11. Juliet Dusinberre points out that

"the small child has a wondrous faculty for picking up the wrong end of the stick, at least from the adult point of view" (65) and then quotes from Ellen Key's *The Century of the Child* the story of the child who, "seeing the pictures of the Christian martyrs in the arena, cried out sympathetically, 'Look at that poor tiger; he hasn't got a Christian'" (302). There is no more apt, nor funny, example of the perversion of the child, of being turned the wrong way.

12. If any one doubts this generalization they would do well to read George Eisen's *Children and Play in the Holocaust* in which he points out that "although human logic cannot easily assimilate this fact, the Holocaust supplies us with ample documentation that play can take place at any time and any place" (79).

13. See *A Thousand Plateaus*, 351–423.

14. This dissatisfaction with progressive theories of play seems to be becoming more prevalent. Cohen also points out that "Piaget noted, and approved of the fact, that as children got older their games became more realistic, more adapted to the real world. That is a Calvinist position if ever there was one. I will ask later on why children stop playing and what might be done, in a changing world, to make adults play so that they don't lose all these skills they built up so cleverly in their infancy" (112).

Chapter 4

1. Cohen describes at some length the way Nicholas played with his younger brother Reuben and uses the same terms to describe that play when he concludes that "to suggest that Nicholas uses play only to tease and put down Reuben would be wrong; often, he is amused but affectionate" (122). "Amused but affectionate" is precisely the attitude that the narrator and narratee take to the protagonist in the Alice books so one might assert that the way that a narrator/narratee play with the protagonist in a children's novel is precisely the way an older sibling plays with a younger sibling. Cohen also noted that part of the pleasure of this kind of play lies in the possibility of regression and that "in dealing with aggressive and obscene games, Reuben also allowed Nicholas the chance to act the baby" (122).

2. It might seem strange that I omit animal fantasy from my analysis considering that it is one of the performance styles isolated by Sawyer and discussed in the previous chapter. I do so for the sake of economy and it is quite easy to see how my rhetorical scheme could be applied to the genre. For example, see "Some Ingredients of Watership Down" and Richard Adams's discussion of the spectrum of affect that is possible in anthropomorphic fantasy (172–73).. Also, John Goldthwaite has already provided an excellent history of animal fantasy in his otherwise idiosyncratic *The Natural History of Make-Believe*.

3. On the other hand, Carroll does use quoted monologue much more often than his contemporaries and this usage does create the effect that Wall subjectively describes. If one counts lines, the proportion of psycho-narration to quoted monologue in the first chapter is 2 to 1 whereas in the domestic novel, whether for adults or children, it plays a considerably smaller role. In the first volume of *Little Women* the proportion of psycho-narration to quoted monologue is 39 to 1 and I suspect one would find about the same proportion in *Pride and Prejudice*.

4. This number is rather arbitrary since some of the paragraphs are ambiguous and some are only one line. I count forty paragraphs of interior monologue in chapter 20 alone but I doubt if anyone else would come up with exactly the same count.

Chapter 5

1. Nikolajeva rather daringly, if reluctantly, suggests that this plot "follows the cycle of the moon" (126) so perhaps we

could call it the periodic plot. If I could be equally daring, and if I were an unskeptical Freudian I would not even hesitate, I would point out that the boy's adventure plot consists of a series of spurts of energy followed by quiescence and re-energization.

2. For example, in chapter four, which describes their first day on the island, the pronoun "we" appears 51 times to the 47 uses of "I."

3. Not surprisingly, the homoerotic suggestiveness of *The Coral Island* and of the boy's school story have recently become explicitly homosexual in Chris Kent's two novellas that are published together as *Boys Will Be Boys: Coral Island Boys, and, Little Big Men* (2003).

4. There might be some debate about chapters twenty and twenty-one but otherwise I suspect that most readers would agree with my attribution of protagonists. Amy only gets half of chapter twenty and Laurie initiates the action in twenty-one but Jo resolves it and it is her consciousness we focalize on.

5. The most concentrated example of the representation of a collective consciousness is in the opening 14 lines of chapter sixteen.

6. I have chosen *Pride and Prejudice* to compare to *Little Women* for obvious reasons but, from the point of view of comparing narrative technique, it is not the best choice. It is an early novel and in Volume One, Austen appears not to have yet discovered the principle of centered consciousness; indeed, it takes a long time to focalize on Elizabeth and it is not until chapter eighteen, when she dances with Darcy, that there is a concentrated focalization on her (156 lines). In Volume One, the comparative percentages of narrative summary, dialogue and consciousness are 31 percent, 50 percent and 18 percent and of the last only 60 percent belongs to Elizabeth. The discrepancy would become more marked if we only considered volumes two and three in which the respective numbers are 25 percent, 45 percent and 30 percent and of the last 85 percent belongs to Elizabeth. I suspect that the discrepancy would become even more marked if we compared *Little Women* to a later novel such as *Emma* and even more marked if we were to compare it to a novel by Henry James.

7. Again it will come as no surprise that Meg, as the eldest sister, despite only getting two chapters, gets almost as many lines as Jo at 201. The younger sisters Beth and Amy get 87 and 92 respectively. Laurie, who exists on the fringe of the collective, gets 75. Also Meg and Jo together as a collective within the collective get 15.

8. This is actually quoted monologue without the quotation marks or what is called "stream of consciousness" and Alcott seems to have chanced upon it unwittingly since she never does it again in the novel.

9. Of course, this is not the case in volume two in which the grown-up Amy comes to almost rival Jo for the role of main protagonist.

10. We do know that in 1879 when she was revising the work, she had read *Through the Looking-Glass* because Merrill, the new illustrator, describes in a letter a meeting with her in which the two of them "recited from 'Jabberwock' line by line, antiphonically" (Alderson, xii).

11. This poem is not included in the Puffin edition I am using, an editorial decision that might reflect modern taste but is unfortunate from a scholarly point of view. Still, considering that the novel was not in print the first time I taught it and seemed to have fallen off the canonical radar screen, its reissue is an important development that properly reflects its importance to the history of the children's novel.

12. According to Gabriella Åhmansson "Montgomery never mentions having read *Rebecca of Sunnybrook Farm* in her journal, but the book was so widely read that it is inconceivable that she did not know

of it at least" (n62, 68). In his article, "L. M. Montgomery and the literary heroine: Jo, Rebecca, Anne, and Emily," T. D. MacLulich demonstrates in some detail just how indebted she is to both Wiggin and Alcott.

Chapter 6

1. In her article "The Development of Consciousness in Lucy Boston's *The Children of Green Knowe*," Lynne Rosenthal accepts the thesis that it is the nuclear bomb that produced the increased "consciousness" of Boston's novels and quotes Boston herself as the source of that belief since in an article in *Hornbook* Boston herself attributes the "present pessimism" of the young and the fact that "all my child heroes ... are dispossessed and looking for what they have lost" to "the lunacy of hydrogen bombs" (261).

2. In "Henry James and the Storyteller: The Development of a Central Consciousness in Realistic Fiction for Children," Lois R. Kuznets is dealing with the same issue that I am and would seem to support my historical generalization when she points out that this narrative technique does not become common until "the mid-twentieth century" (188) and all the examples she analyses are post-war except for Rawling's *The Yearling* (1938). I think Wilder is a better choice for an exception to the rule since Laura starts out as a five-year-old child whereas Jody is an adolescent with a problem.

3. Since I wrote my analysis of Mayne, I have become aware that he has been convicted of sexually molesting young girls so I thought it necessary to note that fact though I hope it is unnecessary to point out that when I say writers for children must be perverts I do not mean that literally.

4. I do not know what Mayne's philosophical background is but he has given a remarkably clear explanation of the difference Deleuze points out in *The Logic of Sense* between Chronos and Aion, the time of bodies and the time of consciousness.

Bibliography

Primary Sources

Adams, Richard. *Watership Down*. 1972. London: Puffin, 1993.
Alcott, Louisa May. *Little Women*. 1868. Oxford; New York: Oxford UP, 1998
Austen, Jane. *Pride and Prejudice*. 1813. Oxford: Oxford UP, 1998.
Ballantyne, R. M.. *The Coral Island: A Tale of the Pacific Ocean*. 1858. London; Edinburgh; New York: T. Nelson, 1893.
Blume, Judy. *Are You There God? It's Me, Margaret*. 1970. New York: Yearling, 1986.
Blyton, Enid. *Five Go Down to the Sea*. 1953. London: Hodder and Stoughton, 1984.
Boreman, Thomas. *The Gigantic History of the Two Famous Giants, and Other Curiosities in Guildhall, London*. London, 1740.
Boston, Lucy. *The Children of Green Knowe*. 1954. London: Faber, 2000.
Bradbury, Malcolm. *The History Man*. London: Secker & Warburg, 1975.
Burnett, Frances Hodgson. *Little Lord Fauntleroy*. 1886. Harmondsworth: Penguin, 1981.
_____. *The Secret Garden*. 1911. Philadelphia; New York: J. B. Lippincott, 1962.
Burney, Fanny. *Evelina*. 1778. Oxford; New York: Oxford UP, 1982.
Carroll, Lewis. *Alice's Adventures in Wonderland*. 1865. Oxford: Oxford UP, 1982.
_____. *The Complete Sylvie and Bruno*. 1889–1893. San Francisco: Mercury House, 1991.
_____. *Through the Looking-Glass*. 1872. Oxford: Oxford UP, 1982.
Conrad, Joseph. *The Heart of Darkness*. 1899. New York: Norton, 1988.
Coolidge, Susan. *What Katy Did*. 1872. London: Puffin, 2004.
Cooper, Mary. *Tommy Thumb's Pretty Song Book*. London, 1744.
Cormier, Robert. *The Chocolate War*. New York: Dell, 1975.
Dahl, Roald. *The BFG*. New York: Farrar, Straus, Giroux, 1982.
_____. "The Champion of the World." 1959. *The Best of Roald Dahl*. New York: Vintage Books, 1990. 377–401.
_____. *Danny, the Champion of the World*. 1975. New York: Puffin, 1998.
_____. *Matilda*. 1988. New York; Puffin, 1998.
Defoe, Daniel. *The Life & Strange Surprizing Adventures of Robinson Crusoe of York*. 1720. 3vols. Oxford: Blackwell, 1927.
_____. *Robinson Crusoe*. Abridged Bob Blaisdell. Toronto: Dover, 1995.
Durrell, Lawrence. *The Alexandria Quartet*. 1962. London: Faber and Faber, 1968.

Bibliography

Fitzhugh, Louise. *Harriet the Spy*. 1964. New York: Yearling, 1984.
Fowles, John. *The Collector*. Boston: Little, Brown, 1963.
———. *The French Lieutenant's Woman*. Boston: Little, Brown, 1969.
Golding, William. *Lord of the Flies*. 1954. Harmondsworth: Penguin, 1960.
Grahame, Kenneth. *Dream Days*. 1898. New York: Dodd, Mead, 1930.
———. *The Golden Age*. 1895. New York: Dodd, Mead, 1922.
———. *Wind in the Willows*. 1908. New York: Scribner, 1960.
James, Henry. *What Maisie Knew*. London: W. Heinemann, 1898.
Jefferies, Richard. *Bevis, the Story of a Boy*. 1882. London: Duckworthy, 1905.
Kent, Chris. *Boys Will Be Boys: Coral Island Boys, and, Little Big Men*. San Francisco: GLB, 2003.
Kipling, Rudyard. *The Jungle Book*. 1894. London: Macmillan, 1907.
———. *Stalky & Co.* 1899. Oxford: Oxford UP, 1999.
Lewis, C. S. *The Lion, the Witch and the Wardrobe*. 1950. New York: Macmillan, 1970.
———. *Out of the Silent Planet*. New York: Macmillan, 1945.
———. *The Silver Chair*. 1953. London: Lions, 1980.
Mahy, Margaret. *The Blood-and-Thunder Adventure on Hurricane Peak*. New York: Macmillan, 1989.
———. *The Pirate Uncle*. 1977. Woodstock, NY: Overlook, 1994.
———. *The Tricksters*. New York: Macmillan, 1986.
Marryat, Frederick. *Masterman Ready*. 1841. London; New York: Dent, Dutton, 1970.
———. *Peter Simple*. 1832. London: J. M. Dent, 1970.
Mayne, William. *Antar and the Eagles*. New York: Delacorte, 1989.
———. *Drift*. London: Jonathan Cape, 1985.
———. *Gideon Ahoy!* New York: Delacorte, 1987.
———. *The Member for the Marsh*. London: Oxford UP, 1956.
Montgomery, Lucy Maud. *Anne of Green Gables*. 1903. Toronto: Seal, 1996.
Nesbit, Edith. *Five Children and It*. 1902. Harmondsworth: Penguin, 1959.
———. *The Phoenix and the Carpet*. 1904. Harmondsworth: Penguin, 1959.
———. *The Railway Children*. 1906. Mineola, NY: Dover, 2000.
———. *The Story of the Amulet*. 1906. Harmondsworth: Penguin, 1959.
———. *The Story of the Treasure Seekers*. 1899. London: Ernest Benn, 1973.
———. *The Would-be-Goods*. 1901. London: Ernest Benn; New York: Coward–McCann, 1958.
Newbery, John. *The Fairing: or, a Golden Toy; For Children of All Sizes and Denominations*. 1768. New York and London: Garland, 1977.
———. *A Little Pretty Pocket Book*. 1744. New York: Harcourt, Brace & World, 1967.
Norton, Mary. *The Borrowers*. 1953. New York: Harcourt, Brace, 1986.
Paterson, Katherine. *Jacob Have I Loved*. 1980. New York: Harper Trophy, 1990.
Pearce, Philippa. *A Dog So Small*. 1962. Harmondsworth: Puffin, 1964.
———. *Here Comes Tod!* 1992. Cambridge, MA: Candlewick, 1994.
———. *Tom's Midnight Garden*. 1958. London: Puffin, 1976.
———. *The Way to Sattin Shore*. Harmondsworth: Kestrel, 1983.
Pullman, Philip. *Count Karlstein*. New York: Knopf, 1982.
———. *The Fire-Maker's Daughter*. New York: Scholastic, 1995.
———. *I Was a Rat*. London: Knopf, 1999.
Ransome, Arthur. *Swallows and Amazons*. 1930. London: Heinemann, 1972.
Spyri, Johanna. *Heidi*. 1880. Trans. Helen B. Dole. 1884. New York: Random, 1946.

Stevenson, Robert Louis. *Treasure Island*. 1883. London: Puffin, 1994.
Thompson, Roger, ed. *Samuel Pepys' Penny Merriments*. London: Constable, 1976.
Twain, Mark. *The Adventures of Tom Sawyer*. Oxford: Oxford University Press, 1993.
Warner, Susan. *The Wide, Wide World*. 1850. New York: Feminist Press at City University of New York, 1987.
Wiggin, Kate Douglas. *Rebecca of Sunnybrook Farm*. 1903. New York: Dover, 2003.
Wilder, Laura Ingalls. *Little House in the Big Woods*. 1932. New York: Avon, 2003.
———. *The Long Winter*. 1940. New York: Harper Trophy, 1971.
Wyss, Johann. *The Swiss Family Robinson*. 1812. Cutchogue, NY: Buccaneer, 1985.
Yonge, Charlotte. *The Daisy Chain, or Aspirations: A Family Chronicle*. 1856. London: Macmillan, 1911.

Secondary Sources

Adams, Gillian. "Medieval Children's Literature: Its Possibility and Actuality." *Children's Literature* 26 (1998): 1–24.
Adams, Richard. "Some Ingredients of Watership Down." *The Thorny Paradise: Writers on Writing for Children*. Ed. Edward Blishen. Hammondsworth: Kestral, 1975. 163–173.
Åhmansson, Gabriella. *A Life and Its Mirrors: A Feminist Reading of L. M. Montgomery's Fiction*. Volume I. Acta Univ. Ups. *Studia Anglistica Upsaliensia* 74, 1991.
Alderson, Valerie. "Introduction." *Little Women*. Oxford: Oxford UP, 1998. vii-xxviii.
Altick, R. D. *The English Common Reader: A Social History of the Mass Reading Public 1800 -1900*. Chicago: U of Chicago P, 1957.
Ariès, Phillipe. *Centuries of Childhood: A Social History of Family Life*. New York: Knopf, 1962.
Avery, Gillian. *Behold the Child: American Children and Their Books 1621–1922*. Baltimore: John Hopkins UP, 1994.
———. "The Voice of the Child, Both Godly and Unregenerate, in Early Modern England." *Infant Tongues: The Voice of the Child in Literature*. Ed. Elizabeth Goodenough, Mark A. Herberle, Naomi Sokoloff. Detroit: Wayne State UP, 1994. 16–27.
Bakhtin, Mikhail. *Rabelais and His World*. Trans. Hélène Iswolsky. Bloomington: Indiana UP, 1984.
Bashevis-Singer, Isaac. "Isaac Bashevis-Singer on Writing for Children." *Children's Literature* 6 (1977): 9–16.
Bateson, Gregory. *Steps to an Ecology of Mind*. New York: Ballantine, 1972.
———. "A Theory of Play and Fantasy." 1955. *Play — Its Role in Development and Evolution*. Ed. Jerome S. Bruner, Alison Jolly and Kathy Sylva. New York: Basic Books, 1976. 119–129.
Bettelheim, Bruno. *The Uses of Enchantment*. New York: Vintage, 1977.
Blake, Kathleen. *Play, Games, and Sport: The Literary Works of Lewis Carroll*. Ithaca; London: Cornell UP, 1974.
Bolter, J. David. *Writing Space: The Computer, Hypertext, and the History of Writing*. Hillsdale, NJ: Erlbaum, 1991.
Boston, Lucy. "A Message from Green Knowe." *Hornbook*. June 1963.
Boswell, John. *The Kindness of Strangers: The Abandonment of Children in Western Europe from Late Antiquity to the Renaissance*. New York: Pantheon, 1988.

Bibliography

Bottigheimer, Ruth B. *The Bible for Children from the Age of Gutenberg to the Present.* New Haven and London: Yale UP, 1996.

Bourdieu, Pierre. *The Logic of Practice.* Tran. Richard Nice. Stanford: Stanford UP, 1990.

Bruner, Jerome S., Alison Jolly and Katy Silva, eds. *Play — Its Role in Development and Evolution.* New York: Basic, 1976. 277–285.

Buchanan, Ian and John Marks, eds. *Deleuze and Literature.* Edinburgh: Edinburgh UP, 2000.

Campbell, Joseph. *The Hero with a Thousand Faces.* Princeton, NJ: Princeton UP, 1968.

Cohen, David. *The Development of Play.* 2nd ed. London; New York: Routledge, 1993.

Cohn, Dorrit. *Transparent Minds: Narrative Modes for Presenting Consciousness in Fiction.* Princeton, NJ.: Princeton UP, 1978.

Corsaro, William A. *The Sociology of Childhood.* Thousand Oaks, CA: Pine Forge, 1997.

Coveney, Peter. *The Image of Childhood: The Individual and Society: A Study of the Theme in English Literature.* Revised ed. London: Penguin, 1967.

Crago, Maureen and Hugh. *Prelude to Literacy: A Preschool Child's Encounter with Picture and Story.* Carbondale and Edwardsville: Southern Illinois UP, 1983.

Crane, Ronald S. "The Vogue of *Guy of Warwick* from the Close of the Middle Ages to the Romantic Revival." PMLA 30 (1915): 125–94.

Cressy, David. *Education in Tudor and Stuart England.* New York: St. Martin's, 1975.

Cunningham, Hugh. *Children and Childhood in Western Society Since 1500.* London and New York: Longman, 1995.

Darton, F. J. Harvey. *Children's Books in England.* 2nd ed. Cambridge: Cambridge UP, 1958.

de la Mare, Walter. *Lewis Carroll.* London: Faber & Faber, 1932.

Deleuze, Gilles. *The Logic of Sense.* 1969. Trans. Mark Lester with Charles Stivale. Ed. Constantin V. Boundas. New York: Columbia UP, 1990.

———. "The Schizophrenic and Language: Surface and Depth in Lewis Carroll and Antonin Artaud." *Textual Strategies: Perspectives in Post-Structuralist Criticism.* Trans. and ed. Josue V. Harari. Ithaca: Cornell UP, 1979. 277–295.

———, and Felix Guattari. *A Thousand Plateaus: Capitalism and Schziophrenia.* 1980. Trans. Brian Massumi. Minneapolis: U of Minnesota P, 1987.

Demers, Patricia. *Heaven Upon Earth: The Form of Moral and Religious Children's Literature, to 1850.* Knoxville: U of Tennessee P, 1993.

Derrida, Jacques. *Of Grammatology.* Trans. Gayatri Chakravorty Spivak. Baltimore: John Hopkins UP, 1976.

Donovan, Ann. "Narrative Strategy in *Drift* by William Mayne." *The Voice of the Narrator in Children's Literature: Insights from Writers and Critics.* Ed. Charlotte F. Otten and Gary D. Schmidt. New York: Greenwood, 1989. 295–307.

Dusinberre, Juliet. *Alice to the Lighthouse: Children's Books and Radical Experiments in Art.* 1987. London: Macmillan; New York: St. Martin's Press, 1999.

Eagleton, Terry. *The Illusions of Postmodernism.* Oxford: Blackwell, 1996.

Eible-Eibesfeldt, Irenäus. *Human Ethology.* Hawthorne, NY: Aldine de Gruyter, 1989.

Eisen, George. *Children and Play in the Holocaust: Games Among the Shadows.* Amherst: U of Massachusetts P, 1988.

Empson, William. *Some Versions of Pastoral.* London: Chatto & Windus, 1968.

Erickson, Erik. *Toys and Reasons.* New York: Norton, 1977.

Fagan, Robert. "Modelling How and Why Play Works." 1975. *Play — Its Role in Development and Evolution.* Ed. Jerome S. Bruner, Alison Jolly and Kathy Sylva. New York: Basic, 1976. 96–115.

Fletcher, John and Andrew Benjamin, eds. *Abjection, Melancholia and Love: The Work of Julia Kristeva.* London: Routledge, 1990.

Foster, Shirley and Judy Simons. *What Katy Read: Feminist Re-readings of "Classic" Stories for Girls.* Iowa City: U of Iowa P, 1995.

Freud, Sigmund. *Beyond the Pleasure Principle.* Trans. and ed. James Strachey. New York: Norton, 1975.

Fuller, Peter. "Uncovering Childhood." *Changing Childhood.* Ed. Martin Hoyles. London: Writers and Readers Publishing Cooperative, 1979. 71–108.

Goldthwaite, John. *The Natural History of Make-Believe.* New York; Oxford: Oxford UP, 1996.

Goody, Jack. *The Interface Between the Written and the Oral.* Cambridge: Cambridge UP, 1987.

Graff, Harvey J. *The Legacies of Literacy: Continuities and Contradictions in Western Culture and Society.* Bloomington: Indiana UP, 1987.

Green, Martin. *Dreams of Adventure, Deeds of Empire.* New York: Basic, 1979.

Griffith, John W. and Charles H. Frey, eds. *Classics of Children's Literature.* 3rd ed. New York: MacMillan, 1992.

Grosz, Elizabeth. "The Body of Signification." *Abjection, Melancholia and Love: The Work of Julia Kristeva.* Eds. John Fletcher and Andrew Benjamin. London: Routledge, 1990. 80–103.

Hamburger, Käte. *The Logic of Literature.* Trans. Marilynn J. Rose. Bloomington: Indiana UP, 1973.

Hanawalt, Barbara. "Childrearing Among the Lower Classes of Late Medieval England." *Journal of Interdisciplinary History*, 8 (1977): 1–22.

_____. *Growing Up in Medieval London: The Experience of Childhood in History.* New York and Oxford: Oxford UP, 1993.

Hardt, Michael. *Gilles Deleuze: An Apprenticeship in Philosophy.* Minneapolis: U of Minnesota P, 1993.

Harris, Judith Rich. *The Nurture Assumption: Why Children Turn Out the Way They Do.* New York: The Free Press, 1998.

Hendrick, Harry. "Constructions and Reconstructions of British Childhood: An Interpretative Survey, 1800 to the Present." *Constructing and Reconstructing Childhood.* Ed. Allison James and Alan Prout. London; Washington: Falmer, 1997. 34–62.

Henkle, Roger. "The Mad Hatter's World." *Virginia Quarterly Review* 49 (1973): 99–117.

Hopkins, Eric. *Childhood Transformed: Working-Class Children in Nineteenth-Century England.* Manchester, UK; New York: Manchester UP, 1994.

Hoyles, Martin, ed. *Changing Childhood.* London: Writers and Readers Publishing Cooperative, 1979.

Hughes, Felicity. "Children's Literature: Theory and Practice." *ELH* 45.3 (1978): 542–61.

Hunt, David. *Parents and Children in History.* New York and London: Basic, 1970.

Hunt, Peter. *An Introduction to Children's Literature.* Oxford and New York: Oxford UP, 1994.

James, Allison and Alan Prout, eds. *Constructing and Reconstructing Childhood: Con-*

temporary Issues in the Sociological Study of Childhood. London; Washington: Falmer, 1997.

Johnson, James E., James F. Christie, and Thomas D. Yawkey. *Play and Early Childhood Development*. 2nd ed. New York: Longman, 1999.

Jones, Gwenyth. "Explorers." *SFEye* 15 (1997). 16 August 2006. <htm>

Kiely, Robert. *Robert Louis Stevenson and the Fiction of Adventure*. Cambridge, Mass.: Harvard UP, 1964.

Kristeva, Julia. *Desire in Language: A Semiotic Approach to Literature and Art*. Ed. Leon S. Roudiez. Trans. Thomas Gora, Alice Jardine and Leon S. Roudiez. New York: Columbia UP, 1980.

Kuznets, Lois R. "Henry James and the Storyteller: The Development of a Central Consciousness in Realistic Fiction for Children." *The Voice of the Narrator in Children's Literature: Insights from Writers and Critics*. Ed. Charlotte F. Otten and Gary D. Schmidt. New York: Greenwood, 1989. 187–198.

Lacan, Jacques. "The Mirror Stage as Formative of the Function of the I as Revealed in Psychoanalytical Experience." *Ecrits, a Selection*. Trans. Alan Sheridan. London: Tavistock, 1977. 1–7.

Lambert, Gregg. "On the Uses and Abuses of Literature for Life." *Deleuze and Literature*. Ed. Ian Buchanan and John Marks. Edinburgh: Edinburgh UP, 2000. 135–166.

Lechte, John. "Art, Love, and Melancholy in the Work of Julia Kristeva." *Abjection, Melancholia and Love: The Work of Julia Kristeva*. Eds. John Fletcher and Andrew Benjamin. London: Routledge, 1990. 24–41.

Lesnick-Oberstein, Karín. *Children's Literature: Criticism and the Fictional Child*. Oxford: Clarendon Press, 1994.

Lévi-Strauss, Claude. *Tristes Tropiques*. New York: Criterion, 1961.

Lewis, C. S. *On Stories and Other Essays on Literature*. Ed. Walter Hooper. New York; London: Harcourt Brace Jovanovich, 1982.

_____. *A Preface to* Paradise Lost. London: Oxford UP, 1959.

Lodge, David. *The Art of Fiction*. New York: Viking Penguin, 1992.

MacLulich, T. D. " L. M. Montgomery and the Literary Heroine: Jo, Rebecca, Anne, and Emily." *Canadian Children's Literature* 37 (1985): 5–17.

Massumi, Brian. *A User's Guide to* Capitalism and Schizophrenia*: Deviations from Deleuze and Guattari*. Cambridge, Mass.: MIT Press, 1992.

McGillis, Roderick. *The Nimble Reader: Literary Theory and Children's Literature*. New York: Twayne, 1996.

McKeon, Michael. *The Origins of the English Novel, 1600–1740*. Baltimore: John Hopkins UP, 1987.

McLuhan, Marshall. *The Gutenberg Galaxy: The Making of Typographic Man*. Toronto: U of Toronto P, 1972.

McMunn, Meradith Tilbury. "Children and Literature in Medieval France." *Children's Literature* 4 (1975): 51–58.

Mead, George Herbert. *The Philosophy of the Present*. Chicago: U of Chicago P, 1932.

Miller, David L. *Gods and Games: Toward a Theology of Play*. New York: Harper, 1973.

Mitchell, Lee Clark. "Introduction." *The Adventures of Tom Sawyer*. Oxford: Oxford UP, 1993. vii–xxxiv.

Mitterauer, Michael. *A History of Youth*. Trans. Graeme Dunphy. Oxford UK; Cambridge, USA: Blackwell, 1992.

Morgenstern, John. "The Rise of Children's Literature Reconsidered." *Children's Literature Association Quarterly* 26.2 (2001): 64–73.
Neuburg, V. E. *Popular Education in Eighteenth Century England.* London: Woburn, 1971.
Newell, William. *Games and Songs of American Children.* 1883. New York: Dover, 1963.
Nikolajeva, Maria. *Children's Literature Comes of Age: Toward a New Aesthetic.* New York and London: Garland, 1996.
———. *The Rhetoric of Character in Children's Literature.* Lanham: Scarecrow, 2002
Nodelman, Perry. "Pleasure and Genre: Speculations on the Characteristics of Children's Fiction." *Children's Literature* 28 (2000): 1–14.
———. *The Pleasures of Children's Literature.* 2nd ed. White Plains, NY: Longman, 1996.
O'Malley, Andrew. "The Coach and Six: Chapbook Residue in Late Eighteenth-Century Children's Literature." *The Lion and the Unicorn* 24 (2000): 18–44.
Ong, Walter J. *Orality and Literacy: The Technologizing of the Word.* London and New York: Methuen, 1982.
Opie, Iona, and Peter Opie. *The Lore and Language of Schoolchildren.* Oxford: Oxford UP, 1959.
Otten, Charlotte F. And Gary D. Schmidt, eds. *The Voice of the Narrator in Children's Literature: Insights from Writers and Critics.* New York: Greenwood, 1989.
Paley, Vivian. "Is the Doll Corner a Sexist Institution." *School Review* 81 (1973): 569–576.
Paterson, Katherine. "From the Newbery Medal Acceptance, 1981: *Jacob Have I Loved.*" *Children's Literature Review,* Vol. 7. Detroit: Gale Research, 1984. 238–240.
Pickering, Samuel F., Jr. *Moral Instruction and Fiction for Children, 1749–1820.* Athens and London: U of Georgia P, 1993.
Pinchbeck, Ivy and Margaret Hewitt. *Children in English Society.* London: Routledge &Kegan Paul; Toronto: U of Toronto P, 1969–73.
Pollock, Linda A. *Forgotten Children: Parent-Child Relations from 1500 to 1900.* Cambridge: Cambridge UP, 1983.
Postman, Neil. *The Disappearance of Childhood.* New York: Vintage, 1994.
Reynolds, Kimberley. *Children's Literature in the 1890's and the 1990's.* Plymouth: Northcote, 1994.
Robeck, Mildred C. And Randall Wallace. *The Psychology of Reading: An Interdisciplinary Approach.* 2nd ed. Hillsdale, NJ.: Erlbaum, 1990.
Rose, Jacqueline. *The Case of Peter Pan: or The Impossibility of Children's Fiction.* London: Macmillan, 1984.
Rosenthal, Lynne. "The Development of Consciousness in Lucy Boston's *The Children of the Green Knowe.*" *Children's Literature* 8 (1980): 53–67.
Rousseau, Jean-Jacques. *Emile: or On Education.* Trans. Allan Bloom. New York: Basic Books, 1979.
Sawyer, R. Keith. *Pretend Play as Improvisation: Conversation in the Preschool Classroom.* Mahwah, NJ: Lawrence Erlbaulm, 1997.
Schlumbohm, J., ed. *Wie Kinder zu Bauern, Bürgen, Aristokraten Wurden 1700–1850.* Munich, 1983.
Schofield, Roger. "Dimensions of Illiteracy, 1750–1850." *Explorations in Economic History* 10 (1973): 437–454.
Scholes, Robert E. *Elements of Poetry.* New York: Oxford UP, 1969.

Schwartzman, Helen B. *Transformations: The Anthropology of Children's Play.* New York: Plenum, 1978.
Scribner, Sylvia, and Michael Cole. *The Psychology of Literacy.* Cambridge, MA: Harvard UP, 1981.
Sedgwick, Eve Kosofsky. *Between Men: English Literature and Male Homosocial Desire.* New York: Columbia UP, 1985.
Shahar, Shulamith. *Childhood in the Middle Ages.* London: Routledge, 1990.
Shavit, Zohar. *Poetics of Children's Literature.* Athens: U of Georgia P, 1986.
Shepher, Joseph. *Incest: A Biosocial View.* New York: Academic, 1983.
Shorter, Edward. *The Making of the Modern Family.* New York: Basic, 1975.
Spufford, Margaret. *Small Books and Pleasant Histories: Popular Fiction and its Readership in Seventeenth-Century England.* Athens: U of Georgia P, 1982.
Steinbeck, John. *The Acts of King Arthur and His Noble Knights.* New York: Random, 1976.
Stevenson, Robert Louis. *The Works of Robert Louis Stevenson.* 24 vols. London: Chatto and Windus, 1912.
Stone, Lawrence. *The Family, Sex and Marriage in England 1500–1800.* New York: Harper & Row, 1977.
Sutton-Smith, Brian. *The Ambiguity of Play.* Cambridge, MA.: Harvard UP, 1997.
Talbot, C. H. "Children in the Middle Ages." *Children's Literature* 6 (1977): 17–33.
Tallis, Raymond. *In Defence of Realism.* Lincoln: U of Nebraska P, 1998.
Thompson, E. P. *The Making of the English Working Class.* New York: Vintage Books, 1966.
Thwaite, M. F. *From Primer to Pleasure in Reading: an Introduction to the History of Children's Books in England from the Invention of Printing to 1914.* Boston: Horn, 1972.
Tolkien, J. R. R. "On Fairy-Stories." *Tree and Leaf.* Boston: Houghton, 1965.
Van Ghent, Dorothy. "On *Pride and Prejudice.*" *The English Novel: Form and Function.* 1953. New York: Harper, 1961. 99–111.
Wall, Barbara. *The Narrator's Voice: The Dilemma of Children's Fiction.* New York: St. Martin's, 1991.
Wardle, David. *English Popular Education, 1780–1975.* Cambridge: Cambridge UP, 1976.
———. *The Rise of the Schooled Society.* London: Rouledge &Kegan Paul, 1974.
Watt, Ian. *The Rise of the Novel: Studies in Defoe, Richardson and Fielding.* Berkeley: U of California P, 1957.
Whiting, Beatrice Blyth and Carolyn Pope Edwards. *Children of Different Worlds: The Formation of Social Behaviour.* Cambridge, MA: Harvard UP, 1988.
Williams, Clare. *Thomas Platter's Travels in England.* 1599. London: Jonathan Cape, 1937.
Wolfenstein, Martha. *Children's Humor: A Psychological Analysis.* Bloomington: Indiana UP, 1978.
Wooden, Warren W. *Children's Literature of the English Renaissance.* Lexington: U of Kentucky P, 1986.
Zipes, Jack. *Fairy Tales and the Art of Subversion: The Classical Genre for Children and the Process of Civilization.* New York: Methuen, 1988.

Index

abjection 52, 56–59, 64–65, 80
Adams, Gillian 7–8, 10–11, 19
Adams, Richard 200, 215n
adventure stories 20, 76–77, 90, 97, 100, 102, 113–115, 121, 123–131, 134–135, 137, 140–141, 159, 170–171, 175, 200–201, 216n
The Adventures of Tom Sawyer (Twain) 134–136, 165, 167
Åhmansson, Gabriella 216n
Alcott, Louisa May 98, 101–102, 108–109, 119, 141–142, 147–149, 151–159, 163–168
Alderson, Valerie 148, 152, 216n
The Alexandria Quartet (Durrell) 198
Alice's Adventures in Wonderland (Carroll) 2, 4, 6, 58–63, 65, 67, 76, 78–79, 91, 93–95, 97–100, 103–105, 107, 116, 124, 140, 152, 179, 192, 196, 206, 208, 215n
Altick, R.D. 14
The American Dream (Mailer) 206
Animal Farm 46
Anne of Green Gables (Montgomery) 90, 109, 126, 165–169, 185
Antar and the Eagles (Mayne) 180, 198–201
anxiety 22, 28–29, 73, 79, 133, 180–182, 187–188, 192–194, 200
Are You There God? It's Me, Margaret (Blume) 113, 180
Ariès, Phillipe 7–8, 11–12, 20–22, 25, 39, 211n
Artaud, Antonin 61–62

Austen, Jane 80, 90, 97–98, 101, 126, 142, 150, 185, 188, 207
Avery, Gillian 7, 211n

Bakhtin, Mikhail 77, 81, 89
Ballantyne, R.M. 97, 102, 128, 131–132, 134
Bashevis-Singer, Isaac 59, 62
Bateson, Gregory 66–68, 70–71, 213n
Bawden, Nina 177
Bettelheim, Bruno 213
Bevis, the Story of a Boy (Jefferies) 102, 136–141
The BFG (Dahl) 96, 197, 208
Black Beauty 206
Blake, Kathleen 95
Blake, William 31–32, 38
The Blood-and-Thunder Adventure on Hurricane Peak (Mahy) 197
Blume, Judy 92, 113, 176, 180, 186
Blyton, Enid 82, 90, 100, 206–207
Bolter, J. David 91
Book of Martyrs 7
Boreman, Thomas 18–19, 211n
The Borrowers (Norton) 197
Boston, Lucy 98, 177–178, 181, 187–190, 197, 199, 213n, 217n
Boswell, John 8
Bottigheimer, Ruth B. 211n
Bourdieu, Pierre 66, 86–87
Bradbury, Malcom 99–100
Bruner, Jerome S. 214
Burnett, Francis Hodgson 100, 178, 181–184, 187, 189

227

Index

Burney, Fanny 37

Campbell, Joseph 125
Carroll, Lewis 29, 58–63, 65, 69, 76, 80, 82, 93–100, 103, 105–106, 108, 114, 119, 135, 140, 156, 178, 180–181, 191, 196, 204, 215n
cartoons 56–58
Cat in the Hat 193
centered consciousness 94, 98, 108–109, 150, 172, 178, 181–182, 184, 186, 188–189, 194, 200–202
Centuries of Childhood (Ariès) 7
chapbooks 9, 14–20, 97, 211–212
The Children of Green Knowe (Boston) 98, 178, 187, 197, 201, 217n
The Chocolate War (Cormier) 177
Christie, James F. 41
The Chronicles of Narnia (Lewis) 46, 49, 57–58, 207
class 11, 13–18, 27–28, 33–34, 36–37, 40–41, 55, 74, 84, 115–116, 137–141, 179, 211–213n
Cleary, Beverley 176
Cohen, David 214–215n
Cohn, Dorrit 89–91
Cole, Michael 26
collective protagonist 108–109, 115, 119, 132–134, 141–143, 152, 156–158, 170
The Collector (Fowles) 198
The Complete Sylvie and Bruno (Carroll) 69
Conrad, Joseph 130
Coolidge, Susan 101–102, 155–157, 159–160, 162–166, 168
Cooper, Mary 18–19, 211n
The Coral Island, a Tale of the Pacific Ocean (Ballantyne) 131–134, 136, 140, 216n
Corsaro, William A. 87, 212n
Count Karlstein (Pullman) 208
Coveney, Peter 32–33, 41
Crago, Hugh 213
Crago, Maureen 213
Crane, Ronald S. 212
Cressy, David 13, 15, 37
Cunningham, Hugh 8

Dahl, Roald 80, 96–97, 108, 176, 180, 193, 195–197, 203, 208
The Daisy Chain, or Aspirations: A Family Chronicle (Younge) 101–102, 109, 151–152
Danny, Champion of the World (Dahl) 195–196
Darton, F.J. Harvey 10, 17
Defoe, Daniel 102, 127–128, 131
de la Mare, Walter 93–94
Deleuze, Gilles 4, 61–63, 65–67, 70–72, 78–82, 84–86, 89, 94
Demers, Patricia 211n
Derrida, Jacques 3, 34, 45–46, 212n
descriptive psychonarration 104, 118–119, 121, 159, 184, 188–189
Dickens, Charles 101, 107, 109, 154, 208
A Dog So Small (Pearce) 192, 201
domestic novel 76, 78, 97–102, 109, 114, 124–126, 141, 149–150, 152–154, 165, 167–172, 174–175, 178–179, 181–182, 201, 215n
Donovan, Ann 198
Dream Days (Grahame) 83
Drift (Mayne) 198–200
Durrell, Lawrence 198
Dusinberre, Juliet 99, 214n

Eagleton, Terry 2
Edwards, Carolyn Pope 212n
Eible-Eibesfeldt, Irenäus 212n
Eisen, George 215n
Empson, William 29–31, 140
Erickson, Erik 214n
Evelina (Burney) 37, 179
Ewing, Juliana Horatia 107, 183

Fagan, Robert 74–75
The Fairing: or, a Golden Toy (Newbery) 17
fairytales 17, 98, 208, 213n
fantasy 63, 67–68, 70, 74, 77, 126, 129, 131, 135–136, 139–141, 149–150, 201, 214n
fantasy (genre) 17, 19, 76–77, 95–96, 98, 114–115, 119, 164, 170, 199–201, 215n

228

Index

The Fire-Maker's Daughter (Pullman) 208
Fitzhugh, Louise 176, 180
Five Children and It (Nesbit) 108, 114, 164
Five Go Down to the Sea (Blyton) 91
folktale 17, 20, 53, 186
Foster, Shirley 101–102, 149, 155, 159, 169, 171–174, 182
Fowles, John 198
The French Lieutenant's Woman (Fowles) 198
Freud, Sigmund 23–24, 32–33, 36, 44–45, 49, 51, 53, 70, 73–74, 82, 85–86, 95, 141, 216n
Fuller, Peter 8, 211n

Gardam, Jane 184
Garner, Alan 178, 197, 200
gender 13, 27, 34, 55, 77, 100–101, 138, 169–171, 184
Gideon Ahoy! (Mayne) 198, 201–203
"Golden age" 98, 101, 108, 180, 186, 208
The Golden Age (Grahame) 82–84, 107, 136
Goldthwaite, John 215n
Goody, Jack 26
Graff, Harvey J. 11, 15
Grahame, Kenneth 82–84, 96, 107, 136–137, 139
grammaphobia 34, 46
Gray, Thomas 31
Great Expectations 197
Green, Martin 126
Grosz, Elizabeth 52–53
Gulliver's Travels 46

Hamburger, Käte 89
Hanawalt, Barbara 8, 12, 211n
Hardt, Michael 66
Harriet the Spy (Fitzhugh) 180
Harris, Judith Rich 23–24, 28–29, 74–75, 212n, 214n
Hartley, L.P. 184
The Heart of Darkness (Conrad) 130, 198
Heidi (Spyri) 154, 208

Hendrick, Harry 27
Henkle, Roger 95
Here Comes Tod! (Pearce) 186
hero myth 125
Hewitt, Margaret 8
Heyer, Georgette 207
The History Man (Bradbury) 99–100
Hopkins, Eric 39–41
horror 3, 56–57, 59, 208
Hoyles, Martin 8
Hughes, Felicity 128–129
humor 79–82, 89, 93–94, 100, 102–104, 107, 109, 111–114, 119, 122, 131–132, 135–136, 145, 153–155, 166, 171–172, 176–177, 180–183, 186, 190, 192–193, 195–197, 199–200, 202–203, 205, 208–209
Hunt, David 8
Hunt, Peter 1–2, 5, 20, 46, 97, 99, 193, 199

I Was a Rat (Pullman) 208
innocence 2, 20–22, 27, 29–33, 38, 42, 55, 65, 70–71, 114, 140, 154, 156, 192, 206
irony 3, 59–61, 63, 65, 79–81, 89–90, 94, 105, 107, 110–112, 136, 141–143, 150, 163, 174, 176, 190–196, 198, 201, 207, 209
Ivanhoe 206

Jacob Have I Loved (Paterson) 113, 180, 194–195
James, Henry 93, 128–129, 182, 184, 216n
Jefferies, Richard 136–137, 139
Johnson, James E. 41
Jones, Gwenyth 100
The Jungle Book (Kipling) 199–200

Kafka, Franz 45
Kiely, Robert 130
Kipling, Rudyard 177, 208
Kristeva, Julia 32–34, 44–46, 51, 53, 58
Kuznets, Lois R. 98

Lacan, Jacques 34, 54, 98
Lambert, Gregg 70

229

Index

Lechte, John 51–52
LeGuin, Ursula 200
L'Engle, Madeline 200
Lesnick-Oberstein, Karín 211n
Lévi-Strauss, Claude 46
Lewis, C.S. 46–50, 53, 56–59, 63–64, 96–97, 108, 115, 118, 200, 207, 212–213n
The Lion, the Witch and the Wardrobe (Lewis) 57, 96, 149, 207
literacy 2, 8–9, 11–16, 18–22, 26–29, 31–32, 34, 36–39, 42–46, 55, 65, 124, 211, 213n
Little House in the Big Woods (Wilder) 184, 187
Little Lord Fauntleroy (Burnett) 100, 154, 181–183, 206
A Little Pretty Pocket Book (Newbery) 17–18, 92, 97
Little Women (Alcott) 98, 101, 106, 141–156, 158, 163, 216n
Locke, John 34, 91
Lodge, David 99–100
The Long Winter (Wilder) 187
Lord of the Flies (Golding) 137

MacLulich, T.D. 217n
Mahy, Margaret 197
Mailer, Norman 206–207
Marchant, Bessie 100
Marryat, Frederick 97, 102, 131–133
Marx, Marxist 8, 18, 37, 44, 85
Mary Poppins 90
Massumi, Brian 66, 213n
Masterman Ready (Marryat) 131–132
Matilda (Dahl) 96, 180, 195–197, 200
Mayne, William 177–178, 180–181, 198–204, 217n
McKeon, Michael 18, 211n
McLuhan, Marshall 42
McMunn, Meradith Tilbury 8
Mead, George Herbert 85–86
medieval children's literature 7–8, 10
The Member for the Marsh (Mayne) 198
Miller, David L. 213n
Mitchell, Lee Clark 135–136
Mitterauer, Michael 22, 25, 28, 39–40, 178–179

mock-heroism 148, 159, 166–167, 169
modern childhood 2, 12, 27, 42, 44, 65, 177
Montgomery, Lucy Maud 82, 102, 150, 165–166, 168–169, 216–217n

narrative asides 104, 106, 123, 143, 162, 166
negative psychonarration 104, 148, 161–162
Nesbit, Edith 80, 82, 92, 94, 96, 98, 100, 102–103, 106–110, 112–116, 123–124, 143, 148, 154–156, 163–165, 169–171, 174, 183, 196, 201, 213–214n
Neuburg, V.E. 14–15
Newbery, John 7, 9, 17–19, 92, 98, 211
Newell, William 4
Nicholas Nickleby 197
Nikolajeva, Maria 20, 90, 108–109, 125–126, 141, 211n, 215n
Nodelman, Perry 1, 4, 22, 28, 32, 76, 79–80
Norton, Mary 197–198, 208
nostalgia 9, 20, 22, 29, 31, 37, 69, 79, 82–83, 85, 95, 107, 134–135, 158, 177, 187, 189, 191
The Nursery Alice (Carroll) 59–60
nursery rhymes 60

objectification 109, 146–148, 154, 157–159, 161–162, 165, 168–169, 173, 181, 199
Oedipus 21–22, 24–25, 45, 51–53, 70, 75, 82, 91, 179
O'Malley, Andrew 211
Ong, Walter J. 21, 26–27, 34, 37, 44
Opie, Iona 60, 213n
Opie, Peter 60, 213n
Out of the Silent Planet (Lewis) 47–51, 213n

Paley, Vivian 214
paradox 4, 45, 54, 67–69, 71, 74, 84, 86
parody 4, 59–60, 74–76, 84, 86, 124, 201, 203
pastoral 32–33, 51
Paterson, Katherine 113, 177, 194–195

pathos 79, 109, 153–154, 165, 170–171, 174, 180–182
Pearce, Philippa 177–178, 181, 184, 186, 189–193, 195, 197, 201
perversity 4, 54, 62, 73, 76, 80–84, 86, 89, 95–96, 102, 104, 106, 111, 114, 119, 125, 132–133, 140–141, 150–151, 153–154, 156, 165, 170, 172, 177, 181–183, 187, 196, 202–203, 209
Peter Pan 140
Peter Simple (Marryat) 131–132
phantasmagoria 3, 65, 70, 75–76, 95, 209
The Phoenix and the Carpet (Nesbit) 114, 177
Piaget 69, 85–86, 95
Pickering, Samuel F. 211n
Pinchbeck, Ivy 8
The Pirate Uncle (Mahy) 197
Pollock, Linda A. 8, 11–12
Pope, Alexander 33
Postman, Neil 42, 177, 179, 212n
postwar novel 172–173, 176, 180–182, 184, 186, 189, 195
Pride and Prejudice (Austen) 98, 141–145, 185, 215–216n
puberty 23, 51, 168, 179–180, 195
Pullman, Philip 208
puritan 27, 30, 85, 151, 213n

The Railway Children (Nesbit) 102, 114, 169–174, 203
Ransome, Arthur 82, 94, 96, 98, 100, 102–103, 108, 115–116, 118, 120, 123–124, 128, 134, 136–137, 139, 143, 160, 197–198, 201
Rebecca of Sunnybrook Farm (Wiggin) 165–168, 216–217n
reluctant psychonarration 120, 145–146, 157, 162, 166, 183
repression 3, 23–24, 32, 45, 52, 70, 82, 141
Reynolds, Kimberley 140
Robeck, Mildred C. 34–35
Robinson Crusoe (Defoe) 83, 90, 97, 117, 122–123, 127, 130, 133
Rose, Jacqueline 47, 50, 140
Rosenthal, Lynne 217

Rousseau, Jean-Jacques 31–33, 38, 41, 51

satire 59–60, 83, 90, 95, 107, 135, 170–172, 208
Sawyer, R. Keith 76–77, 85–87, 101, 215n
Schlumbohm, J. 25
Schofield, Roger 14
Scholes, Robert E. 72
school 8–10, 12–13, 15–16, 21–22, 24, 26–29, 34, 36–39, 41–42, 45, 88, 97, 115, 135, 137, 146, 153, 166, 177, 179, 207, 211n, 216n; pre-school 3, 13, 22–24, 41–42, 71–72, 75–76, 78, 88, 96, 101, 176, 179, 186, 202
Schwartzman, Helen B. 71
Scribner, Sylvia 26
The Secret Garden (Burnett) 102, 173, 181–184, 187–188
Sedgwick, Eve Kosofsky 77
Seuss, Dr. 82, 96
sex, sexuality 3, 29–30, 42, 51, 56, 59, 61, 82, 138–140, 150, 180, 212n, 214n, 216n
Shahar, Shulamith 8
Shakespeare, William 10, 15, 35, 37
Shavit, Zohar 7, 47, 59, 63, 196, 212n
Shepher, Joseph 214n
Shorter, Edward 8
The Silver Chair (Lewis) 59
Simons, Judy 101–102, 149, 155, 159, 169, 171–174, 182
socialization 3, 23–24, 44–47, 53, 55, 57, 74, 78, 81, 126, 172
Spufford, Margaret 9, 14, 211–212n
Stalky & Co. (Kipling) 177
Steinbeck, John 35–36, 45
Stevenson, Robert Louis 127–130, 134
Stone, Lawrence 8, 12
The Story of the Amulet (Nesbit) 114–115, 170
The Story of the Treasure Seekers (Nesbit) 106–112, 116, 165
Sunday school 152, 157, 168
Sutton-Smith, Brian 3–5, 69, 85
Swallows and Amazons (Ransome) 100–101, 115–124, 134, 136

Index

The Swiss Family Robinson (Wyss) 131

Talbot, C.H. 8
talking animals 3, 19, 46–50, 55–59, 64, 78
Tallis, Raymond 99
Thompson, E.P. 212n
Through the Looking Glass (Carroll) 93, 155, 191, 216n
Thwaite, M.F. 10
Tolkien, J.R.R. 96, 200, 213n
Tom's Midnight Garden (Pearce) 184, 189–192, 194–195, 201
Trease, Geoffrey 206–207
Treasure Island (Stevenson) 90, 97, 117, 127–130, 134–135
The Tricksters (Mahy) 197
Twain, Mark 102, 134–136, 165–167

Ullyses 91

Van Ghent, Dorothy 171
violence 57, 160, 196
Vygotsky 85–86, 91

Wall, Barbara 1, 91, 91–95, 101–103, 106–108, 110–111, 113, 115–116, 123, 127–132, 135–137, 143, 152, 164, 181–184, 187–190, 192, 198, 203, 215n
Wallace, Randall 34–35
Wardle, David 13, 39

Wardle, Francis 24
Warner, Susan 101–102, 149–150, 164
Watership Down (Adams) 200, 215n
Watt, Ian 14–15
The Way to Sattin Shore (Pearce) 193–195
What Katy Did (Coolidge) 101–102, 106, 150, 155–165
What Maisie Knew (James) 93, 182, 195
Whiting, Beatrice Blyth 212n
The Wide, Wide World (Warner) 101–102, 149–151, 156
Wiggin, Kate Douglas 165, 167–168, 217n
Wilder, Laura Ingalls 178, 180, 184–188, 199, 217n
Williams, Clare 38
Wind in the Willows (Grahame) 2
Wolfenstein, Martha 61
Wooden, Warren W. 7
Woolf, Virginia 99
Wordsworth, William 31–32, 38, 82–83
The Would-Be-Goods (Nesbit) 107, 213n

Yawkey, Thomas D. 41
Yonge, Charlotte 101–102, 151–152

Zipes, Jack 36

www.ingramcontent.com/pod-product-compliance
Lightning Source LLC
Chambersburg PA
CBHW051220300426
44116CB00006B/657